The New City

ECONOMICS TODAY
Edited by Andrew Leake

The *Economics Today* series surveys contemporary headline topics in applied economics. Each book in the series is written by an expert in the field in a style that is fluently readable. It serves the student of introductory economic principles while also making the subject accessible to a more general reader. The series embraces the problem-solving skills of the new generation of students and stresses the importance of real-world issues and the significance of economic ideas.

Published

Andrew Leake: **The Economic Question**
Jean-Louis Barsoux and Peter Lawrence: **The Challenge of British Management**
Andy Beharrell: **Unemployment and Job Creation**
Frank Burchill: **Labour Relations**
Kenneth Durham: **The New City**
S.F Goodman: **The European Community**
Jenny Wales: **Investigating Social Issues**

Forthcoming

Margaret Wilkinson: **Taxation**

THE NEW CITY

Kenneth Durham

M
MACMILLAN

First published 1992

Published by
MACMILLAN EDUCATION LTD
Houndmills, Basingstoke, Hampshire RG21 2XS
and London
Companies and representatives
throughout the world

ISBN 0–333–55149–4 hardcover
ISBN 0–333–55150–8 paperback

A catalogue record for this book
is available from the British Library.

Typeset by
Ponting–Green Publishing Services,
Sunninghill, Berkshire

Printed in Hong Kong

Contents

List of Tables and Figures

Tables

Figures

List of Abbreviations

AFBD	Association of Futures Brokers and Dealers
ARIEL	Automated Real-Time Investments Ltd
BIS	Bank for International Settlements
BZW	Barclays de Zoete Wedd
CD(s)	Certificate(s) of Deposit
CHAPS	Clearing House Automated Payments System
DTI	Department of Trade and Industry
ECU	European Currency Unit
EFTPOS	Electronic Funds Transfer at Point of Sale
ERM	Exchange Rate Mechanism
ESCB	European System of Central Banks (Delors plan)
FIMBRA	Financial Intermediaries, Managers and Brokers Regulatory Association
FRN(s)	Floating Rate Note(s)
GDP	Gross Domestic Product
IDB	Inter-dealer broker
IMRO	Investment Management Regulatory Organisation
ISE	Interantional Stock Exchange (London)
ISRO	International Securities Regulatory Organisation
JMB	Johnson Matthey Bank
LAUTRO	Life Assurance and Unit Trust Regulatory Organisation
LFOX	London Futures and Options Exchange
LIBOR	London Interbank Offered Rate
LIFFE	London International Financial Futures Exchange

LME	London Metal Exchange
LTOM	London Traded Options Market
MLR	Minimum Lending Rate
OFT	Office of Fair Trading
OTC	Over the Counter
PSBR	Public Sector Borrowing Requirement
PSDR	Public Sector Debt Repayment
SEAQ	Stock Exchange Automated Quotation System
SEC	Securities and Exchange Commission (USA)
SIB	Securities and Investments Board
SRO(s)	Self-Regulatory Organisation(s)
TAURUS	Transfer and Automated Registration of Uncertified Stock
TSA	The Securities Association
USM	Unlisted Securities Market

1 Tales of Two Cities

Old and New

Picture this: you are standing outside the Bank of England, somewhere near the hub of the City of London. Above the roar of the traffic, you can almost hear from the offices and dealing-rooms around you the expensive hum of the very latest microelectronic technology. Millions of pounds are changing hands as you stand and stare. You are staring at a pair of middle-aged men who stride purposefully and unselfconsciously towards the rather grand doorway of the Bank. They are: unaccountably, wearing top hats. Nobody else has given them more than a passing glance. They are representatives of the London Discount Houses Association. Discount houses act as intermediaries between the Bank of England and the other banks that form the London money market. The men have come to talk with the Governor of the Bank about the movement of funds to and from the banking sector. This will have significant implications for short-term interest rates. In a sense, then, the meeting affects every one of us in a direct and important way.

The business could, presumably, be transacted as effectively over the telephone, or, at least, without the benefit of eccentric headgear. Until fairly recently the Deputy Governor was charged with the weighty responsibility of dropping a penny into each of the upturned hats while their owners were closeted with his boss. In a brutal bid for modernity this ritual was abandoned in 1981. The hats remain – highlighting, in their way, the contradictions that characterise the City today.

Perhaps it is not particularly surprising to see men in top hats strolling in the City of London. One image of the City is of tradition and public-school manners. This version places it somewhere fairly high up the list of eccentric but peculiarly endearing British foibles, along with roast Sunday lunches and the last night of the Proms. This City is populated by 'gentlemen' who knew one another at boarding school, conduct their business over long lunches or rounds of golf, wear bowler hats and live in pleasant homes in Surrey or Berkshire.

But another image is rapidly emerging. The City is becoming brash, exciting, sexy. It was possible in 1990 to see on British television a soap opera-cum-drama series set in the City of London. The characters were not 'gentlemen', indeed, many of them were not even 'ladies'. Lunches were for plotting and propositioning. Work was apparently conducted at fever-pitch and very high volume on two or three telephones simultaneously, confronted by banks of unintelligibly flickering computer screens. Men wore sharp suits and braces, women were in slinky designer two-pieces and home was a converted warehouse in Rotherhithe. There was not a top hat, nor even a bowler, in sight and absurd rituals with pennies would have looked like historical drama. This was, of course, fiction and not many people would honestly pretend, hand on heart, that it accurately reflected life and work in the City of London. It undoubtedly does reflect, though, the City's new image in the popular imagination and, in part, genuine changes that have occurred in a fairly brief space of years.

An article in *The Independent on Sunday* in early 1990 reported on the efforts made by Citicorp, the massive American-based international bank, to infiltrate the City establishment. Advisers and consultants were employed, but to no avail. If there is a City establishment today, the ground is shifting so fast that it is hardly worth infiltrating. In the same article Lord Swaythling (previously David Montagu, of the merchant bankers Samuel Montagu – now owned by Midland Bank) was quoted speaking with some nostalgia of the days when one could trust one's colleagues and when the pace of City life was more casual. 'It's no longer a gentleman's profession,' he said. Jacob Rothschild of the famous banking family and founder of Rothschild Investment Trust has pronounced, with rather more approval, that 'the City's becoming a shirt-sleeve business'.

Signposts to the New City

If we were to ask for signposts on the road to this new City, we should probably be directed first to the Big Bang of October 1986. This was the not-so-quiet revolution which received such publicity and which, if we are to believe what we read, introduced the City to computers, yuppies, monstrous salaries and Japanese bankers – as well as making one of its major tourist attractions, the Stock Exchange floor itself, entirely redundant. Big Bang was certainly a major event in the development of securities markets in the 1980s and 1990s, but the road to the new City starts a little earlier than 1986.

Just as the West Midlands used to be regarded as the home of the British motor industry, and textiles were woven in Lancashire, so the City of London is really no more than the concentrated centre of one specific industry – financial services. Like all service industries, the growth of the financial sector depends first (and, in some cases, always) upon the growth of other sectors. Banks will only develop when there are individuals and companies with money to deposit and others who want or need to borrow. The insurance industry requires not just risks, but risks where a great deal of money is at stake, if it is to grow quickly and successfully. Britain was a major trading nation as long ago as the sixteenth century and with the expansion of trade – much of it passing through the port of London itself – came the savings and the borrowings as well as the risks upon which the financial sector could thrive. Surprisingly, perhaps, Amsterdam remained the world financial centre until late in the seventeenth or early in the eighteenth century. It was, significantly, the development of a particularly close and mutually beneficial relationship between the City and the government that finally enabled London to eclipse Amsterdam. The City was able to raise massive loans to support a series of military adventures which themselves laid the foundations for a trading empire that was to keep the City supplied with funds and with customers (and thus with expertise) until well into the twentieth century.

Even from this cursory analysis two factors can be isolated that will prove particularly significant in tracing the development of the new City. First, the real growth of the City was based upon international business. By the middle of the nineteenth century, London was the banking centre of the world, helped by the fact that more than half of the world's trade was conducted in sterling and by the remarkable willingness of Victorian entrepreneurs to risk their savings in speculative ventures overseas. As late as 1913 over half of British savings were, amazingly, invested abroad. It is no accident that when the City was pursuing largely domestic business, it did not outshine the world. Access to international business is not enough, though: the second factor to remember is that the success of a financial sector in attracting and retaining such business depends crucially upon the restrictions placed upon it or privileges granted to it by its domestic government. Much of the City's success can be attributed to the fact that governments were sympathetic to its activities (in part because they relied upon it for their own increasingly complex financial needs) and paid it the greatest compliment that any financial sector can receive – they did not interfere.

The City of the 1920s and 1930s is still a far cry from the new City of today. It is after the ending of the Second World War that we begin to see glimpses of the future. These were extremely inauspicious times. It must have seemed likely to some observers that the post-war City could do nothing but decline. The fragmentation of the empire considerably reduced the significance of sterling in world trade and a new regime of fixed exchange rates elevated the dollar to sterling's old role. At the same time increasingly fierce competition in international trade reduced and ultimately destroyed the balance-of-payments surpluses whose reinvestment abroad had been so important to the City's earlier growth. Most ominously of all, perhaps, the British economy declined in international importance. The UK manufacturing sector was no longer the workshop of the world. Other countries, particularly West Germany and Japan, consistently outperformed the UK industrially and thus generated the customers and the funds (not to mention the balance-of-payments surpluses) upon which a financial sector thrives. Surely the financial services industry could not survive the decline of those whom it was employed to service? Other brash young financial centres would be bound to emerge in the newly dominant trading nations and allow the City of London a dignified and elegant retirement. Such centres did emerge, most prominently in Tokyo, and yet the City was not quite ready for a twilight home in the shadows cast by the sun rising in the East.

The Clearing-House of the World

To understand the City's resilience it is necessary to go back to our earlier points. The City's expertise in international business enabled it to benefit from the very factors that might have destroyed it. It was in 1904 that Joseph Chamberlain described the City as 'the clearing-house of the world' and it was true then but, if anything, it actually became truer with the astonishingly rapid development of international banking during the 1960s and 1970s. This was not the work of British banks in particular (though they were of course involved) but rather of the banking industry itself – but it occurred in the City of London. The success, if we choose to call it that, is really the success of the institution of the City for its ability to attract a fairly spectacular inflow of foreign banks during these years. By 1970 there were more American banks in the City of London than in New York. In 1988 overseas banks were responsible for over 83 per cent of the international lending conducted in the City of London.

The growth was in 'wholesale' banking. This involves transactions between companies or countries or financial institutions rather than private individuals (whose business is described as 'retail'). It was in non-sterling business too. The new economic conditions led to the hitherto unknown phenomenon of large currency balances being held outside their country of origin. The first such balances were in dollars and came to be known as Eurodollars, but Euromarkets soon developed in many other currencies. The recycling of these balances to form huge loans to governments or to multinational companies became a massive industry based in London. In 1963 when the Euromarket is said to have been born, $100 million of such loans were organised in the City of London. By 1986 the figure had risen to over $186 billion. It is currently estimated that more than $2 trillion is held in the form of Eurocurrency bank deposits.

The 1970s, such a dismal period for so much of the British economy, saw the most rapid growth in the London-based Euromarkets – a growth that was helped, perversely, by some of the very factors that were holding back other industries. The breakdown of the fixed exchange rate system in 1972/3 led to increased volatility in the movement of currencies and gave greater incentive to large savers and borrowers to move their business from one currency to another. At the same time the oil crisis of 1973/4 generated huge balance-of-payments surpluses for oil-exporting countries which could be recycled by the Euromarket to form massive loans – many to the governments of developing countries (laying the foundation of the international debt problem that was to dog the 1980s).

It was not just expertise in international banking that attracted the Euromarket to London, though. Once again, the relationship with the government proved crucial. London boasted one of the most open, unregulated markets for foreign money in the world. Foreign currency could move in and out virtually unfettered. This was particularly ironic since the existence of tight exchange controls limited the movement of sterling to a very considerable extent. Thus there emerged in the 1960s and 1970s two Cities – an international City that was successful, unregulated and dominated by overseas firms (not unlike the new City of today) and a domestic City that was the province of British firms and was more tightly regulated, most significantly by exchange controls. Perhaps it was this City that actually most closely represented the old City of nostalgic cliché.

The Old City Feels the Cold

The new City that forms the subject of this book could be said to be no more than the fusion of the domestic and international Cities of the 1970s, or, more precisely, the absorption of the domestic by the international City.

The success of the 1970s was the success of international wholesale banking. Retail banks in the UK – the well-known clearing banks – were quite heavily controlled by government through ratios that forced them to hold proportions of cash and other liquid assets. A far more effective control, though, was the cosy, mutual back-scratching relationship that they had with the Bank of England. In very simple terms, the Bank was determined to maintain the security of the financial system and so was not especially concerned with competition that might threaten this security – especially if the banks were cooperative in assisting the Bank of England to fund central government and smooth the money markets. This relationship extended beyond the retail banks to all the institutions of the domestic City. When the government was keen to avoid interest rate increases in the mid-1970s despite large increases in its own borrowing, the Bank of England only had to nod meaningfully to the important investment institutions for them to bid happily for a twofold increase in their holdings of government gilt-edged stock.

The price of such cooperation was protection from competition. Building Societies, for example, were not able to compete directly with banks in the provision of loans. Membership of the Stock Exchange was closed to incorporated companies and to foreigners. Stockbrokers operated a system of fixed minimum commissions which reduced the discomfort of competition over price. The existence of exchange controls of course was the best protection of all, for it prevented British savings finding their way into overseas financial markets in any volume. The domestic City was playing in a game where the opposition were not allowed to touch the ball – it was just a matter of the home team passing to one another all day, so perhaps it is no wonder if their ball-skills grew a bit rusty.

Towards the end of the 1970s it was being whispered that, despite the huge success of the Euromarkets, London was slipping. There was no market to speak of in financial futures and options. America had picked up that ball and was running with it very effectively. The London Stock Exchange had already fallen behind both America and Japan in terms of the value of stock quoted and dealt. Deregulation of international banking in New York would divert business there. To make matters worse, the debt crisis was making large-volume international lending a great deal less attractive, which was very bad news for an international banking centre whose entire reputation was based upon just that.

Deregulation and the Challenge of Technology

The final steps along the road to the new City were taken purposefully, though not entirely intentionally, by the Conservative government which was elected in May 1979. Within weeks of their election exchange controls were abolished and the domestic City was exposed to the sudden chill draught of real competition. The rationale for abolition actually had more to do with the impact of North Sea oil than with competition in the City. The thinking was

TABLE 1.1
Recent Deregulation and Liberalisation of Financial Markets in Selected Countries

Deregulation	*United Kingdom*	*United States*	*Japan*	*Germany*	*France*
Exchange controls	Abolished	Non-statutory restrictions on foreign currency bank accounts to be abolished 1990	Largely abolished	—	Phased abolition to be completed 1990
Interest rate controls	—	Largely abolished	Progressive abolition on large time deposits	—	—
Credit controls	Abolished	—	Quantitative controls abolished	—	Quantitative controls abolished
Restrictions on establishment	Entry of foreign securities houses under Big Bang	—	Entry of foreign firms in stock exchange (in limited numbers,) and to trust banking	—	—

Restrictions on activity	Banks allowed to purchase/set up brokers under Big Bang. Access to discount market liberalised	Limited securities underwriting by securities subsidiaries of bank holding companies	Limited deregulation of banks' securities operations, Banks allowed to deal in JGBs and JGB futures	—	Financial institutions allowed to purchase stockbrokers
Restrictions on secondary markets	—	Banks allowed into discount broking	Seasoning period on eurobonds reduced. Warrant trading liberalised	—	—
Offshore banking	—	Establishment of IBFs permitted	Japan Offshore market established	—	—
Fiscal restrictions	Reduction of stamp duty	Abolition of withholding taxes on bonds and equities	Reductions in transactions taxes – more comprehensive capital gains tax	Abolition of withholding tax	Abolition of withholding tax on interest payments to non-resident bond-holders

TABLE 1.1 (continued)
Recent Deregulation and Liberalisation of Financial Markets in Selected Countries

Deregulation	*United Kingdom*	*United States*	*Japan*	*Germany*	*France*
Modernisation of existing markets	Electronic screen based stock market. Abolition of minimum commissions	Proposal for after-hours trading by some exchanges	Increased computerisation. Reform of short-term money markets	Links between regional stock markets: planned screen-based trading system	Electronic screen based stock market. Removal of fixed brokerage commissions
Establishment of new markets	LIFFE – futures; LTOM – options; commercial paper market	Full range of markets already established	TIFFE – futures. Stock index options and futures. Bond lending market. Commercial paper market	Establishment of futures and options market (1990)	MATIF – futures. MONEP – options. New short term markets

ABBREVIATIONS: IBFs International Banking Facilities
JGBs Japanese Government Bonds

SOURCE: *Bank of England Quarterly Bulletin*, November 1989.

that exports of oil would generate surpluses on the British balance of payments and thus push up the value of sterling. This would make life hard for British exporters. With exchange controls removed, there would be nothing to stop the extra funds from being invested overseas, reducing some of the upward pressure on the pound. Certainly, between 1979 and 1984, British investment institutions spent some £18 billion on foreign securities.

Predictably, the exposure to foreign competition that resulted from the abolition of exchange controls was merely the first step along the deregulation road. It certainly exposed the weaknesses of some of the institutions of the domestic City. By 1984, in a famous statistic, more shares in ICI were traded on the New York Stock Exchange than in London, presumably because it was cheaper to deal there. Once the abolition of exchange controls allowed British investors a taste of other markets the days of the old City were numbered – it became a case of deregulate or die.

Developments in technology were crucial too. The revolution in telecommunications has made it possible to deal in any national market that one chooses with more or less the same ease. The abolition of exchange controls made it legal to move money from one market to another – but without the technology to move it easily, cheaply and immediately, the effect could not have been nearly so dramatic. The market has become, in an overworked phrase, global. The domestic City suddenly found itself not simply having to let the opposition touch the ball, but actually having to play against half a dozen teams at once.

The pressure to remove regulations that hindered domestic firms in their ability to compete in this global market became understandably intense (though not always from the firms themselves). The Stock Exchange's Big Bang is only the best-known example of this trend which began with the abolition of exchange controls. Once the process of deregulation was begun, it almost became a matter for international competition itself – financial centres have been falling over themselves to remove the rules that prevent their firms from getting the biggest share of this huge and suddenly accessible international market: the Japanese have removed restrictions upon international banks in Tokyo, have reformed taxes on capital gains, have admitted foreign firms to their Stock Exchange; the Americans have largely abolished interest rate controls and have opened up after-hours trading; the Germans have introduced a futures and options market; a fuller list is given in Table 1.1.

The new City, then, is, above all a deregulated City. It is important to realise too that this process of deregulation was really no more than an extension to the old domestic City of the atmosphere and attitudes that had always characterised and accounted for the success of the international City. The chairman of America's Chase Manhattan Bank once explained why international banks such as his were so attracted to the City by describing it as 'a very warm place for doing business'. I suspect that we all know what he meant by that. The 'warmth' of the international City lay in the reluctance of the authorities to interfere by anything more than a sidelong glance or a disapproving frown. Nor should we underestimate the importance of the technological revolution in the establishment of the new City. Only when the domestic City's most powerful protection of all – the privacy and convenience of its national boundaries – had been infiltrated by microelectronics could the real necessity of deregulation be appreciated.

The emergence of the new City has been rapid and, in many ways, painful. It has involved, almost literally, a clash of cultures as the ways of the international City have met head-on with those of its domestic counterpart. There have been many casualties. The City of middle-aged men who stroll the streets in top hats does not always sit easily with the City of yuppies in Armani suits who are yelling down the phone to Tokyo at 7a.m. and are still dealing on Wall Street by computer long after the sun has set on suburban gardens in Surrey and Berkshire. Whether the new City is still as 'warm' – in every sense – as the chairman of Chase Manhattan believed is a matter that we must consider later for, paradoxically, the process of deregulation has carried with it a completely new and complex system of regulation. Before looking at this, though, we should investigate the markets that actually comprise the phenomenon of the new City.

The City at Work 2

Divine Services?

Whilst public attitudes to the City may have changed a lot in terms of youth, glamour, and excitement over the 1980s, it still has image problems. Indeed, in one sense, they are worse now than ever. The basis of a good deal of the resentment of the City of London is that it does not seem to 'do' anything. According to this argument, references to the 'financial services industry' are a contradiction in terms. Industries are thought of as furnaces from which physical output is wrought in ways that are smelly, sweaty and probably dangerous. The City of London is not like that. Its output is not physical (though this does not of course mean that there is no output at all). There is an implication, too, that the City's work is somehow parasitic: that it makes itself rich by living off the backs of real producers; that, far from helping these producers, it probably deceives them and certainly overcharges them. It is admitted that the City is clever but (disapprovingly) 'too clever by half'. We do not understand what goes on there and are probably better off not knowing. At its most basic the argument comes down to the idea that making profits simply by moving other people's money around is probably dishonest and is surely no job for right-thinking young women and men – nor even, perhaps, for middle-aged ones.

In the United Kingdom we have been very slow to accept the decline of the manufacturing sector and to recognise that wealth-creation and manufacturing are not synonymous terms. This is, perhaps, especially remarkable for an economy whose service sector developed and became internationally established considerably earlier than those of most of our industrial rivals. The service sector, of course, produces output just as valuable as physical goods and, in many cases, just as tradeable. Traditional economic theory teaches us that countries should concentrate resources in those industries in whose production they have a comparative advantage relative to their trading partners. Experience seems to show that the UK has such an advantage in financial services. Clearly such services are genuinely demanded – for the City's success over three centuries and the development of similar centres in New York, Tokyo and elsewhere can hardly be put down to a monstrous confidence trick or to clever advertising. It will help if we can specify these services more precisely.

What the City Does

Business needs money. Any production is, in a sense, speculative – goods must be produced in advance of demand. Materials must be paid for and workers must be hired before goods and services are sold in the market. Where is the money to come from? Even if you have some cash from goods that you sold last week or last month, you may want to produce more this time. How can you pay for it? Bills may not neatly coincide with your stream of earnings. Some are quarterly, some monthly, some weekly, some may even be yearly. There are bound to be times when a bill must be paid without sufficient money to cover it. How can it be done? Business expansion exposes the speculative nature of production and the consequent need for cash even more obviously.

There is, of course, no shortage of cash, for there are thousands of individuals (or other firms) who want to put some of their money on one side for a while – saving for a house or a car or a holiday, for their retirement or their daughter's wedding, to pay a phone bill or to buy a new machine, or for any number of other reasons. The secret lies in transforming these savings into available cash for the productive sector. This is an essential task and one whose efficiency will help to determine the efficiency with which the entire economy can perform. It is not quite as simple as it appears, either. The needs of the borrowers and the lenders are not the same. A lot of savers want to save for only a short period, they want to have access to their savings so that they can withdraw them when they go on holiday or when the bills arrive. Firms are likely to want money for a long time; it can be many years before a new enterprise can pay off development costs. Similarly, savers want their money to be safe whereas much production is, as we have seen, speculative and risky. Most private individuals would be extremely reluctant to lend their hard-earned savings to most firms – the two sides would be unable to agree terms.

The role of the financial services industry is to channel the savings to the borrowers whilst at the same time meeting the needs of the lenders. This is a most valuable service and requires considerable skill and experience. For the time being a few simple examples will serve to show some of the technicalities involved – the rest of the book, of course, furnishes many others.

Perhaps a building society shows the principle most clearly. Borrowers want twenty-five year loans for house-purchase. Lenders want virtually free access to their savings. The experience of the building society allows them to satisfy both by ensuring that there is a constant flow of small savings into the Society to continue to cover outstanding loans. This is, of course, why interest rates to savers must be competitive – if the Society fails to attract new savings, then it not only limits its ability to lend more, but actually threatens existing loans.

A merchant bank effectively does exactly the same thing. It might advance £1 million to a company to be repaid in fifteen years' time. The bank itself finances the loan by borrowing a series of smaller sums in the London money markets. Each of these loans might last for only a year but, provided that the bank can replace each loan with another as it falls due, then they have succeeded in transforming short-term savings into a long-term loan. Clearly, they will charge the firm interest for the service they have offered.

A firm that is expanding needs an enormous sum of money for a very long period of time. By issuing shares and selling them to the public, they receive the cash. The buyers, though, do not have to leave their money tied up for years – by using the Stock Exchange, they can sell their shares whenever they like. The company gets very long-term cash. The investors get access to their money whenever they wish.

A company can borrow smaller sums by issuing a commercial bill

– an IOU that promises payment on a particular date in the future. Markets exist in the City where such bills can be sold (the buyer is in effect lending to the issuing company) and where holders can resell to other investors in order to obtain cash quickly. Once again, the firm has the money for a longer period, but City markets enable lenders to recover cash if necessary. These bills can clearly be risky – the firm might not be able to repay it when it falls due. Merchant banks can help here too – they can 'accept' the bill, promising payment if the firm fails. This makes the bill far easier to sell. The firm gains by being able to borrow more easily. The lender faces a vastly reduced risk. The bank, of course, will charge a fee to the issuing company.

Firms dealing in international markets need to exchange currencies. The City not only provides facilities for this but enables companies to reduce their exposure to sudden changes in exchange rates by making use of markets in currency futures.

Altogether, then, the services provided by the City are of genuine value to other producers in the economy. We might summarise the services thus:

- the City translates private savings into productive loans – the 'broking' function of bringing together the two sides to a deal;
- in doing this the City must provide a wide and attractive array of savings instruments in order to attract the savings;
- the City reduces financial risks to both borrowers and savers by bearing some of the risks itself, as well as using its expertise to calculate these risks;
- it also, more mundanely, offers financial advice to borrowers and lenders based upon its own experience and accumulated expertise.

City Markets Today

Now that we know what financial services are, we are in a position to look at the major markets and firms of the City and see how they reckon to provide such services. The 1980s, as we saw in Chapter 1, were years of great change in the City. This book will return time and again to the far-reaching effects of *internationalisation* and *deregulation*. It is time now to add a third ugly word to this pair: the early 1980s was also a period when large companies chose (for reasons that we shall consider in detail in Chapter 4) to replace traditional borrowing from banks by borrowing in the money markets of the City through the issue of negotiable securities (such as the commercial bills that were outlined earlier or longer-term bonds). This phenomenon, which sadly came to be known as *securitisation*, has had a major impact on banks (who found themselves losing business) as well as on markets and firms that traditionally deal in securities (who stood to gain). In considering how the City actually operates today, these three developments – internationalisation, deregulation and securitisation – crop up continuously.

The International Stock Exchange

The market that most readily comes to mind when the City of London is mentioned is probably the market in stocks and shares – or 'equities' as they are known in the financial world. This market is the most widely reported and probably one of the most easily understood areas of City activity. The securities bought and sold here represent shares in the ownership of companies. The market can be seen to serve two major functions:

1. it allows firms to raise finance by the issue of new shares to the public;
2. it provides a secondary market in shares where investors can buy and sell easily.

The trend towards securitisation in the 1980s certainly had an impact on the Stock Exchange as increasing volumes of shares were issued and dealt. This trend is illustrated in Figure 2.1. The increase in the issue of shares to finance industrial expansion from 1983 to 1987 is in the order of 637 per cent; between 1986 and 1987 new issues rose by a staggering 137 per cent. We shall consider the reasons for this trend, and its implications, in Chapter 3 but it surely must indicate that the costs of a share issue were highly competitive relative to formal loans. It may also reflect a general increase in interest in Stock Exchange activity, boosted no doubt by the publicity given to the huge privatisation issues of the middle 1980s, and the Big Bang of 1986. After 1987, as the table shows, new share issues fell substantially, illustrating the sudden loss of confidence in stock

FIGURE 2.1
Value of New Share Issues by UK Industrial and Commercial Companies, 1983–7

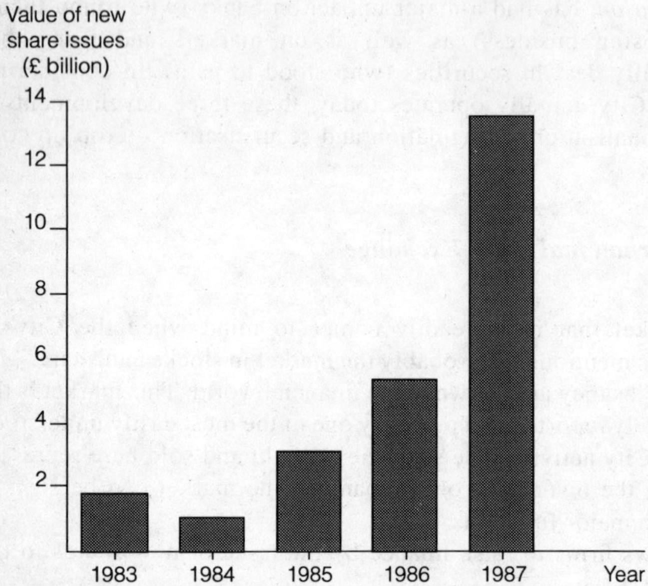

SOURCE *Financial Statistics* (London: HMSO).

markets that followed the 1987 crash. Financial markets can be disturbingly volatile.

As we have already seen, Big Bang was not the first example of deregulation in the City nor was it by any means the last. Its effect, though, has been immensely far-reaching. As a result of Big Bang it is no longer possible to divide the firms and institutions of the City into neat categories according to their precise specialisms. In a remarkably far-sighted speech delivered at a *Financial Times* conference in 1983, Jacob Rothschild (from whom we heard briefly in Chapter 1) predicted a financial world dominated by immense conglomerate organisations competing to offer every service from loans and share-dealing to bond finance, insurance, and foreign exchange. He foresaw a world controlled by 'two broad types of giant institutions, the worldwide financial service company, and the international commercial bank with a global trading competence'. There were probably those who heard him in 1983 who regarded this as science fiction. By opening membership of the Stock Exchange to outside companies, Big Bang brought the vision into reality. We talk now of a company having a market-making division which looks after its share-dealing operations while other divisions look after corporate banking, insurance broking, foreign exchange dealing and so on. Big Bang also introduced foreign competitors into the domestic City, particularly some fierce Japanese conglomerates, and was the excuse for some of the absurd salary-bidding that got the City such a bad name in the middle 1980s. All these developments are considered in detail in Chapter 3.

The internationalisation of the Stock Exchange does not end with the influx of foreign members in the wake of Big Bang. We have only to remember the impact that a fall on Wall Street had on the London market in October 1987 to appreciate that there is now a continuous market in shares. As one exchange closes another opens and improvements in telecommunications allow easy access to each of them. It used to be the British Empire upon which the sun never set; now, rather more prosaically, it is the international financial community.

Table 2.1 shows the importance of international business on the London Stock Exchange. Ranked in terms of the value of domestic shares listed, the London exchange seems a minor player by world standards. It is the scale of its foreign business that gives it international status. Over a quarter of the transactions taking place in London involve foreign equities. This well outstrips comparable activity in New York and Tokyo (turnover from foreign equity trading in London in 1988 totalled some £40 billion, one and a half times that of New York and ten times that of Tokyo). Nearly half the shares bought and sold outside their own countries are bought and sold in London. In comparison, though, our domestic stock exchange is small by international standards. London's share of total trade in equities within their own national boundaries is a mere 5 per cent. This, of course, largely reflects the small size of the UK economy. One of the less exciting side-effects of Big Bang was a merger in December 1986 between the Stock Exchange and the International Securities Regulatory Organisation. Whilst this may not have captured the popular imagination, it did introduce the word 'inter-

TABLE 2.1
Comparison of Major Stock Exchanges at End of 1988

Exchange	*Market value of domestic shares ($)*	*Number of domestic firms listed*	*Number of foreign firms listed*	*Foreign as percentage of total*
Tokyo	3840	1571	112	7
Osaka	3270	1091	0	0
New York	2367	1604	77	5
London	711	2054	526	20
NASDAQ*	355	4179	272	6
Frankfurt	230	355	310	47
Paris	224	459	217	32
Zurich	141	161	219	58

* National Association of Securities Dealers Automated Quotation System – a computer-based dealing system in the USA separate from the New York Stock Exchange

SOURCE *Quality of Markets Bulletin* (London: ISE) Spring 1989.

national' into the exchange's formal title. It is an appropriate description.

Unlike many of the markets of the City, the Stock Exchange actually is a physical location – just up the road from the Bank of England. This at first seems rather comforting, when so much City activity is disconcertingly abstract. Sadly, though, a visit to the Stock Exchange is not as much fun as it once was. The impact of telecommunications technology has removed virtually all dealing from the floor of the exchange itself. It now takes place in the already rather clichéd surroundings of vast dealing rooms where ranks of video screens report second-by-second developments in the market.

Retail Banking

Banking is another of the more accessible of the City's activities. Banks clearly provide the widest range of financial services – by attracting private savings and lending to business, they offer perhaps the most basic service of all. Increasingly, though, in the manner predicted by Jacob Rothschild, they offer a far wider range of services to their customers.

The word 'retail' in financial markets describes activities involving private customers rather than other financial players. The retail banks that most of us know and that are at the heart of the domestic financial system are the UK clearing banks. These include the 'big four' – National Westminster, Lloyds, Midland and Barclays – as well as the Scottish banks and newer additions such as the Cooperative Bank and the Trustee Savings Bank. Table 2.2 shows the relative sizes of the largest of these banks in 1988. They are known as the clearing banks because of their membership of the London Clearing House, an institution which exists simply to settle transactions between its member banks. For example, if on one day a Lloyds customer pays £50 to someone who banks at Barclays, and another Barclays customer pays £30 to someone who banks at Midland, the clearing house would arrange for Lloyds Bank to pay £20 to Barclays Bank and £30 to Midland Bank to settle all of that day's transactions. The clearing process has been much improved in the 1980s with the development in 1984 (surprisingly late) of an automated system for clearing cheques and with the establishment in 1985 of three separate clearing companies (for large payments, small automated payments and for cheques). These systems now extend considerably beyond the 'big four' to include building societies, and so the term 'clearing banks' can be rather misleading. It will grow even more so if other building societies follow the example of the Abbey National which, in July 1989 (when it was Britain's second largest building society), converted to banking status.

These domestic banks are distinguished by their immense branch networks which enable them to attract the huge sums in retail deposits that they use to fund lending to other, often corporate, customers. Over 80 per cent of British adults now have an account at one of them.

The 1980s have been a complicated period for the big four. They have been exposed to increasingly fierce competition at home from the building societies and, to a lesser extent, from foreign banks after the abolition of exchange controls in 1979. They have benefited from deregulation as cumbersome systems of control were abandoned in the early 1980s and yet have come under considerable pressure from

TABLE 2.2
The Major UK Clearing Banks and their Competitors in 1989

	Assets (£bn)	*Profits (£ million)*	*Number of branches*	*Number of staff*
Nat Westminster	116.2	404	2 997	86 600
Barclays	127.6	692	2 645	85 900
Lloyds	57.5	–715	2 184	62 400
Midland	62.5	–261	2 042	47 500
TSB	25.5	155	1 538	25 100
Standard Chartered	24.7	67	14	1 900
Royal Bank of Scotland	27.4	228	842	20 500
Bank of Scotland	14.1	179	527	12 100
Abbey National	37.2	501	678	13 600
Cooperative Bank	2.7	19	109	4 600
Girobank	2.5	22	21 030	6 600
Yorkshire Bank	4.0	113	251	6 000
Clydesdale	4.3	59	356	7 500
Building Societies*	188.8	—	6 915	80 148

* Figures for Building Societies are for 1988. No profit is recorded since they are not profit-making institutions.
SOURCE Banking Information Service, *Abstract of Banking Statistics*, May 1990.

the Bank of England to adopt lending policies that are thought to benefit the economy, as well as having been subject to private taxes on their profits. The Big Bang of 1986 gave them the opportunity, which all grabbed, to enter the securities market and offer share-dealing services to their customers. Midland acquired the brokers, Samuel Montagu, to form Midland Montagu which has since closed its dealing operations. Lloyds decided to build a more modest in-house dealing department but has had to withdraw from gilt-edged and Eurobond dealing. County NatWest was designed as an integrated securities house but had its problems, losing £116 million in

1987/8. Barclays was most ambitious, merging with prominent stockbrokers and jobbers to form Barclay de Zoete Wedd, which so far seems the most successful of the enterprises.

Although known in the UK primarily as domestic retail banks, each of the big four also has a merchant banking and international banking capacity. These have presented problems too. All were affected by their exposure to Third World debt in the 1980s, and Midland – the world's largest bank in 1947 – misguidedly tried to expand its international operations through acquiring part of the California-based Crocker National Bank. The losses were devastating and although Midland managed to pass Crocker on to the Wells Fargo Bank in 1986 the adventure cost a great deal – Midland is now itself part-owned by the Hong Kong and Shanghai Bank. Lloyds has hardly escaped more lightly, having to close Lloyds Bank International amidst rumours of fraud.

Deregulation has also encouraged these domestic banks to expand into less obvious areas. Lloyds has come from nowhere to own the largest chain of residential estate agents in the country. Barclays, Lloyds and TSB have become highly active in the life assurance market – selling their own products. We shall look into the changing face of banking and its implications in Chapter 4, as well as considering its role in the huge expansion of personal lending which occurred in the later 1980s, and which is shown in Figure 2.2.

Merchant Banking

While most people have heard of merchant banks, comparatively few could name many or describe their activities convincingly. Despite their more glamorous reputation, they are smaller and less well-known than the retail banks. They are not deposit-takers and so they have no need of extensive branch networks nor of a high profile with the general public. They are wholesale bankers. They lend to companies, to government institutions and to other banks.

The main function of merchant banks for many years was the acceptance business described earlier. By lending their name to commercial bills they accept the risk and thus make the bills more readily saleable. This task was not originally performed by banks at all but by prosperous and well-known merchants. Their service became so highly demanded that they specialised and developed into merchant banks.

FIGURE 2.2
Lending by UK Clearing Banks to the Personal Sector, 1983–9

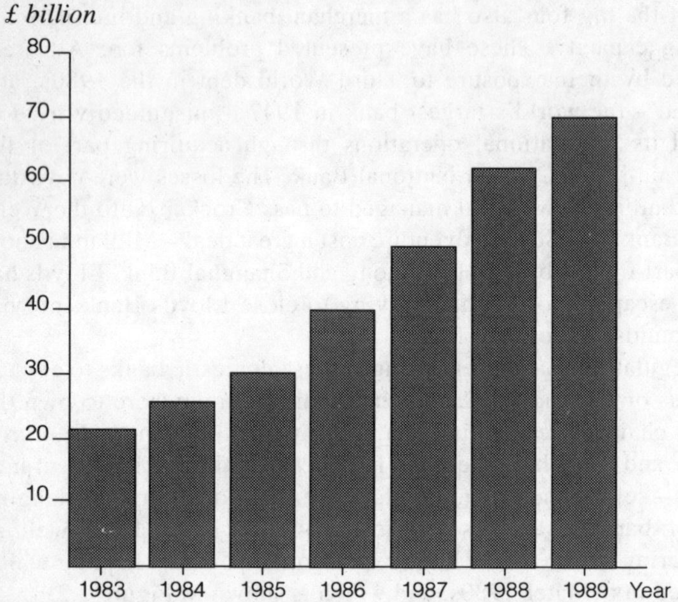

SOURCE Banking Information Service, *Abstract of Banking Statistics,* May 1990.

The banks have now established other areas of financial expertise – especially the issue of new shares (for which they are often known as issuing houses) and the provision of corporate financial advice. They have experience in putting together complex financial deals that aim precisely to meet the needs of their clients. The fees from these activities (handling a large privatisation issue, for example, or looking after the daily business of a multinational company) more than supplement their earnings from lending.

The 1980s have shaken up the merchant banking world too. Internationalisation, deregulation and securitisation affected all operators in the new City, but merchant banks in particular. They were traditionally 'niche' players – offering very specific services to very specific types of customer. They had always faced foreign competition but now they found themselves up against the vast banking houses of America and Japan. Big Bang on the Stock Exchange broke down further barriers and gave them full access to every aspect of securities business (if they wanted it).

The movement towards financial conglomerates has altered the role of merchant banks far more than that of their retail cousins who already had fingers in a great many pies. Some merchant banks have tried to carve themselves a role by forming the very sort of company to which Jacob Rothschild referred: S. G. Warburg has merged with major stock and gilts brokers and jobbers to form Mercury Securities; Kleinwort Benson and Morgan Grenfell have followed similar routes. Barings (once described as equal in importance to a national government) have, on the other hand, chosen to concentrate on their niche market.

The boom in mergers and takeovers in the mid-1980s provided a very handy opportunity for many banks to use their skills in corporate financial advice. Such corporate advice has become a boom industry in the City. The quality of the advice may have suffered as a result. In Chapter 4 we consider whether the 1980s have seen the demise of traditional merchant banking, and whether corporate clients are as well-served by their successors.

International Banking

For any trading nation a large portion of the financial needs of businesses will be international in nature. This will usually revolve around foreign currency dealing. The huge growth in international banking which, as we saw in Chapter 1, has been such a feature of the City for at least a century is based on more than this. It represents the first steps in the internationalisation of the financial community. Certain types of financial business – particularly the arrangement of large loans for multinational companies or national governments – could take place anywhere. London's traditional supremacy has attracted them here – along with the banks who wish to participate. One side-effect of the technological revolution may be to reduce the need to be located within the City in order to conduct this business. Some international banks have already begun to leave.

Nonetheless London's position seems fairly secure. It accounts now for around 20 per cent of all international banking business. The number of foreign banks has continued to grow (from 330 in 1975 to 521 in early 1989). American banks are the most numerous (at about 75) though Japanese representation is growing fast (there were 52 in 1989) and Western Europe also has a major presence (219 altogether).

Over the 1980s, though, London's position has been threatened. In 1980 over 25 per cent of all international banking business was transacted in the City. By 1989 it was down to 20 per cent. The main challenger, hardly surprisingly, has been Japan. Tokyo's share in 1989 was also 20 per cent – up, astonishingly, from just 5 per cent in 1980. The USA currently has 10 per cent of such business (down from 13 per cent in 1980). Table 2.3 gives a full account of these trends.

International bankers conduct two distinct types of business: foreign currency business for one's domestic customers, as distinct from genuinely cross-border business, where the customers as well as the business are international. Much of Japan's increase has been in the first category – arranging foreign currency deals for Japanese citizens. Nonetheless, Japan runs London very close in cross-border

TABLE 2.3
International Banking by Major Centre: Outstanding Lending as percentage of Total Market

	1975 (%)	*1980* (%)	*1985* (%)	*1989* (%)
Belgium	8.8	4.2	3.8	3.5
France	9.1	10.8	7.1	6.7
W. Germany	7.1	5.5	3.2	3.7
Italy	3.4	2.3	2.2	1.8
Switzerland	5.7	4.5	2.6	2.2
United Kingdom	27.1	27.0	25.4	20.5
Japan	4.6	5.0	10.8	20.6
United States	13.5	13.4	13.3	10.0

SOURCE Bank for International Settlements, quoted in *Bank of England Quarterly Bulletin*, November 1989.

business too – London has 19 per cent of the world market while Tokyo can boast 16 per cent.

There is no doubt, then, that this element of the new City faces a very real threat from Japan – even more so when it is recognised that Japanese banks in London were responsible for 36 per cent of the City's international bank lending in 1988, up from just 13 per cent in 1975. The assault is on two fronts: Tokyo rivals London as a centre and, at the same time, Japanese banks are coming to dominate lending out of London.

The Foreign Exchange Market

The nearest that most of us think that we get to the foreign exchange market of the City is changing currency before we go on holiday. Even then, our innocuous transactions seem far-removed from the world of international finance. Actually, we are more closely involved than we think. Whenever goods or services are traded across national boundaries – if we are buying goods manufactured overseas, or selling exports in foreign markets – currencies will need to be exchanged. The producer wishes to be paid in his or her domestic currency, while the consumers want to pay in theirs. Once again, then, the City is providing an essential financial service to other producers in the economy, enabling international trade to occur. Nor is the service restricted to clients within the British economy. The City is the world's largest centre for foreign exchange trading. Most of the customers are foreigners and, inevitably, much of the business is conducted by foreign firms who are located in the City.

The foreign exchange market has no physical location. Along with an increasing proportion of the City's markets, trading is conducted by telephone from large open-plan trading rooms in retail, merchant or foreign banks. As well as these dealers (called 'principals') the market also involves the services of specialist brokers whose job is to arrange deals with principals on behalf of clients. Brokers do not deal themselves but earn commissions by setting up deals. You will have noticed that virtually all the markets that we have considered have spawned their own brokerage communities which, it is claimed (by brokers at least), help the markets to work efficiently by bringing buyers and sellers together and by overcoming the understandable mystification of inexperienced outsiders. Others might suggest that their existence adds an extra layer to this mystification, as well as an extra layer to the final bill. About 38 per cent of foreign exchange business in London is conducted through brokers, and that proportion seems to be gradually falling (it was 43 per cent in 1986).

A survey conducted by the Bank of England (itself a major principal in the market) in 1989 estimated that approximately $187 billion worth of foreign exchange business is transacted in the City each day. This is an alarmingly large figure and seems to be increasing rapidly (up from $90 billion in 1986). London is still ahead of New York ($129 billion worth of business a day) and Tokyo ($115 billion), although they are catching up. Between them, the six major foreign exchange centres of the world (which include Switzerland, Singapore and Hong Kong) account for some $600 billion worth of daily business. Common sense tells us that these deals cannot possibly all relate directly to international trade in goods and services, the sums are far too large. There are other indicators: over 90 per cent of the business conducted in London involves the US dollar while only 30 per cent involves sterling and a similar proportion involves the Deutschmark. While these figures may tell us something, they certainly do not reflect the relative importance of the countries in Britain's trade. Straightforward international trade can acccount for only a small proportion of currency exchange in the City.

This can lead all too readily to pious and knowing references to the activities of speculators. One of the issues that will be addressed in Chapter 5 is the question of whether such speculators exist and, if they do, of the effects that they have in the market. There are, in fact, a variety of foreign exchange markets in the City. Currencies may be bought for delivery at once on the 'spot' market. This is still the largest element of currency dealing, though its share is declining (it was measured at 64 per cent of the total in 1989 compared with 73 per cent in 1986). Currencies may also, though, be bought for delivery in months or even years from the date of the deal. These are known as 'forward' contracts. Are such dealers speculating on future changes in rates? Or are they, as they would say, taking out a form of insurance against the same fluctuations? We will try in Chapters 5 and 6 to unravel some of the mysteries of forward markets (and of the dealing in options and futures that are still to be considered). We must also face up to the implications for currency markets of an inexorable tendency towards greater stability of exchange rates –

first through the Exchange Rate Mechanism (ERM) of the European Monetary System and thereafter, perhaps, through movements towards European Monetary Union (a single currency within the EC).

Futures and Options

If the Stock Exchange and banking represent the most accessible areas of the financial services industry, then dealing in futures and options contracts must surely be among the most obscure. It falls to few of us to experience any part of these markets directly and, inevitably, we tend to feel suspicious of their value and even of their morality when we are introduced to them.

A futures contract is simply a deal to deliver something – we shall call it the product – on a specific future date but at a price set today. An option, on the other hand, gives the buyer the right to buy the product on a future date at a price set now. The difference is small but significant: a futures contract is dealing the product at a future date while a traded option is dealing the right to buy or sell it rather than the product itself. Futures markets developed initially, like the forward currency market outlined above, as a means of hedging against price fluctuations that might affect the profitability of a deal. The first attempts were in agricultural markets in the USA where prices could swing wildly from year to year. By making a future deal at a fixed price it was possible for buyer and seller to sleep easily at night. Inevitably, of course, one of them was likely to have lost and the other won – since prices would actually be higher or lower than on the contract that they had agreed. This made it possible to gamble in such contracts, agreeing perhaps to sell goods at a certain future price in the hope that the market price would actually be lower and that it would therefore be possible to buy the goods in the future at a low price and sell immediately to the holder of the futures contract at the agreed higher price. In this way, futures dealing ceased to be so closely related to markets in the products themselves and became a quasi-speculative activity. Dealers in wheat futures on the Baltic Exchange in the City today are unlikely to have come any closer to their product than their breakfast toast. They are dealing in pieces of paper rather than in wheat, and only a tiny proportion of the deals lead to actual deliveries of wheat being made. They would be quick to insist, though, that the basic purpose is the same as ever it was.

Businesses still use futures markets as a means of hedging against future changes in the prices of products – be they commodities, exchange rates or financial instruments.

The USA is the international centre of futures and options dealing, with the major exchanges being in Chicago. Table 2.4 shows that London, Amsterdam, Paris and Tokyo are creeping up but that Chicago still boasts almost 80 per cent of the world market. There are six separate markets in the City where such contracts are traded: the Baltic Futures Exchange which trades agricultural and freight futures (the last as an extension of its original function as a centre where ship-owners could meet merchants with cargoes to be carried and vice versa); the International Petroleum Exchange (IPE) where contracts in fuels are bought and sold; the London Futures and Options Exchange (LFOX) which trades sugar, coffee and cocoa; the London International Financial Futures Exchange (LIFFE) where financial instruments including exchange rate contracts and loans at specified interest rates are traded; the London Metal Exchange (LME) which, of course, handles contracts for base metals; and the London Traded Options Market (LTOM) which trades options in shares, in gilts, in currencies and a new product based on changes in the *Financial Times* Ordinary Share Index.

Whilst the products traded in these markets may be obscure, the markets themselves are amongst the most colourful and hectic that remain in the City. Trading still takes place by the 'open outcry' system; the scene fluctuates from periods of total inactivity, to trading so noisy, chaotic and aggressive that it is difficult to believe that anyone has much idea of the deals that have actually been made. Much dealing, as in so many other financial markets, relies upon the services of specialist brokers.

These markets are, in a way, the clearest evidence of the existence of a new City. Dealing in futures and options contracts had been happily left to Chicago. It was a brash and pushy business to which Americans seemed naturally suited and which would have sat unhappily in the heart of the old City. London firms might deal, but the markets were not British. Table 2.6 shows that London's real growth in this area has been the trade in financial futures conducted at LIFFE – an exchange which has only been in existence since September 1982. Many of its members represent international banks and most of its dealing is in international instruments. We look at it in Chapter 6 and whilst it would be wrong to describe such a

TABLE 2.4
Futures and Options Exchanges: Shares of World Trade, 1985–9

Exchange	*1985* (%)	*1987* (%)	*1988* (%)	*1989* (%)
London:				
Baltic	0.1	0.1	0.1	0.1
IPE	0.1	0.2	0.3	0.5
IFOX	0.6	0.4	0.7	0.6
LIFFE	0.8	2.0	2.5	3.1
LME	0.7	0.7	1.4	1.4
LTOM	0.7	1.9	1.5	1.8
Total:	3.1	5.2	6.6	7.5
Chicago	94.1	84.0	80.7	78.1
Amsterdam	1.7	1.7	1.6	2.1
Paris	0.0	1.9	3.0	4.0
Tokyo	0.1	2.9	3.9	3.2

SOURCE *Bank of England Quarterly Bulletin*, November 1989.

comparatively small and specialised City market as a representation of the new City itself, nonetheless its youth, vigour, lack of regulation and internationalism centred as they are in the old Royal Exchange building oppposite the Bank of England and in the very heart of the old City make it as handy a symbol as any.

Money Markets

The money markets of the City represent to some the more obscure aspect of the financial services industry. Indeed, the very notion of a market in money may seem rather strange at first. In fact, it describes nothing more than the traditional features of so much City activity – borrowing and lending. Key players in the money markets of the City are the bankers – retail, merchant and international – that have been outlined above. The markets do not exist in a physical sense, dealing is conducted by telephone and loans can vary from the very short term (overnight, perhaps) to a far longer time-horizon of a number of years.

If the loans are arranged in sterling, then the activity is on the sterling money market, where borrowers are likely to be British firms or the British government or British local authorities. Loans may, on the other hand, be arranged in foreign currency, in which case the Euromarket is involved. The loans here are likely to be larger and the borrowers may be national governments, or, perhaps, multinational companies. The Euromarket, though, is simply a market that lends and borrows funds that are being held outside their home country.

The processes of these markets are broadly similar. Borrowing takes the form of selling a security, sometimes called a financial instrument or, more commonly, a bond or bill. The seller of such a security promises annual interest payments over a given number of years in exchange for a lump-sum payment when the security is sold. If it is denominated in sterling, then it will be dealt with in the sterling money markets of the City. If it is in a foreign currency then it will be in the Euromarkets. In many cases the dealers are the same, all that differs is what is being dealt.

The sterling money market is of most interest to outside observers as the medium through which the government, through the agency of the Bank of England, seeks to influence short-term interest rates. It is also here that those peculiarly British institutions, the Discount Houses, operate. As well as explaining their role, Chapter 7 will look at their prospects in the wake of deregulation which has removed their privileged dealing relationship with the Bank of England.

The Government is also involved in the sterling money market as a major borrower. It issues a specific security of its own for this purpose known as a gilt-edged security. The market in gilts forms its own subsection of the sterling money market and it has undergone more than its share of development over the 1980s. Most obviously, the supply of gilts has dried up considerably as a result of the government reversing its need to borrow to finance current expenditure and instead running a sizeable budget surplus. As well as this, deregulation has had its impact on the gilts market, for Big Bang allowed more firms to deal in gilts – many of these firms have since had to withdraw as satisfactory profits eluded them. The Government has even experimented with entirely new techniques of gilt issue. These are explained in Chapter 7.

Predictably, securitisation has had a major effect on these markets. As formal loans were increasingly rejected in favour of the sale of securities, the business of the markets grew correspondingly hectic. The Eurobond market based in the City was especially affected. Eurobonds are simply bonds denominated in a foreign currency which thus enable the borrower to tap into the huge volume of Eurocurrencies being held in deposits outside their country of origin. In 1989, 65 per cent of such bonds were issued in London and an even larger proportion of secondary dealing (dealing in bonds that are already issued) took place there. Out of 114 recognised dealers in such securities, 80 were located in London. We saw in Chapter 1 that much of the success of the City was based on the development of this market. In Chapter 7 we consider what it holds for the future.

Insurance

Insurance is another of the areas of the financial service industry that is readily recognisable. Most of us at some time insure a car or a house or our life. The insurance companies and markets of the City are involved in this same business, though on the grand scale. Insurance offers the service, of immense value to all customers but especially businesses, of reducing risks. While the insurers take on the risks of fire, theft, accident or whatever, businesses can concentrate their attentions on the commercial risks of their enterprise. The City frequently boasts of its contribution to the British balance of payments, but special credit should be given to the insurance industry. The City's overall international surplus in 1988 was reckoned to be some £10 billion of which the insurance industry contributed £4 billion.

The insurance market can be subdivided in a number of ways. One method appropriate to the City is to distinguish between the insurance companies (many of them familiar: Prudential, Legal and General, Norwich Union, General Accident, Sun Alliance, etc.) and Lloyd's of London which is a separate and unique insurance market. Lloyd's is not an insurance company, nor is it in any way connected with Lloyds bank. It is an organisation which enables risks, often very valuable ones, to be insured by syndicates of wealthy individuals. Clients with risks to insure contact brokers. Brokers usually specialise in particular types of business and do not themselves bear any of the risk. Their role is to find business to bring to the market. In the increasingly competitive world of international insurance they frequently have to travel a long way to find such business – especially to the USA which can boast over half of the whole world's insured risks. Brokers do not, of course, have to take the business to Lloyd's. They can place it with one of the companies if they wish. Lloyd's is particularly suited to the insurance of large and unusual risks. The broker wishing to bring business to Lloyd's must find an underwriter who will take on the risk. Underwriters are the people who actually offer insurance, but since the risks are great they do not take them on alone but as a member of a group of individuals called a syndicate. Our broker will approach underwriters in the underwriting room of the extraordinary Lloyd's building in the City. He will know the syndicates and their specialisms and thus have an idea of whom it is best to approach first. The underwriter will examine the risk and decide whether to accept it on behalf of his or her syndicate. In accepting it, the underwriter also sets the premium (the cost to the client). If the risk is large, the underwriter may well only accept a part of it, in which case the broker must approach other syndicates to cover the rest. Behind any insurance deal, there must somewhere be a large sum of money that is available if the worst happens. The curious aspect of Lloyd's is that this financial backing actually comes from wealthy individuals who join the syndicates in the hope that their share of premium income (which can, of course, be invested to bring a greater return) will considerably outweigh their share of the claims that have to be paid. These non-professional syndicate-members are known as 'names' and include sporting and show-business personalities as well as rich businessmen. Ultimately, their success or failure depends upon the skill of their professional underwriting agent who decides whether or not to accept the risks and what the premiums will be.

Lloyd's remains an important and successful part of the British insurance market. Its share of world insurance business is falling – it stands now at less than 1 per cent – but it still reckoned to contribute £1 billion of the £4 billion earned by the industry as a whole in its international work in 1988. The 1980s were a trying time, though. A series of scandals (which are outlined in Chapter 9) seemed to expose weaknesses both of organisation and regulation. Huge broking companies have come to dominate the market and, by acquiring underwriting businesses, conflicts of interest seem increasingly likely. In 1988 the number of Lloyd's 'names' began to decline for the first time in twenty years, presumably in alarm at some of the stories emerging from the market. A new regulatory framework has been in place since 1982 but it has not been universally welcomed and it is not yet clear that the troubles of Lloyd's are over.

Another distinction in the world of insurance is between primary insurance (which is the sort of direct insurance of risk that we have so far considered) and reinsurance. Reinsurance, which has been a major growth area in recent years, is a wholesale activity that occurs when underwriters (whether at Lloyd's or elsewhere) take out insurance themselves against a particular claim being made upon them. It is, effectively, a way of spreading risk ever more widely. Without a thriving reinsurance market, some of the high-value risks that arise from activities such as oil exploration and space technology could not be easily underwritten. Most reinsurance is carried out by specialists (some Lloyd's syndicates specialise in it) and many of them are located in London. A new reinsurance centre is planned to open in London in 1991 and, if successful, should complement Lloyd's to make the City the centre of the rather dramatically named high-value catastrophe market.

International competition in the insurance world is fierce, particularly from America, Japan and Germany. Changes in European markets after 1992 may well intensify competition from German companies. Offshore centres are developing (untroubled by domestic regulation) in Guernsey, Luxembourg and Bermuda. London's share of the market is falling. Risks are changing too. A number of underwriters have made serious losses on business involving new risks such as AIDS, asbestosis, environmental pollution and American litigation. The City is still a major insurance centre but it will have to fight hard if it is to remain so.

Fund Management

There is a further side to the insurance market. Life insurance is customarily considered separately from the more general areas that were addressed above. Since death is a certainty and, thus, not technically a risk, life insurance is unlike other insurance. This is why it is often described as assurance rather than insurance (death, unfortunately, is assured). There are many vast life insurance companies in the City of London (Prudential, Legal and General, Commercial Union, etc.) From our point of view, they represent a separate financial service altogether. They collect together immense funds from their customers in the form of premiums which can then be invested in and lent to industry in order to earn the returns that provide the lump sums and endowments that are guaranteed when policies mature or clients die.

There are other investing institutions. Pension funds are among the largest. A boom in private pension plans over the 1980s has helped them to grow further. Investment and unit trusts are also very important. In each case, small savers are invited to buy shares (or 'units') in the trust. A huge fund is thus accumulated, which professional managers administer. The theory is that the fund is large enough, and the managers sufficiently skilful, to balance risk and profitability in such a way as to achieve a far higher return than savers could manage alone.

These institutional investors spread their enormous funds around a variety of assets – property, gilt-edged securities and equities are the most popular. Over 80 per cent of the shares quoted on the Stock Exchange are owned by institutions. Private saving in this way is actively encouraged by the tax system (payments are tax- deductible) and so the influence of the managers of the funds becomes ever greater. Such funds represent a higher proportion of GDP in the UK than in any comparable country. Fund management is therefore an important element of City activity and an increasingly international one. British fund managers look after funds from Europe, America and Japan. Institutional investors have been criticised in the past for taking too little interest in the companies in which they invest and for starving certain areas of cash altogether. They are, nonetheless, highly influential; in Chapter 3, we consider their influence.

The City's Contribution

So, the City serves the business community in a variety of ways. It was summed up neatly in *The Bank of England Quarterly Bulletin* of November 1989: 'Developed capital markets contribute to the efficient allocation of funds and hence the supply side of the economy more generally, as well as offering effective payments services and a spectrum of choice for savers'. Exactly how efficient these markets really are is a matter to which we shall return frequently in this book. James Tobin wrote in the *Lloyds Bank Review* of July 1984 on the efficiency of the financial system. He came to no startling conclusions and he certainly welcomed the process of deregulation, but his article was penetrating. Regulations had led to a standardisation of financial products. Deregulation has therefore vastly increased choice in the market. But standardisation is cheap, so deregulation is likely to have increased costs too. His conclusions about advancing technology were similar: 'I suspect that the immense power of the computer is being harnessed to this "paper economy", not to do the same transactions more economically but to balloon the quantity and variety of financial exchanges.' He went on to voice his fear that the increased ease of dealing in a greater variety of financial instruments had its greatest effect in facilitating further and more complex types of speculation rather than benefiting the productive economy. This is clearly another matter that requires investigation.

It is only fair that we should add here that the financial sector is an industry in its own right and thus that as well as servicing other producers, employers and exporters, it is a major producer, employer and exporter itself. Table 2.5 shows that financial services (represented by the classification 'Banking, finance, insurance, business services and leasing' in National Income accounts) have increased their share of GDP from around 10 per cent in 1975 to over 18 per

TABLE 2.5
Financial Sector's Share of GDP, 1975–88

	1975 (*£ billion*)	*1985* (*£ billion*)	*1987* (*£ billion*)	*1988* (*£ billion*)
Financial sector (BFIBsL)*	10.0 (10%)	48.5 (15%)	65.6 (17.5%)	76.9 (18.5%)
Rest of economy	88.1	273.4	309.3	416.8

* Banking, finance, insurance, business services and leasing
SOURCE National Income and Expenditure (CSO).

cent in 1989. Shares of total employment have grown similarly, from 8 per cent in 1981 to almost 12 per cent in 1989. It is true that employment in the securities industry fell after the 1987 crash; banking and insurance have continued to experience an astonishing increase, though. There were 154 000 more jobs in these sectors in 1990 than at the time of the crash – a 20 per cent increase in three years.

The City's trading performance is already fairly well publicised. It is a major source of the UK's invisible earnings, contributing some £6 billion in 1989, to a total net invisible earnings of £11.7 billion. Table 2.6 shows the contributions of other major invisible earners. These figures show gross earnings; they are, in almost all cases, smaller than the net contribution of the financial sector. The city's performance did appear to drop off towards the end of the decade. The £6 billion surplus of 1989 should be compared with one of £7.3 billion in 1988. The reasons lie in some large pay-outs by the insurance industry, and interest payments by bankers to the many overseas savers attracted by high UK interest rates. The City is at pains to interpret this as a purely temporary phenomenon. It might be the first sign of some weakening in our competitiveness, though. The UK's positive balance is, certainly, relatively greater in this sector

TABLE 2.6
Other Major UK Invisible Earners, 1979–89

	1979 (£ million)	*1988 (£ million)*	*1989 (£ million)*
Tourism	2797	6184	6877
Shipping	3807	3526	3870
Civil Aviation	1755	3192	3578
Expenditure by overseas students	306	743	792
Telecommunications and postal services	154	692	788
Films and television	112	324	363
Land freight	74	230	302
Advertising	40	128	125

SOURCE British Invisibles, *Statistical Card*, September 1990.

than those of any of our major competitors. It seems, then, that the UK does genuinely have a comparative advantage in the provision of financial services and that it has in the 1980s been able to exploit this advantage in an expanding market. This success, as was pointed out earlier, is in many ways the success of the institution of the City itself in attracting international business (along with international practitioners to conduct it), rather than specifically of the British firms operating there. The City's international role was curiously illustrated by Iraq's annexation of Kuwait in 1990; the exiled Kuwaiti government was able to carry on the country's financial business virtually as normal since its assets were largely held in the City of London. The global market has produced a supranational financial sector based around centres like London.

Why London?

Finally, it is worth wondering exactly why London seems to have such a disproportionately large share of much of the world's financial business. In part, of course, the reasons are historical and were addressed in Chapter 1. As the fastest growing economy and the most important trading nation of the world for many years, the UK was ideally placed to develop an expertise in financial services. More recently, though, other factors have become more important in explaining the City's ability to attract international business. London has a pool of suitably trained labour, a reasonable tax regime, a tendency towards less regulation, a good supply of office premises, a widely respected legal system and, importantly, political stability. The English language is traditionally the language of finance. All these items have helped to develop external economies of scale for financial operators in London. Firms can benefit from close business contacts with each other and from the specialist ancillary services of lawyers, accountants and so on. Additionally, financial markets are thought to be among those that become more efficient with more participants and so the process becomes circular.

There is another reason, for the City's success that is more fortuitous. London lies in a central time zone between the USA and the Far East. Inevitably, with the USA, Europe and Japan representing the world's major economic blocs three financial centres are bound to dominate. New York, Tokyo and London are so placed around the world that an hour or two before one closes the next opens. A dealer in London can watch Tokyo in the morning and New York in the afternoon. The crash of 1987 showed graphically how waves of pessimism could follow the globe on its axis like the setting sun. There is a sense, then, that, while it may be discomforting, competition from New York and Tokyo does not genuinely threaten the City. Competition from mainland Europe, from Germany for instance, might. Greater integration within Europe after 1992, along with steps towards monetary union and the possibility of a prominent role for the Bundesbank need to be taken seriously. Salaries, property prices, rents and rates within the City rose dramatically over the 1980s and must have made it less attractive to international operators than it once was. Germany, even after unification, is unlikely to be able to eclipse the City but the threat should not be too readily dismissed.

3 Crazy Years at the Stock Exchange

The Market Goes Mad

The 1980s can lay a substantial claim to having been the most extraordinary period in the long history of the London Stock Exchange. Most people can remember the crash of 1987, at the height (or depth) of which 100 000 deals were conducted on the Exchange in a single day and prices were changing so fast that the computer screens that display them went blank. Many would also recall the Big Bang of 1986 which drove an international juggernaut through the country village that was the traditional London Stock Exchange. Some might even point out that the monster privatisation share issues – British Telecom, British Gas, the local water companies, the regional electricity suppliers – must have contributed to the decade's particular profile.

It goes back earlier than all this, though. There was more to the 1980s than Big Bang, even on the London Stock Exchange. The decade saw one of the most prolonged and dramatic bull markets that has ever occurred. In the strange jargon of the Stock Exchange this refers to a period when the prices of shares are, in general, rising. It contrasts with a bear market, when prices are falling. Changes in share prices are measured by the *Financial Times*-Stock Exchange Share Index (the FT–SE Index) which is an average of the prices of shares in one hundred of Britain's largest, most prestigious companies. The hope is that the companies reflect such size and range of activity that, between them, they give a fair indication of what is happening on the market in general.

Figure 3.1 shows movements of the FT–SE Index over the 1980s. Starting from round about 600 in 1981, the Index rose steadily to about 1600 in the period before Big Bang. This represents an approximate tripling of share prices in five years. It is, indeed, dwarfed by the 60 per cent increase in prices (from 1600 to 2600) that took place in less than a year between Big Bang and the summer of 1987. Nonetheless, the sustained increase in activity after 1981 is

FIGURE 3.1
The *Financial Times*–Stock Exchange 100-Share Index 1979–90

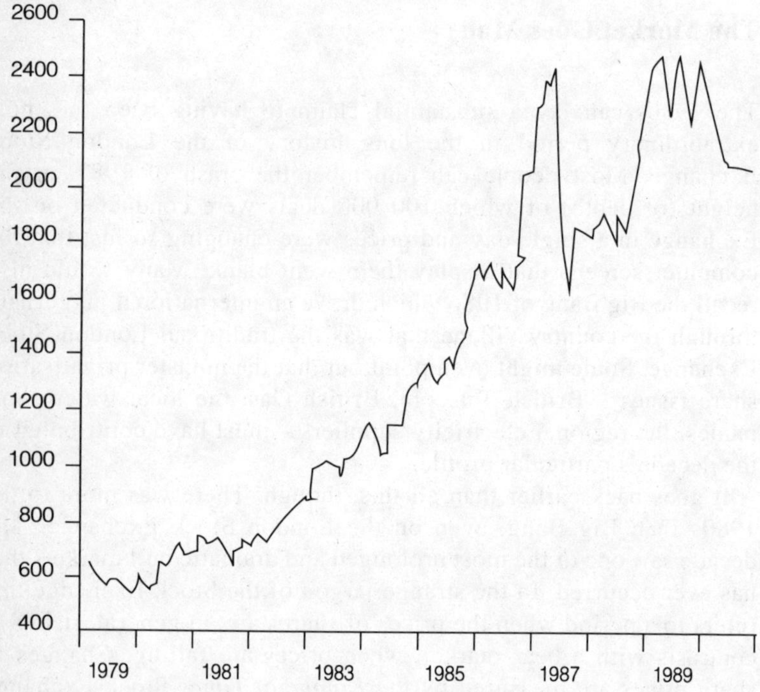

SOURCE Datastream.

quite remarkable. It cannot be attributed to privatisations – the first large flotation (British Telecom) was not until 1984. Nor can it be explained by Big Bang, which did not occur until October 1986. Even after the crash, which reduced the FT–SE Index by 22 per cent in four days, it was back up to 2200 in October 1990, a day or two after the UK joined the Exchange Rate Mechanism of the European Community.

The extraordinary increase in activity is not only reflected in price rises. Average daily turnover on the London Stock Exchange increased from £128 million in 1981 to £716 million in 1986. Even allowing for the effect of increases in prices (which, as we have just seen, roughly tripled over this period), this still means that the volume of business more than doubled in five years. In 1981 there were, on average, 15 600 deals conducted per day. By 1986 this had risen to 30 200. The actual number of shares traded in the year rose from a modest 24 billion in 1981 to 78 billion in 1986. This all predates Big Bang which caused a further surge in market activity. It suggests that even before Big Bang rocked the boat the stock market was already going through a crazy period. We saw in Table 2.1 that the growth in new issues on the market was also remarkable – from £1.7 billion worth in 1983 to over £12.7 billion worth in 1987. The impact of Big Bang itself seems to have been to cause a market that was already buoyant to become positively intoxicated. Daily business increased by an astonishing 50 per cent in the first six months of 1987, easily passing the £1 billion mark. The average size of share deals rose from £91 000 to £250 000 over the same six months, presumably as a result of increased institutional dealing. Altogether, both up to the crash of 1987 and, after a period of adjustment, beyond it, the level of activity in the London stock market increased phenomenally. In 1981 dealing in shares constituted only 17 per cent of the activity on the Stock Exchange (the bulk of the remainder being in gilt-edged stock). By the middle 1980s, interest in shares had revived sufficiently to raise this figure to a creditable 28 per cent.

Do these developments of the 1980s mean that we have witnessed a major transformation in the London stock market? Or was all this a temporary madness? To find answers to these questions, we need first to look back to the market of the early 1980s, and investigate the origins of Big Bang.

According to Cecil

The most well-publicised element of Cecil Parkinson's three-month stay at the Department of Trade and Industry in 1983 was the manner in which it ended. A seamy sex scandal breaking during a Conservative Party conference is bound to eclipse the more humdrum work of a departmental minister. In any case, three months is not a long time in which to stamp lasting change upon the industrial landscape. Nonetheless, the Accord reached in July 1983 between Mr Parkinson and the Chairman of the Stock Exchange, Sir Nicholas Goodison, was to form the basis of what came to be described by many as a revolution. This was the origin of Big Bang and an important signpost along the road to the new City. Ironically, the Accord was seen by many at the time as a political fix.

The job of the Office of Fair Trading (OFT) is to investigate any practices which it suspects are being used by firms as a way of restricting competition and thereby denying benefits to the consumer. In the middle 1970s, it began to take an interest in the Stock Exchange. The system in those days was one in which dealing was done on behalf of customers by stockbrokers who charged a commission for their services. They did not hold shares themselves, but dealt with another group, stock-jobbers, who did. Jobbers' profits came from selling to brokers at a higher price than they bought from them (the so-called 'jobbers' turn'). What interested the OFT was the system of fixed minimum commissions that the Stock Exchange allowed brokers to operate. The simple result of this was that brokers did not compete with one another by price. As the institutional investors (such as insurance companies and pension funds) took over from private shareholders, brokers found themselves dealing with fewer and fewer customers but making larger and larger deals. A fixed commission system made this most lucrative. At the same time, the larger brokers came to offer their services as fund managers on behalf of these institutional investors. They offered the service free of charge but of course took a commission on every deal that they themselves advised. The temptation to 'churn' their clients' portfolios (buying and selling shares unnecessarily, simply to generate commission) was also enough to raise the suspicions of the OFT.

Brokers did attempt to practise some non-price competition by offering research services or, more mundanely, long lunches and generous days out. But competition was clearly restricted. Membership of the Exchange was restricted to private individuals. Incorporated firms could not join. This meant that all broking and jobbing firms had to take the form of partnerships (like so many accountants and lawyers). Profits were distributed amongst the partners, which was most attractive for them but made it hard for the firms to accumulate much capital for expansion. Indeed, there seemed little or no advantage in doing so. Member firms were all small – especially so when compared with the huge organisations that dominated other City markets in banking, insurance and so on – and, predictably, British.

In 1979 the Director General of Fair Trading referred the Stock Exchange to the Restrictive Practices Court for a ruling as to whether or not its practices were against the public interest. Fear extended beyond the Exchange itself. This challenge might only be a foretaste of what was to come for other City markets. Perhaps this was why the Bank of England tried so hard to persuade Cecil Parkinson (as they had failed to persuade his predecessors) that the case against the Stock Exchange should be dropped in place of the 1983 Accord by which the Exchange agreed to abandon the scale of minimum commissions and to relax some of the rules covering membership.

On the face of it, the accusation of a political fix does not seem too wide of the mark. The real origins of that Accord, though, lie not in local difficulties with politicians and bureaucrats, but rather in a more deadly threat from the USA.

Straws in the Wind

It was pointed out in Chapter 1 that the abolition of exchange controls in 1979 was a major cause of the changes that were to come in the 1980s. It certainly affected the securities market. The existence of controls had made it hard for the Stock Exchange to compete satisfactorily for international business. With a thriving domestic market, this may not have seemed especially serious. Competition was gathering, though. The abolition of fixed commissions on Wall Street in 1975 encouraged the institutional investors of the USA to deal in vast quantities of securities, since they were now able to negotiate considerably reduced commissions. This in turn led to the establishment of huge brokerage houses, fat with the earnings from this enormous increase in business. These houses, along with their Japanese equivalents, were naturally attracted to the international scene and came to dominate the London Eurobond market. For now the combination of exchange controls and the restrictive membership rules left the Stock Exchange apparently safe from them. It was a safety that could not last.

The abolition of exchange controls allowed British investors to deal in an international market. Between 1979 and 1984 they spent some £18 billion on foreign securities. As much as 95 per cent of these overseas investments were handled by foreign firms who could simply offer a cheaper service than their British counterparts. Foreign brokers may not have been allowed to join the Exchange, but there was nothing to stop them from locating in London to be close to the newly unfettered institutional investors of the City. British life insurance companies raised the proportion of their assets invested in foreign securities from 2.9 per cent in 1979 to 9.2 per cent in 1983. Over the same period British pension funds increased their proportion from 5.5 per cent to 14.7 per cent. As early as 1980 the Stock Exchange began to make concessions in the light of these developments. Jobbers, in particular, were allowed access to outside dealers in the market for international equities. If they had not been, then London would have lost access to this lucrative international business.

The huge market in Eurobonds was dominated at this time by American brokerage houses who were not restricted by the distinction between broking and jobbing capacities. They could buy and sell bonds on their own account and then deal from their own stocks with clients. This gave them a major advantage over their small and cumbersome British competitors. In recognition of this, British firms were allowed to operate 'dual capacity' in the Eurobond market – operating as both broker and jobber. The abolition of exchange controls made it only a matter of time before this would have to be extended to Stock Exchange operations. If single capacity could not compete in Euromarkets, then neither could it in equity markets. Nor was it competing: in 1982 the combined profits of the entire London Stock Exchange were smaller than the $500 million earned by a single New York dealer, Salomon Brothers. In the process of competitive deregulation that has come to dominate the 1980s, if the

Americans can operate more cheaply than the British, then the British must change to the American rules or they will lose their market. The British *were* losing their market too. By the early 1980s, over five times as many shares were being traded in New York as in London. Most gallingly, this included shares in prominent British companies like ICI, BP, Glaxo and British Telecom. Indeed, British institutions who were disappointed to be allocated such a small portion of the huge British Telecom privatisation issue in 1984 were happy to find afterwards that they could buy most of what they wanted on the Wall Street market through the dealer Morgan Stanley.

Viewed from this angle, the 1983 Accord and the Big Bang which followed in 1986 were not so much directives from above as simple acknowledgements of the way things were. Big Bang, in fact, was merely the work of international market forces.

Indeed, many of the key changes of Big Bang were actually under way well in advance of the great day in 1986. Many of the small jobbing firms had been merging throughout the 1960s and 1970s in an attempt to increase their capitalisation. The number of jobbers declined over these two decades from 104 to thirteen. The Stock Exchange was forced to allow brokers and jobbers to be part-owned by outside companies simply to allow them to raise sufficient capital to ensure a reliable market in large quantities of shares. Big Bang led to a vast increase in this activity, but it was going on before. Similarly, commissions were reduced in 1976 and again in 1982 before becoming fully negotiable in 1986. Brokers and jobbers were already conducting much business, particularly in foreign equities, off the flooor of the Exchange by telephone and were even signalling the end of single capacity by deals in which brokers found both buyers and sellers and passed the deal through a jobber (at much reduced cost) simply for form's sake. In 1984 insistence on single capacity was relaxed for Stock Exchange members dealing in international equity and bond markets.

Perhaps what is most surprising about Big Bang in the light of all this is that it should have been so long in coming. As we can see, it was inevitable and was actually well under way before 1986. The 1983 Accord referred to nothing more than a phased end to minimum commissions and slight changes to the rules governing outside involvement. Had they stuck to this (and as late as 1985 Stock Exchange members still voted against extending membership to foreign firms) then the days of the Stock Exchange would indeed have been numbered.

Big, But Not Much of a Bang

If Big Bang was so obvious, so inevitable, so unremarkable, you could be forgiven for wondering how it appeared to cause such dramatic changes in the City of London.

The reasons are complicated. First, the combination of changes that Big Bang represented was remarkable for it embodied not only the deregulation that was, in many ways, overdue but also the technological change that was to alter the entire manner in which these markets operated. So the Stock Exchange was reforming everything at once. Second, developments that appear inevitable with the benefit of hindsight may well have seemed crazily extreme at the time – particularly in markets that had been protected from some of the harsher aspects of the real world. Third – and again with the benefit of hindsight – it can be argued that Big Bang need not have caused all the drama that it did. Perhaps the City did overreact. Perhaps the crash of 1987 was in part a result of this overreaction. Perhaps the City got it wrong.

Big Bang embodied five separate changes in the operation of the Stock Exchange:

- the abolition of minimum commissions;
- the ending of single capacity;
- the extension of membership to corporations;
- permission for outsiders to own up to 100 per cent of member firms;
- the replacement of face-to-face dealing by a computerised system.

Taken on their own, these reforms are by no means surprising. Minimum commissions had to go if the Exchange was to compete for international business. Without minimum commissions, existing member firms would not be able to generate sufficient capital from single-capacity trading to offer a reliable market in large quantities of shares. Dual capacity (operating as both broker and jobber) would be more profitable. If the market was to compete internationally, though, the members would need an even larger capital base – hence the need to allow corporate membership as well as funding from outsiders. Finally, developments in information technology meant that a market could operate with far greater efficiency if it was computerised. Once again, the rigours of international competition made this essential and the cost of the necessary investment provided a further reason to extend membership to well-capitalised corporations and to attract money from outsiders.

It is worth noticing in passing that a major development at the back of all these changes was the rise of the institutional investor. These monsters can trade shares in batches as large as a million at a time. An efficient market requires dealers who can happily buy shares in these huge quantities. Traditional London jobbers were too small for the task. The rise of the institutions quickly exposed the under-capitalisation of the London market and was, in a sense, directly responsible for the eventual abolition of single capacity and all the other changes that went with it. It was these same institutional investors, of course, who were also most directly hurt by the system of minimum commissions.

Predictable and necessary though they may have been, the reforms of Big Bang were a great deal more penetrating than the mild tinkering implied by the 1983 Accord. The post-1986 market is entirely different from its ancestor:

- Dealers are not small but, for the most part, are divisions or departments of huge financial conglomerates.
- Where once all dealers were British, now many are owned by Japanese or American parent companies.
- Rather than the strict, slightly unnatural distinction, between brokers and jobbers, member firms are now all broker-dealers who deal both on behalf of clients and on their own account. In addition, many agree to be market-makers in specific classes of share – meaning that they will readily trade with any other broker-dealer wishing to buy or sell.
- If you wish to buy shares today, you will contact a broker-dealer who will check a computer screen to see the current prices being offered by the various market-makers. The broker-dealer may either sell you shares himself or arrange the deal for you from the most keenly priced market-maker. In either case, he must be able to prove that he secured you the best possible deal.
- Thus trading no longer takes place on the floor of the Stock

Exchange but by telephone in vast City dealing-rooms equipped with banks of computer screens.

So, Big Bang did revolutionise the market even if the revolution was a long time coming.

Musical Chairs in the Madhouse

A major part of the revolution was that incorporated firms (even foreign-owned ones) could now join the Stock Exchange. The era predicted by Jacob Rothschild in his 1983 speech was suddenly upon the City. Conglomeration became the name of the game. A period now began in the crazy 1980s which makes the other developments seem positively well-balanced. It was widely believed that deregulation would liberate the London stock market and that business, particularly from overseas and from institutions, was bound to increase. The belief was, of course, quite correct. The action taken on it was not altogether well-advised.

Before the ink from Cecil Parkinson's pen was dry on the 1983 Accord, large financial institutions outside the Exchange (particularly banks) were looking around for ways of cashing in on this great new opportunity. The story goes that Lord Camoys, vice-chairman of Barclays Merchant Bank, rang London from his holiday in Ibiza on the day of the Accord to instruct his staff to start looking for an appropriate stockbroker for the bank to acquire. Lord Camoys was ahead of the field. Merger activity was subdued during 1983. It became absurdly hectic in 1984. Hardly a week passed without an announcement of some new grouping being formed. By Big Bang itself over 100 such alliances had taken place. The Bank of England reported in February 1987 that 65 outside entities had taken stakes of various kinds in Stock Exchange members. The vast majority of these were British, European, or American banks. Membership of the Exchange rose from 200 firms before Big Bang to 360 afterwards – and these member- firms were bigger, better-capitalised and, perhaps, more ambitious than their predecessors. Every jobbing firm finished within one of these newly formed conglomerates, and only one broker (Cazenove) chose to remain independent. The increase in dealing capacity on the London Stock Exchange was extraordinary – 13 smallish jobbers were replaced by 31 large and bullish equity market-makers. The details of the various mergers that occurred are recorded fully elsewhere, a few examples will serve here: in 1984 Barclays bank acquired 85 per cent shares in the stockbroker de Zoete & Bevan and the jobber Wedd Durlacher Mordaunt to form Barclays de Zoete Wedd (BZW), the most ambitious move by a British commercial bank; the merchant bank, S. G. Warburg, put together another particularly ambitious merger when they acquired the stockbroker Rowe & Pitman, the government gilts broker Mullens and the jobber Ackroyd & Smithers to form Mercury Securities; the huge American bank, Citicorp, picked up a couple of brokers (Vickers da Costa and Scrimgeour Kemp-Gee) and a Discount House (Seccombe Marshall & Campion).

Some of these deals seemed odd even at the time. Morgan Grenfell failed to acquire a stockbroker at all, but instead spent £10 million on the small gilts broker, Pember & Boyle. They appeared to believe that one broker was much the same as another. With hindsight, it just seems to illustrate how little the bankers knew of the market they were so crazy to enter.

The sums paid in many of these acquisitions by supposedly hard-nosed investment bankers also seem, on the face of it, examples of some form of collective hysteria. Warburg paid £42.5 million for Rowe & Pitman whose assets were valued at around £9.6 million. The Barclays deal cost some £200 million – the combined asset value was less than £100 million. The costs did not end when new businesses were acquired. Dealing-rooms had to be set up complete with the necessary computer technology. The largest rooms in the City have positions for about 700 traders. It was reckoned at the time that the necessary financial investment came to about £30 000 per trading position.

Nor was there any real doubt that a good deal of this investment must ultimately be ill-advised. Whilst everyone expected the market to grow after Big Bang, few believed that this would justify the increase in capacity that had actually occurred. Everyone knew that there would be losers. Everyone thought it would not be them. The way to win was to get the best team in your dealing and market-making departments. The way to get the best team was to offer the silliest salaries and inducements. Not only did they pay over the odds for companies, but also for individuals. This was the origin of so much of the folk image and the colourful vocabulary of the 1980s City – golden hellos (lump-sum payments to attract new employees), golden handcuffs (payments dependent upon a given length of service), the mobile marzipan layer (dealers just below partnership level who were not receiving the icing on the cake when companies were acquired and were thus ready to move if the inducement was right) and so on.

In the cold light of reality, the market did go temporarily crazy. Decisions were made about acquisitions, employment and salary structures, which could not possibly all be justified. County NatWest, for example, paid over £20 million for the jobbers, Bisgood Bishop, and then watched the bulk of the market-making team leave just one week later, poached by rivals. It is tempting to suggest that if their customers were to behave in the manner in which many bankers behaved between 1984 and 1987, they would be quick to receive stiff-necked criticism.

At the opening of this chapter, we wondered whether the remarkable behaviour of the stock market over the 1980s was the result of a genuine and permanent transformation or simply a temporary hysteria. The realignment in the light of Big Bang shows that it was both. Big Bang itself was an extremely important, if long overdue and inevitable, development. It transformed the Stock Exchange by dragging it into the international securities market. It also permanently altered membership of the Exchange in a huge way. Dealers today are operating on behalf of immense international financial corporations. As we shall see, huge dealers attract huge customers. Nonetheless, the extent of merger activity in the wake of Big Bang was excessive and temporary. When the market settled, some form of normality and sanity would have to return. It did.

Beware of the Bull

It is worth remembering that the crazy years of the London Stock Exchange predated Big Bang. We have already seen that many of the reforms and liberalisations that constituted the Big Bang package were actually well under way before 1986. We have also seen that prices on the market had been roaring since the early 1980s. The extraordinary price increases in the wake of Big Bang tend to eclipse the enormous increase in activity that occurred before it. Was this bull market all part of the madness?

Once again the removal of exchange controls in 1979 had its part to play in boosting the market since it allowed British investors to deal in international shares with far greater ease. Increased opportunities are bound to generate increased business. Similarly, the government's privatisation policy increased interest in equity markets and successfully introduced a whole new category of small investor to the market.

The real reasons for the extraordinary developments of the 1980s are probably more mundane. For years, in the 1970s, UK stocks had been undervalued. In the end this was bound to lead to an increased demand for them as they were perceived to be potentially profitable, especially as progressive deregulation attracted voracious international institutions to the scene. High interest rates in the early 1980s encouraged firms to consider other ways of raising capital. Share issue was high on the list. This helps to account for the boom in new issues at the start of the decade and may itself have generated interest in equity markets. A similar boom in new issues can be detected over the later 1980s when, once again, companies faced very high rates on traditional bank borrowing. The securitisation boom had its effect too. Companies rediscovered the use of securities (mainly bonds) as a means of borrowing. These had distinct advantages (which are explained fully in Chapter 4) over bank loans. The main impact of securitisation was an astonishing increase in the issue of bonds. Nonetheless, one by-product was that it reinvented the fashion for active dealing in pieces of paper. It is a small step for dealers in bonds to perceive the profit potential of shares. Similarly, securitisation encouraged City dealers to take a more active interest in the company sector. Again, this is likely to encourage share dealing. Once it begins, of course, active share dealing can become self-sustaining – particularly during a bull market. A period of rising prices makes shares a very attractive investment, since it comes increasingly to appear that one cannot lose from buying them. This fuels further buying and further price rises. The market spirals upwards until a sudden crisis of confidence (as occurred in October 1987) blows it down like a house of cards.

Further to this, renewed interest in the equity market and a rediscovered passion for security dealing helped to fuel a boom in mergers and takeovers. An active market, with specialist observers, makes it easy to spot companies who are currently undervalued by their share price. A bull market allows one to pay for an acquisition with shares issued for the purpose. During 1986 and 1987 about

1800 companies were acquired in the UK. These deals were paid for with some £8 billion in cash and £18 billion worth of shares. A good deal of the increased stock-market activity of the 1980s can be put down to the merger boom which, as well as thriving from the bull market, also helped to sustain it.

There are other factors: the Conservative government reduced and, for a period in the late 1980s, abandoned the issue of gilt-edged stock. Dealers looked around for something else to trade – shares represent one option among many. Nonetheless, the great bull market was really a temporary phenomenon easily explained in terms of the peculiar circumstances in which it occurred.

The enormous increase in activity between 1986 and 1987 must have been largely a consequence of Big Bang itself. Table 3.1 shows how dramatically prices rose at this time. During the first six months of 1987 business was nearly 50 per cent above the level of the months immediately before Big Bang. The average size of a share bargain tripled to around £250 000. Daily turnover reached over £1 billion. The reasons for all this are not hard to find: there was already a bull market;in addition, Big Bang increased the number of dealers considerably; and, most significantly of all, it introduced intra-market trading to the London market in a big way. The new market-makers needed to carry large quantities of their chosen stocks (classified into *alpha*, *beta*, *gamma* and *delta* categories) in order to be ready to deal. As well as acquiring these from outside customers, they could, of course, buy from other market-makers. The growth in this type of business was alarming. It was sufficiently large to spawn a whole new breed of trader: the inter-dealer broker. These are brokers who deal on behalf of market-makers but do so anonymously, so that other market-makers are not aware of how their rivals may be adjusting their holdings. It is reckoned that all this intra-market dealing amounted to 40 per cent of total turnover in the months after Big Bang. The market-makers and dealers involved were now all part of large, well-capitalised financial conglomerates, eager to establish strong positions in their chosen stocks. Inevitably, this boosted the bull market further.

Big Bang also liberated the institutional investors. In the days of minimum commissions they had been subject to high charges on the London market. Once commissions became negotiable – and some market-makers were prepared to deal with large customers on a 'net' basis, charging no commission at all and relying upon buying and selling alone to generate profit – the incentive to deal on a much larger basis was obvious. It is worth noting that, while the size of the average share deal rose to £250 000 after Big Bang, about 80 per cent of deals were still for less than £10 000. This implies that the remaining 20 per cent (from the institutions for the most part) must have reached immensely large sums, well into the millions of pounds.

Viewed from this angle, the crash of 1987 was inevitable. Share prices theoretically represent the value of the companies quoted. It is hard to put this to the test, but one method is to calculate price/earnings ratios. This seeks to relate the price of a share to the profits of the company. Profits are divided by the number of shares to establish the earnings per share. This is then divided into the share price to give the price/earnings ratio, which effectively tells you how many years it will take to recover the cost of the share. The higher the answer, the more expensive shares are deemed to be. Average price/earnings ratios in the UK rose some 50 per cent between 1982 and 1987. Economic prospects may have been improving with faster growth and slower inflation, but this surely suggests that the increasing prices of the early and middle 1980s were only partly due to circumstances affecting the companies themselves. Much of this bull market was more to do with developments within the market itself (both pre- and post-Big Bang) than with events in the wider economy.

The Crash Restores Sanity

The specific causes of the crash have been well-documented. They lay in doubts about the US federal and trade deficits and in fears of future interest-rate increases (to support the dollar) pointing the world economy towards a recession. There were other, more mundane, factors at work in London, though.

It was well known that there was excess market-making capacity on the London Exchange. Dealers were expecting some form of cataclysm. When Wall Street started it off in October 1987, it was widely believed that the time had come. Greenwell Montague had already withdrawn from equity trading after losing £6 million in five months. The Midland bank withdrew after even greater losses. Competition had reduced profit margins. The crash created further losses. BZW were said to have lost £50 million as a result of it. Warburg lost £4 million in a week. This did not directly cause many liquidations but it did lead to a rationalisation of some of the decisions taken in the heady days of Big Bang. It had to – business in 1988 fell to some 65 per cent of pre-crash levels. Total market losses in 1988 were estimated at around £500 million, and the figure for 1989 is not much lower. An attempt by Citicorp to revive business by means of a price war in 1988 met with little success. If anything, it made the losses bigger. Ten thousand redundancies were announced in 1988 alone. Salary structures and bonus systems were restored to sanity. There were other casualties – Morgan Grenfell withdrew from the market in 1988 and Chase Manhattan followed in 1989. It would be wrong to think that these withdrawals were caused by the crash, even though the market remained fairly sluggish for much of 1988. Far more importantly, they were the result of the excessive optimism and mistaken decisions that preceded Big Bang. The losses made by major banks in the decade following the pre-Big Bang mergers of the early 1980s beggar belief: Barclays and Citicorp are each reckoned to have lost £300 million on securities dealing; NatWest just £200 million.

There are other aspects of the crash that reveal characteristics of the new market. The first, and perhaps most obvious, is that the equity market is now global. Panic was transmitted from time zone to time zone in a most dramatic way. Much of the loss of value of UK stocks actually occurred when the London market was closed. This suggests that we should be prepared for wilder fluctuations in share prices in the future as markets feed off one another's behaviour and give rise to cumulative international waves of optimism and pessimism. We should not conclude, though, that all national market developments will automatically be transmitted internationally. In 1990 the Tokyo market experienced one of the most sustained and dramatic falls in recent history, yet New York and London survived virtually unscathed. Waves of optimism and pessimism *can* now be easily transmitted from centre to centre but, if dealers believe that price changes have specific local causes, then they will treat them as such. The new market circumstances can certainly create global volatility but we should be wary of the conclusion that they always will.

The isolation of dealers in the new market can exaggerate such waves though. At the height of panic during the crash, it was believed that certain market-makers were deliberately failing to answer their telephones. This heightened the panic in a way that might not have occurred with traditional face-to-face trading. Prices were falling so quickly that the SEAQ (Stock Exchange Automated Quotation System) screens could not record them and displayed a 'fast market' symbol. This may well have contributed to panic too. It was believed that 'programmed trading' – triggered by computer programmes – added to the mayhem as well. We shall look at this in the context of trading in share options in Chapter 6.

Although the crash was an unusual event, it might still be claimed that it was simply the means by which the new equity market came finally to terms with itself. It was the watershed between the crazy optimism of the previous seven years and the more measured good sense that dominated the market afterwards. Any rising market must come to an end. Study of Figure 3.1 could lead to the conclusion that the sudden boom of 1986–7 took share prices way above their long-term trend line and that the crash was, therefore, necessary to restore prices to trend.

After the Smoke has Cleared, What Changed?

It is palpably true from what we have covered so far that the new Stock Exchange differs dramatically from its distant ancestor that was dozing happily in 1979. It is now a major part of an international securities market. It is dominated by huge international member companies. Its organisation (with broker-dealers and market-makers rather than brokers and jobbers) is entirely new. Their method of dealing (by telephone and computer) is also completely different from the face-to-face work of the old Exchange. The floor of the Stock Exchange is now virtually empty and, with the merger of the London Traded Options Market with LIFFE, will become redundant. Ironically, all that remains of the old market is an archaic settlement system whose computerisation (by means of TAURUS) has been much delayed (its latest deadline is late 1990) and which is still markedly slow and paper-heavy.

Behind all this, though, there are more significant questions to ask:

- Has the new market reduced costs for customers?

- Has it helped to restore the small investor to equity markets?
- Does it serve the needs of the quoted companies any better?

Taking costs first, we know that Big Bang was born out of a need to reduce commissions and thus attract business back to London. Table 3.1 shows that the average commission did indeed fall over the 1980s. This was, however, as a result of commissions coming down on deals valued at £20 000 or more. The costs of smaller deals actually rose. The real gainers, then, have been the institutions who have been able to negotiate cost savings as a result of the immense volume of their business. In 1986 there was a strong move towards dropping commissions altogether for institutional investors, but the investors themselves reacted against it when they discovered that it deprived them of access to the research service provided by dealers. Nonetheless, in 1988 24 per cent of deals were executed net of commission. The institutions provide less than 40 per cent of dealers' commission revenues. The other cost element in a share deal

TABLE 3.1
Stock Exchange Commissions, 1983–8

Bargain value (£)	*March 1983* (%)	*July 1986* (%)	*July 1987* (%)	*July 1988* (%)
0–600	3.83	6.81	6.45	5.69
601–2000	1.65	1.53	1.93	2.00
2 001–10 000	1.38	1.26	1.43	1.46
10 001–20 000	0.79	0.72	0.86	0.86
20 001–50 000	0.56	0.58	0.52	0.47
50 001–100 000	0.49	0.41	0.34	0.31
100 001–150 000	0.41	0.32	0.27	0.25
250 001–1 000 000	0.35	0.31	0.25	0.23
1000 000+	0.22	0.14	0.20	0.20
Average rate	0.58	0.43	0.45	0.37

SOURCE *Quality of Markets Quarterly* (London: Stock Exchange).

FIGURE 3.2
Ownership of Shares, 1957–89

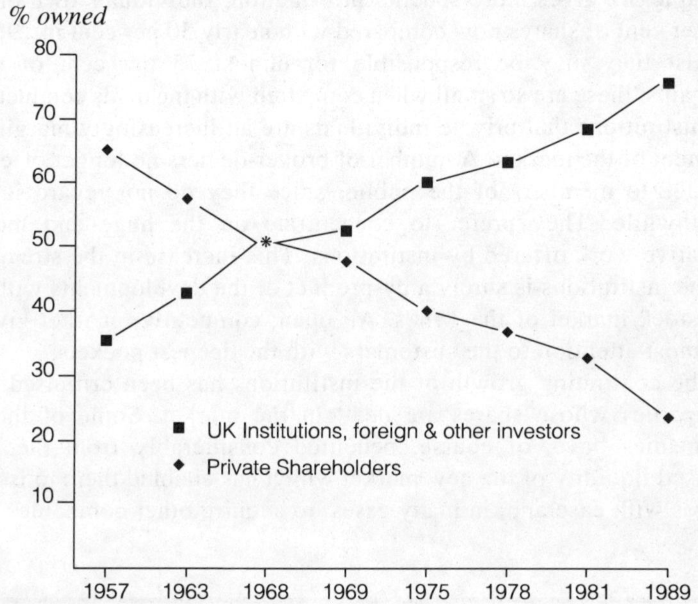

SOURCE *Who owns the Blue Chips? Stock Exchange Surveys*, (UBS Phillips & Drew); *Economic Affairs*, November 1990.

is the spread between buying and selling prices offered by a market-maker. These have fluctuated considerably over the decade, principally due to changes in market activity. When the market is very busy, spreads can be small. In the dull period after the crash, though, they inevitably widened again. There is little firm conclusion to draw here about the nature of the new market.

On the question of the small investor the conclusion is clear and predictable. Privatisation issues have certainly led many private individuals to purchase shares who had never done so before. The government estimated in 1988 that 20.5 per cent of the adult population owned shares of some kind, 15 per cent in privatised companies. Sadly, as Figure 3.2 shows, the trend away from private share ownership and towards the domination of the institutional investor has not only been maintained duriung the 1980s but has, in fact, gathered pace.

Table 3.2 gives more specific information. Individuals own only 20 per cent of shares now compared with nearly 30 per cent in 1983. Whilst they may be responsible for almost 75 per cent of the bargains, these are so small when compared with the deals conducted by institutions that private individuals are an increasingly marginal element of the market. A number of broker-dealers no longer offer a service to members of the public, since they do not regard it as worthwhile. They prefer to concentrate on the huge and more lucrative work offered by institutions. This increase in the strength of the institutions is surely a by-product of the developments within the stock market of the 1980s. An open, competitive market gives the most attention to the customers with the deepest pockets.

The continuing growth of the institutions has been criticised by companies whose shares are dealt in the market. Some of these companies have, of course, benefited considerably from the increased liquidity of the new market which has enabled them to issue shares with ease and, in many cases, to acquire other companies by

TABLE 3.2
Ownership and Dealing of Shares in the UK, 1983–8

	Value (%)			*Bargains(%)*			*Average bargain size (£ thousand)*		
	1983	*1986*	*1988*	*1983*	*1986*	*1988*	*1983*	*1986*	*1988*
Major institutions	29.6	33.6	34.9	5.8	7.8	7.3	56	113	156
Other institutions	30.1	26.5	28.4	9.3	9.7	9.8	35	73	85
Others*	11.9	21.3	17.3	8.0	9.0	11.2	15	52	50
Individuals	28.4	18.6	19.4	76.9	73.5	71.7	4	7	9

* Authorised dealers and market-makers in the UK and overseas
SOURCE *Quality of Markets Quarterly* (London: Stock Exchange).

judicious use of equities. Others, though, reckon that the market serves them ill. They complain that dealing is concentrated disproportionately in *alpha* stocks (those of the largest, most prominent companies) which causes excessive volatility for them and becalms shares in smaller, less fashionable companies. They say that the market is only interested in short-term developments and does not consider longer-term possibilities. Thus it can unfairly mark down share values in companies whose long-term prospects are good. It is said that institutional researchers are interested only in applying statistical rules of thumb to company accounts, rather than taking an interest in the particular circumstances that may be affecting a company or an entire industry. The institutions are thought to watch one another too closely and thus produce an identity of view that can lead to wide swings in share prices unjustified by circumstances. The institutions are so large, of course, that their combined deals can cause genuine concern in the market. The new market makes dealing easier for them and they deal in even larger quantities as a result. Most seriously, fund managers have been accused of fuelling hostile takeovers. Since their only interest is profit, they are likely to accept attractive offers for shares regardless of the actual strengths and weaknesses of existing and potential company managers.

Altogether, a number of entrepreneurs have become outspoken in their criticism of behaviour in the new market – by which they generally mean the interaction of market-makers and institutional investors. Richard Branson withdrew the Virgin Corporation from the stock market believing that these important dealers were not sufficiently concerned with the best interests of the company. Andrew Lloyd Webber did the same with his Really Useful Group. These accusations are very serious for, if the reform of the market actually makes it less effective at serving the needs of the company sector, then the supposed benefits of the new market must be questioned very hard.

Criticisms of the new equity market do not end there. Immediately after the crash of 1987, new issues of shares fell off dramatically. There is no great surprise in that, for confidence in the market was bound to have taken a knock. New issues remained low in 1989 and 1990. The volatility of the market since the crash has led a number of companies to fear that a Stock Exchange quotation could leave them vulnerable to hostile takeover. This is more worrying. One of the major functions of an equity market is to provide a reliable means of valuing companies. If entrepreneurs fear that the market may underprice shares and thus needlessly expose their companies, then it is failing in this responsibility. Price volatility has also caused underwriters to increase the cost of insuring new issues against failure. This must further discourage use of the market.

Some aspects of dealer behaviour have led to criticism too. 1990 is said to have seen the introduction of 'bear raiding' to the London market. Unscrupulous dealers circulate a rumour (which they know to be untrue) about a company with the intention of driving down its share price. They sell shares in the company, which they do not yet own. They then watch the price fall as the rumour takes hold. When they judge the price to have fallen far enough, they buy sufficient shares to honour their previous commitment to sell. In this way they have bought at a low price and sold at a high one, but in an unusual order. In the meantime they have done considerable damage to the standing of the unfortunate company. The market's concern may quickly extend to corporate bankers, clients and beyond. Asil Nadir attributed the collapse of his Polly Peck Corporation in 1990 to behaviour of this kind. Rumours on that occasion were said to have included the suggestion that Mr Nadir himself had been shot. Of course, such rumour-mongering is notoriously difficult to prove. It is especially worrying for the fact that, if the rumours are to be believable, they presumably have reputable and respected sources. The new market may be more susceptible to behaviour of this kind, for traders isolated at computer terminals are thought by some to be more gullible and more liable to panic than they used to be. Perhaps it was harder to lie when dealing face-to-face.

It was long believed that the Stock Exchange did too little to help smaller companies. The increasing power of investing institutions is bound, as we have seen, to concentrate dealing in the shares of well-known, well-respected 'blue chip' corporations. Attempts have been made to redress this imbalance. In 1980 the Unlisted Securities Market (USM) was established. About 600 shares are quoted and turnover is respectable. In January 1987 the Third Market was set up catering for newer companies (only a year of revenue-earning is necessary). Interest has not been great. There are few dealers and they themselves are small.

Further To Go

The comparative failure of the Stock Exchange to cater satisfactorily to the needs of smaller companies and smaller investors – a failure which may actually have been reinforced by the dramatic developments of the 1980s – has led to the suggestion that the greatest reform of all may be on the way: competition for the Exchange itself. There is nothing to stop others setting up a service to arrange dealing in equities. It has been tried. In the middle 1970s a group of merchant bankers established ARIEL (Automated Real Time Investment Ltd) which offered a computerised dealing system some ten years before the Stock Exchange. It did not last (perhaps because the Bank of England refused permission for the quotation of gilts). It only managed 1 per cent of the equity market. Nonetheless, the impact of competition was sufficient to induce the Stock Exchange to reduce commissions in 1976.

In 1984 Robert Fleming, a merchant bank, took on the Exchange by offering a market in certain specified UK shares. By 1985 they had won 10 per cent of dealing in some industrial categories. Others followed: the European Banking Company, for example, specialised in chemical and pharmaceutical shares. In the end, Big Bang brought all these activities within the Exchange again. Nonetheless, a principle was established. The Bank of England had not instructed these companies to cease their activities. Indeed, the merger between the Stock Exchange and the International Securities Regulatory Organisation (ISRO) in 1985 (to form the International Stock Exchange) was really founded in a need to prevent the ISRO from competing directly with the Stock Exchange to provide a market in international equities.

The Exchange may have something to fear from foreign competition too. The movement towards a single European market in financial services in time for 1992 is bound to encourage overseas centres to practise the sort of deregulation that has characterised London in the 1980s. The London market has certainly won business as a result of the arthritic nature of some of the equity markets of Europe. It may be that, as the drive towards a single market helps to cure the arthritis, some of this business will return home. Of course, there will also be improved opportunities to compete for business that has previously been trapped within national boundaries by domestic regulations. Nonetheless, London has less scope for improvements in efficiency than most of the other European centres and so it can only win business by concentrating on its traditional skills and reputation. It can no longer rely upon inefficiencies abroad. The London Stock Exchange's proposal to centralise European equity trading (presumably along lines similar to London's own) unaccountably failed to find favour elsewhere in Europe.

In August 1990, John Redwood, the Government Minister for Corporate Affairs, raised the issue of the Stock Exchange's monopoly on equity trading by suggesting a new market to cater specifically for the needs of smaller companies and small investors. Such a market would operate in a different way from the current Stock Exchange. The existing market is 'quote-driven' – it is based on dealers who advertise the prices at which they will buy and sell. A new market might be 'order-driven' – based on investors themselves who offer specific deals to the market. This should provide more scope for dealing in shares whose market is currently small.

Mr Redwood was at great pains to preface his comments with colourful praise of the international achievements of the Stock Exchange in the Big Bang decade. He would like to see 'a bigger drive for domestic business'. There is an extravagant irony within all this if we care to look for it.

The Stock Exchange of the 1970s was becalmed in a largely domestic market, unable to meet the challenge of gathering foreign competition. A process of rapid and traumatic deregulation changed it almost beyond recognition. The systems have changed, the dealers have changed, the investors have changed, even the stocks traded have changed (involving far more foreign stocks than before). The inadequacies of the market have changed as well. We now have a market in which a number of huge international corporate dealers encourage a smaller number of huge international corporate investors to turn over huge quantities of shares in a fairly small number of huge international corporations. It seems to be extremely efficient and competitive at what it does. But there have been costs:

- Company ownership is concentrated in the hands of investors who may not have the best long-term interests of the companies at heart.
- Research and broking facilities that are so valuable to the small

investor are expensive, and have been reduced in favour of increased institutional and intra-market dealing.

- Costs for small investors have increased anyway.
- Trade in less-fashionable shares has declined. The difference between buying and selling prices of *gamma* stocks was reckoned to be 8.5 per cent in June 1990 – about twice as high as the level prior to Big Bang, implying riskier, reduced business.

All in all, the market may actually be less suited to the needs of many domestic companies than it was before Big Bang. The fact that the developments of the 1980s were inevitable and overdue should not hide the ironic possibility that they may have left the market less efficient at catering to the needs of quoted companies.

Sir Kit McMahon said archly in 1990 (when he was Chairman of Midland Bank) 'We are only halfway from Big Bang to where we are going.' If we are aiming towards a market that is fully efficient both domestically and internationally, then 'halfway' may be verging on the optimistic.

4 The Death of Banking

Other People's Money

Sad to say, but to most people, banks are boring. They may be necessary, handy, reliable, even helpful but they are not much fun. Advertisers have pillaged the imaginations of popular film-makers in a doomed attempt to give bankers a credibility that veers ever so slightly towards the dashing and modern, but it does not seem to work. In the end, apparently, there is a limit to the thrill that can be got out of looking after other people's money.

Surprisingly, though, this perceived dullness does not seem to extend throughout the profession. It is mainly the prerogative of the commercial banker. These are the ones with whom we deal on a day-to-day basis. As well as being known as 'commercial banks', they are also variously called 'clearing' and 'high street' banks. They are characterised by extensive branch networks. They attract deposits from private individuals and private companies and they use this cash to back loans to other private individuals and private companies. They are huge (the 'big four' account for some 44 per cent of private deposits between them), solid and worthy. If banks were represented as private cars, then the commercial bank would be a large, sensible family saloon – a Ford, perhaps, or, at its most exciting, a Volvo. There are other banks, though. And some of them enjoy a very different sort of image. Merchant banking has become almost a by-word for the brash, buccaneering, jet-set world of high finance. Where commercial bankers are staid, sober and respectable, their colleagues in the merchant-banking arm of the profession are thought to be bold, wild and dangerous. If commercial banks are represented by a sensible family saloon, their merchant cousins would be a dashing two-seater sports model – an MG or, more appropriately, a Porsche.

Somewhere in between these two images – a Jaguar or a Mercedes, perhaps – is the international banker. International banking is generally regarded as more exciting than domestic commercial banking, presumably because it involves foreign travel and high-level negotiation in the plush board-rooms of random continents. But it still lacks some of the dash of merchant banking. After all, it is still just looking after other people's money, even if some of the people are foreign.

It is my sad duty to inform you that these perceptions and judgements are today entirely without foundation. Perhaps once, in the halcyon days of the old City, it was all true (though I doubt it). Not any more. I will not go so far as to say that banking is interesting – that will be for you to decide. But the notion that there are different types – classes, even – of banking is no longer the case. The old distinctions between commercial and merchant, domestic and international, even retail and wholesale (the one that we introduced innocently in Chapter 2) will not do any longer. In the new City, banking, as we used to think of it, is dead. There was always more to it than looking after other people's money. The single simple word 'banking' is really a shorthand term for a wide range of financial services. Even so, over the 1980s the nature of the provision of these services has changed virtually out of all recognition. To all intents and purposes, there are no longer different types of bank, just different companies, some of which call themselves banks. By the same token, we can no longer separate with ease those financial services that fall naturally within our shorthand 'banking' category. Banking today covers every type of financial service: deposit-taking; lending; dealing in securities; market-making; broking; advising; foreign exchange dealing; even supplying insurance. Every single aspect of the industry now falls within its ambit, along with a number of services whose relationship to traditional banking is, at best, marginal: estate agency, specialist legal services and so on. This is not to say that all banks do everything, nor that every company that gingerly dips its toes into the water of financial services is automatically a bank. The simple truth is that the traditional image and categories of banking have ceased to exist. In that sense at least, banking is dead. What we must now seek to discover is why this has happened, and what it means for the future.

The World's Banker – or Landlord to the World's Bankers?

There is another story that runs alongside this one and that must also form a theme and backbone to this chapter. We touched on it in Chapter 2. It concerns the status of the City as an international banking centre. It is no exaggeration to say that the City's reputation as a financial centre has been based more than anything else upon its ability to secure an enormously large share of international financial business. A great deal of this falls within the general category of banking. The process goes back hundreds of years, but the most acute period of growth was in the 1960s and 1970s when the development of Euromarkets based in London led to a vast increase in international financial business. The statistics are hardly credible: in the early 1960s the value of Eurobonds issued in London (by borrowers who wish to tap into the large deposits of Eurocurrencies that exist) totalled some $100 million; by the middle 1980s the figure was in excess of $200 billion.

The fact that these international markets became centred in the City is a matter of some pride for London. It reflects the high regard in which the accumulated skill and experience of City operators is held in the financial world. It also reflects some other factors which are more accidental: London's central position in world time-zones and the status of English as the language of international finance. More than all these, it reflects the generous regulatory system that for years distinguished the City from its overseas rivals. The domestic markets of the City may have been protected by exchange controls and hedged around by a strict set of rules operated by the Bank of England. As far as international business was concerned, though, the City was able to operate as a giant off-shore banking centre. The transfer of non-sterling assets and liabilities in and out of London could be managed with virtually complete freedom. This obviously made the City a considerably more attractive home for international bankers than most other financial centres.

The growth of international banking in the City was always more a concentration of foreign banks than a recognition of the superiority of the British. UK banks do of course conduct their share of international business, but it has been regarded by some as a surprisingly small share. To describe the UK as the world's banker was always to exaggerate. The situation is rather that a remarkably large proportion of the world's bankers have located themselves in London (where they employ British specialists as well as benefiting from the generous British regulatory system). In the late 1950s there were about eighty foreign banks in the City. By the late 1980s, the figure was over 500. In this sense, then, London's international success was more as landlord to bankers than as banker itself.

It looks, though, as if this might all be about to change. The City's success was based upon its comparative lack of regulation. Over the late 1970s (with the development of International Banking Facilities in New York) and the 1980s (when the Japanese followed suit and established the Japanese Offshore Market) deregulation has caught on everywhere. The so-called 'level playing field' (where rules are much the same in all financial centres and competition is genuinely keen) appears to have arrived in the field of international banking. This could be very bad news for the City whose success in this area was built on a 'playing field' that, from the British point of view, was downhill all the way. Table 2.3 shows very clearly that the UK's share of international lending, which in 1975 was over twice as large as that of our closest rival (the USA), is now smaller than that of Japan. The influx of foreign banks into the City has slowed to a trickle. Some American banks have left. Deregulation has (as we shall see) reduced the need for a Euromarket at all.

There is another sense, then, in which we can talk of the death of banking. International developments seem to spell the end of London's supremacy as a world banking centre. Is this as serious as it sounds? If so, what does the future hold? These questions form a secondary theme that will be addressed in this chapter.

To recap, then, we are seeking to explain two separate but linked phenomena: the changing face of traditional banking in the UK; and the future of London as an international banking centre. A number of individual factors – international debt; securitisation; Big Bang; international and domestic deregulation – are in part responsible for both of these developments. We must consider them.

The Shadow of Debt

International finance is dogged on the grand scale by the problem facing countries with balance-of-payments deficits who need to find some means of financing them. The traditional manner in which this has occurred has been for wealthy private individuals in other countries to buy stock issued by the deficit nation. The 1980s saw a particularly clear example of this when the USA's huge deficit was in part funded by the sale of large quantities of government securities to savers in Japan – enabling the Americans to accumulate yen with which to buy more Japanese imports. The system can create problems (as in the late 1980s when the supply of Japanese savings began to dry up) but it is broadly reliable.

In the middle 1970s, circumstances conspired to develop a new system. The oil crisis of 1973–4 generated huge balance-of-payments surpluses for the oil-exporting states of the Middle East. These sums were in dollars (still far and away the most important currency for international trade, and especially trade in oil) and found their way, unsurprisingly, into the huge Eurodollar market based in London. This inflow of currency was one factor that enabled the Eurodollar market to increase in size twentyfold during the 1970s. These markets are the province of private banks rather than international agencies and so the international banking world found itself able and eager to lend sums on a scale that had previously never even been contemplated. The sums inevitably were recycled to the biggest borrowers – nations with balance-of-payments deficits (caused ironically by the need to pay vastly increased prices for oil supplies). Most of these countries were from the developing world.

The principle of private banks lending to sovereign states was a new one. Previously such lenders had either been smaller (private individuals buying government stock, as explained earlier) or larger (international agencies such as the IMF or the World Bank). High inflation helped to fuel the lending. Deficit countries reckoned that real interest rates were likely to be low (or negative) and were therefore happy to borrow on a large scale. Countries with surpluses sought the highest possible rates of return and were therefore attracted to the Eurodeposit markets where interest rates were generally higher than elsewhere. The recycling process was handled by international banks through the form of syndicated lending. The money was not lent by individual banks but by syndicates. One bank would 'lead' the deal (taking responsibility for attracting others) and the risks would be shared. The City became the centre for this syndicated lending. It had every advantage: it was the centre of the Euromarkets where the funds were being generated and it boasted the greatest concentration of international banks in the world. Where could a syndicate be more conveniently arranged? The City's primacy is shown most readily by the fact that the rate of interest charged on these loans was fixed according to the London Interbank Offered Rate (LIBOR), the rate at which City banks lend to one another. The lending was vast. Volume increased from $5 billion per year in the early 1970s to over $130 billion in 1981, the peak year.

British banks were themselves involved in this lending – though usually as members of a syndicate rather than as lead banks. They were estimated to be responsible for some 10 per cent of syndicated lending in the late 1970s. This sounds high but should be set in context: the share of the big four British banks was actually smaller than that of one American bank (Citicorp, the market leader), and while they may have beeen responsible for 10 per cent of the lending, over 60 per cent of it was actually put together in London. So a great deal of the activity in the City by-passed British banks.

The next part of the story is well-known. Continuing inflation pushed up interest rates and world recession made balance-of-payments problems worse. By the early 1980s it was clear that many countries were unable to repay their debts. It has been suggested that lending banks must have realised that the loans could only ever have been repaid by increased borrowings. But banks who, by now, felt heavily exposed and extremely nervous, were most reluctant to allow increased borrowing. The conclusion was inevitable. Mexico and Brazil were actually the first countries to suspend repayments (in 1982) but it soon became clear that rescheduling of loans would have to occur and that, in the end, a good deal of the money would never be repaid.

Clearly this episode (and it is far from over) has had a serious effect upon the developing countries involved and upon the international agencies (most importantly the IMF) who have attempted to wrestle with it. We are concerned here, though, with its effects on the banks who lent.

The problem was eased slightly by the world recovery of the

middle 1980s which boosted the export revenues of some of the borrowing countries and (helped by marginally lower interest rates) enabled them to make partial repayments. For all that, banks – including the British big four – still faced a number of decisions. First, they must avoid making the same mistake again, which meant that they must look for other borrowers. Second, a world recession could expose them further. This fuelled a desire to win new business quickly. Third, the sheer volume of unpaid debt involved left banks looking severely under-capitalised. Close scrutiny of their balance-sheets might shake confidence in individual banks or even in the entire banking system. The way to offset this was to raise capital quickly. Share issues were one method employed, but the implications went deeper into banking behaviour.

These three points can be seen to lead in a single direction. The debt crisis has led British commercial banks to seek new types of business with a view to increasing their profitability and thus accumulating capital.

Where was this new business to be found? The banks concentrated at first on financial services for which fees can be charged. Unlike lending this does not use up much capital. So the big clearers started to muscle in on areas such as the arrangement of bond sales and share issues – previously the province of the merchant (or wholesale or investment) bankers. It did not stop there. The big four developed or acquired their own merchant banking subsidiaries and were soon offering an ever-increasing range of investment banking products. Competition was intense. Fees were cut and the market grew – interest rate swaps, floating rate Euronotes (both explained in Chapter 7) and other innovations were all part of the keen search for profitability. The development of new products became frenzied. Banks that could previously have been safely described as 'retailers' moved so heavily into the wholesale market as to make the traditional distinction almost meaningless.

Of course, these developments become bound up with the impact of securitisation, Big Bang, and other examples of deregulation to leave us with commercial banks who are stockbrokers and estate agents as well. It is nonetheless clear that one of the major causes of the breakdown of the traditional distinctions within British banking during the 1980s, and particularly the fusion of retail and wholesale operations, lies in the domestic implications of the debt crisis.

Securitisation

A peculiar feature of financial markets, particularly during the 1980s, is the glee with which they take up new and ugly pieces of jargon. A trend towards the replacement of traditional bank borrowing with the issue of tradeable securities quickly becomes known as 'securitisation'. In no time its effect on the structure of lending has been dubbed 'disintermediation'. Ugly or not, both have been key features of the markets in the 1980s. They have significantly changed the role and behaviour of banks. Ironically, banks were themselves largely responsible for the development.

Governments have always been major issuers of securities as a method of borrowing. UK government securities are called 'gilt-edged stock' but the principle behind all such instruments is the same. A piece of paper (usually called a bond) promises the holder a fixed annual rate of return and repayment of a principal sum after a given period has elapsed. The bond is then sold. The buyer is effectively lending, the seller is borrowing. Of course, the buyer can sell the bond to someone else whenever he or she wishes to – so securities have the same advantage as shares that they are fully negotiable without affecting the liquidity of the company that issued them. The rate of interest that the bond offers is fixed when it is issued (meaning that the annual return to the holder is fixed too) but the price of the bond in secondary markets (after it has been issued) will vary according to changes in the market rate of interest. Bonds usually have a maturity of some years (the British government issues 'undated' ones that have no date of maturity at all), but similar short-term instruments (called bills) exist that enable firms to borrow for a matter of months. Bills (called commercial bills or commercial paper when issued by companies) promise the holder a fixed sum on a specified date and are sold for a figure lower than that sum.

Markets in bills and bonds have always been a feature of financial centres. Advice on the details of an issue and the finding of willing buyers has been a major function of investment or merchant banks. Figure 4.1 shows that the growth in the issue of bonds in the 1980s has been spectacular. The total value of new bonds issued rose from $44 billion worth in 1981 to almost $200 billion worth in 1989. Companies have increasingly come to prefer the issue of securities to traditional bank borrowing. The reasons give a clear insight into

FIGURE 4.1
Gross Value of New Bond Issues, 1981–9

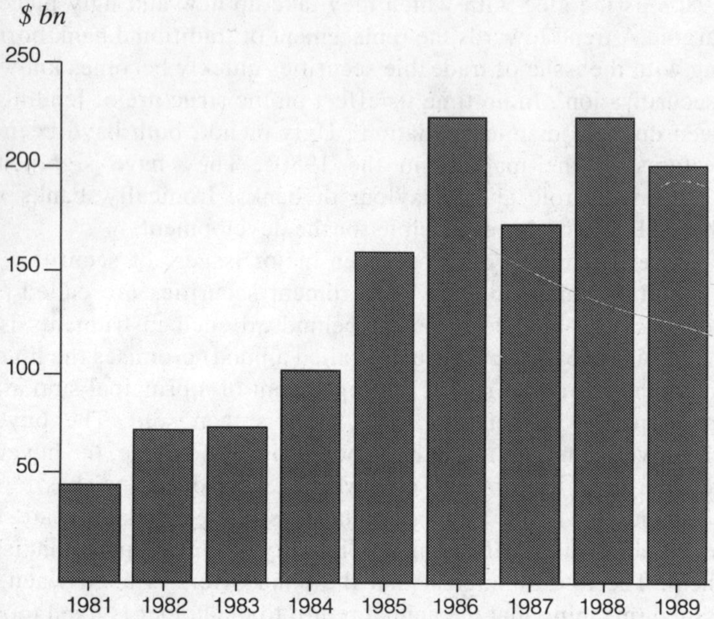

SOURCE *Bank of England Quarterly Bulletin*, May 1988, 1989 and 1990.

some of the changes in financial markets in recent years.

Paradoxically, banks themselves helped to champion this movement away from formal bank lending. As we have seen, their exposure in the debt crisis left them eager to increase profits without endangering capital. Traditional lending requires capital. Arranging the issue of securities simply involves a fee. Active securities markets also generate commission income whenever the securities are bought and sold, so banks had even more to gain from the growth of such markets. Once again, commercial banks were insinuating themselves into markets that were traditionally the province of merchant bankers. The distinction was further broken down.

There is another way in which the debt crisis precipitated securitisation. The crisis made banks a worse credit risk themselves.

They were likely to face higher rates of interest when they borrowed, and so would have to charge higher rates of interest when they lent. Large corporations on the other hand were better credit risks. If the corporation could borrow direct without using the bank as an intermediary, then it could almost certainly borrow more cheaply. So the corporations issued securities which they sold direct to investors such as pension funds. The process came to be known as 'disintermediation' (since the bank, as intermediary, was being by-passed) and has been regarded by some as a serious development for bankers. This is to miss the point. Banks were still involved in these deals, but as brokers earning commission rather than as direct lenders. They were behaving as merchant bankers again. In fact, it enabled banks to arrange more lending because the regulations under which they operated until the early 1980s restricted formal lending, but did not control the issue of securities. Disintermediation is actually a major reason for the abandonment of credit controls on banks as a means of monetary policy.

Developments in Japan and the USA fuelled the securitisation boom. The propensity to save in Japan is especially high and the rapid growth years of the 1970s through to the middle 1980s led to the accumulation of a huge savings mountain in Japan. The highly developed securities markets of the USA provided a natural home for this money. Inevitably, this boost to the American market, leading to ever more creative innovation, had a knock-on effect in the securities markets of London.

Some of the innovation was of dubious value to genuine economic activity but, having been fuelled by highly active securities markets, then managed to fuel them further. Active bond trading helped to create the boom in mergers and takeovers that has characterised the entire 1980s. The sale of bonds could raise the capital that was needed to pay for an acquisition. Sale of assets could then generate the revenue to pay off the bonds. At their worst, these securities came to be known as 'junk bonds' since, although they offered ludicrously high rates of return, they had no genuine security. Their value was simply to acquire short-term liquidity with which to indulge in asset-stripping.

Finally, the decline in inflation helped to foster securitisation. High inflation makes fixed interest loans risky. Changes in the inflation rate are bound to leave either the borrower or the lender worse off when interest payments are compared with the fall in the real value of money that has occurred. So securities markets (which involve fixed interest rates) are bound to be depressed at such periods. As inflation falls, though, the markets recover – just as occurred in the 1980s.

As with the debt crisis, the securitisation boom has had many important side-effects. The one that concerns us is the permanent change that it has wrought in the nature of banking. Traditional bank borrowings still, of course, occur. But the trend towards the issue of securities, happening as it did at a time when commercial banks were keen to find new types of business, has been a major cause of the blurring of the distinction between retail and wholesale banking. The boom was in wholesale business (at a time in the early 1980s when the retail market was depressed anyway) and commercial banks were quick to use their size and market power to get their share. They set up new departments and these supposedly sober and conservative bankers helped to develop an ever more complicated and creative array of products: interest-rate swaps (allowing borrowers to gamble on the choice between fixed and variable rates), floating-rate notes (a new type of bond whose rate of interest is not fixed) and so on. What were merchant banks to do?

From Big Bang to Big Banks

It would be neat and tidy if, faced with increased competition in wholesale markets from their retail rivals, merchant banks had themselves moved into the retail market. It would not have been very sensible. The costs of a successful retail banking operation are vast, since it relies upon an extensive branch network from which to collect deposits and an efficient cheque-clearing system through which to settle transactions. Merchant banks are small, niche operators in the realm of corporate banking. They did not want to get involved in the high-cost retail end of things.

Jacob Rothschild had the answer. You will remember that in his 1983 speech he foresaw a situation in which there was no place for niche operators – a world dominated by 'the international commercial bank with a global trading competence' which would itself finally amalgamate with others to form 'the ultimate, all-powerful, many-headed financial conglomerate'. The transformation of the

British merchant bank into something along these lines must have seemed in 1983 like some ghastly exercise in genetic mutation.

It was, of course, deregulation that provided the stimulus. As we investigate further it becomes increasingly clear that regulations had served to separate markets from one another in a manner that seemed entirely natural at the time but can be seen with the aid of hindsight to have been artificial . The tight rules of the Stock Exchange made the UK equity market into a sort of private function. The relaxation of these rules in the Big Bang of 1986 (and, as we saw in Chapter 3, earlier than that) was to issue party invitations to every financial operator in London, and quite a few from overseas as well.

British merchant banks did not get involved simply because Jacob Rothschild had hinted that they should. This was a natural extension of their existing business. They are investment bankers. Their job is to help corporate clients with all of their financial needs. They were already involved in almost every share issue that occurred in London – advising, arranging and advertising the shares on behalf of their client. There is virtually no company that seeks a quotation on the London Stock Exchange without the support of a merchant bank. As we have seen, they were already involved in the issue and dealing of other securities (bonds and bills) on behalf of their customers. As part of their interest in corporate finance, they were continually monitoring developments in equity markets and, when it came to advising clients on merger and takeover activity, had to be completely *au fait* with the behaviour of all types of security including shares. Indeed, one of their largest areas of growth in recent decades has been that of fund management – looking after the investments (many, of course, in shares) of pension funds, unit trusts and insurance companies. The move into active equity dealing was an entirely natural development. It simply enabled merchant banks to complete the range of services that they offered to customers.

The same can, of course, be said of commercial banks. They were already moving rapidly into the investment banking field and so precisely the same arguments applied to them. In addition they had millions of private customers for whom, among other things, they served as adviser and even broker in the equity market. They too could complete the service offered to their customers by gaining a foothold at the Stock Exchange.

We already know what happened. Of the major commercial banks, Barclays, National Westminster, Midland and the Royal Bank of

Scotland all acquired combinations of brokers and jobbers to give themselves a broking and market-making facility. The Royal Bank of Scotland actually went so far as to pick up a merchant bank, Charterhouse Japhet (bought, ironically, from Jacob Rothschild). Lloyds chose to build their own in-house market-making division at their merchant-banking arm. Merchant banks behaved similarly. Virtually all the members of the prestigious Accepting Houses Committee of prominent merchant bankers – S. G. Warburg, Kleinwort Benson, Morgan Grenfell, Schroders, Hill Samuel, Hambros, N. M. Rothschild, Barings, Guinness Peat – succeeded in forming alliances with various brokers and jobbers. Some of the smaller merchant banks even found themselves to be targets for acquisition.

Once again, the traditional distinctions within the banking world have been eroded. This can be seen first from the fact that commercial and merchant banks have behaved in exactly the same ways to become elements (in some cases leading elements) of broad-based financial conglomerates. Second, this very broadness of base spells the end of the days when banking activities could be neatly summarised and distinguished from those of other financial operators. Jacob Rothschild's predictions seem to have been entirely validated. The term 'bank' may tell you more about where a particular financial operator came from than where it is now going.

This fusion of roles may have been necessary – even inevitable – but it has caused a good many problems. We know now that some of the mergers and takeovers that occurred before Big Bang were ill-advised. The process of broadening the scope of banking may have been carried out in a way that was short-sighted and over-hasty.

Culture Shock

Mergers are the commercial equivalent of marriages. It is far from certain that partners who seem ideally suited from the outside will actually hit it off. The mergers that took place within the financial sector in the middle 1980s were further complicated by the fact that they were between different sorts of company. We may confidently assert that the differences between retail banks and wholesale banks and between banks and brokers were artificially created. It is still true that the institutions had developed along different lines and had different cultures. The results were something like a marriage between a party-goer and a stay-at-home or a socialist and a conservative.

Commercial banks and merchant banks tended to be very conscious of budgets (especially after their international debt problems), were reluctant to take risks and were run by systems of committees. Merchant banks, of course, saw themselves as a good deal more enterprising and less stuffy than their colleagues in commercial banks. But they were still culturally very different from the brokers and jobbers alongside whom they now worked. Stockbrokers were salesmen, used to concentrating on a short time-horizon and without much medium- or long-term planning. Jobbers, on the other hand, were gamblers who worked on their own account and had little understanding of, or sympathy for, company administration and hierarchy.

The problems of knitting these disparate elements into single corporations were (and still are) hard to accommodate. At the most basic level, salary structures presented difficulties. Brokers and jobbers, as partners in their businesses, were often used to payments considerably greater than were the norm in banking. Perhaps this is another reason for some of the absurd salary hype that occurred before the crash of 1987. The real concern, though, was how to structure the new organisations without giving overdue prominence to the security-dealing arm which was, of course, the cause of all the change in the first place. Merchant banks in particular were aware that similar developments in the middle 1970s in America had caused a major downgrading of traditional corporate finance as the security dealers became more powerful. It is difficult to tell how far these fears proved groundless, but there have surely been casualties. Ironically, a number of British securities dealers found it equally hard to come to terms with the traditional practice of American bankers. Both Security Pacific and Citibank have now withdrawn from the London securities market.

The most prominent bankers to suffer in the securities markets have been Midland (who withdrew in 1987 after announcing losses on market-making of some £5179million), and Morgan Grenfell (who gave up late in 1988 having lost £22 million since the start of the year). Lloyds has withdrawn from gilt-edged market-making. Hill Samuel, the merchant bank, lost its independence as a result of troubles in the securities market. Towards the end of 1990, the future of Kleinworts was in doubt after sustaining heavy losses on market-making in oil shares. Other banks have persisted in some extensive loss-making (total market losses in 1988 and 1989 were estimated at somewhere around £500 million per year), but cling on in the hope of future profits.

These excursions into securities dealing illustrate the clash of cultures within the British banking conglomerates disappointingly well. The skill of bankers has traditionally lain in the use that they can make of other people's money, not their own. Market-making in the securities industry involves the different talent of risking your own capital. It begins to look as though the most sensible of the merchant banks, at least, were the ones who ignored the lure of the new market. There were precious few of them. Morgan Grenfell is perhaps the bank with greatest cause to regret the changes through which it put itself. It has always enjoyed a rather more buccaneering reputation than some of its colleagues but has been dogged by disaster and scandal in the late 1980s: it was forced to withdraw from securities dealing; a senior executive was successfully prosecuted for insider dealing; and it was one of the banks involved in the Guinness affair. It has now lost its independence. One might conclude that the broadening of its business through acquisition had been insufficiently regulated from within and that the bank was the victim of, at best, the excessive enthusiasm of some its employees. Perhaps the same phenomenon has occurred elsewhere on a smaller scale and in a way that receives less obvious publicity. To some extent, it must have. The expansion into securities dealing, then, has also caused fundamental changes to the culture as well as the face of British banking. It is also just one market in which UK banks face fierce competition from overseas – at a time when international circumstances are changing very quickly.

The International Challenge

If a single theme can be said to emerge from study of the recent developments in financial markets, it is surely the theme of deregulation. The relaxation of rules governing the conduct of business in financial centres has become a competitive sport between governments. Table 1.1 is evidence of this. The end-result, supported by developments in communications technology, should be the true global market where firms throughout the world compete on merit alone. The international banking sector of the City ought, you might think, to be a great winner from all this. Sadly, it has turned out to be a bit more complicated than that.

The City's success as an international banking centre was founded, as we saw earlier, on its very generous regulatory framework. International business could be carried on with almost complete freedom. This attracted a record catch of foreign banks (most of whom employed British specialist staff) and a huge share of international banking business (27 per cent of the total in 1975, compared with 13 per cent for the USA – the next major centre). The source of the City's international supremacy lay in the Euromarkets which developed with astonishing rapidity from about 1960 onwards and which quickly came to be based in London – largely due to that same friendly lack of regulation that was noted above.

The Euromarket is explained in greater detail in Chapter 7. For now, it is enough to know that a Eurocurrency describes money that is being held in a deposit outside its country of origin (dollars held in Europe, for example). The market can apparently claim its origin in the Soviet Union – not otherwise noted for pioneering developments in international capitalism. In the late 1950s the Russians were nervous of holding their precious dollars in deposits in the USA, where an unkind government might freeze them. Instead they deposited them in Paris at the *Banque Commerciale pour l'Europe du Nord*, whose telex address was *Eurobank*. The Euromarket was born.

The Soviet Union may have have been an unknowing midwife at the birth, but the true parents of the market were the UK and USA. Interest-rate regulations operating in the USA in the early 1960s meant that Americans could get a far better return on their dollars overseas. Regulations on banks normally take the form of a requirement to keep a fixed portion of total assets in very liquid form. Having to tie up capital in this way leaves banks unable to afford to pay very high rates of interest to depositors. The international bankers of London were subject to no such restrictions. So London could offer far higher rates of interest on these Eurodollars than the USA, or anywhere else for that matter. This is why the market really took off.

Eurodeposits form the basis of this market. They are recycled by international bankers and borrowed by others in the form of straightforward Euroloans or by the issue of Eurobonds. The syndicated loans discussed earlier in this chapter were a type of Euroloan. The size and growth of this market in the City have been astonishing. The volume of Eurodeposits grew in the 1970s at a rate of around 20 per cent per year. It was reckoned in the middle 1980s that the gross volume of Eurodeposits exceeded $2 trillion. In the later 1980s over $180 billion worth of Eurobonds were being issued per year. Altogether, international lending was thought to total somewhere in excess of $6000 billion per year at the end of the decade. 75 per cent of this was in the form of Eurocurrencies.

The Euromarket, then, is central to the international banking industry as a whole and to the City's pre-eminence in particular. It is worth noting in passing that, whilst the City is the home of the Eurobond market, the top five international bond managers in 1988 included three Japanese banks (Nomura, Daiwa and Nikko), the Deutsche bank of Germany and Crédit Suisse First Boston. The Japanese became a major force in international banking during the 1970s, being virtually unscathed by the debt crisis and keen to expand beyond their overcrowded domestic market.

The success story of the Euromarkets was based upon the existence of tougher regulation outside the UK. Competitive international deregulation must call into question the City's continued ability to lead the field. The USA and Japan have relaxed restrictions on international banking, putting themselves more or less on a par with the City. Europeans have not been far behind. We know from Table 2.5 that the UK is no longer the largest international banker in the world. It has been overtaken by Japan. Figure 4.2 shows the international market shares of banks located in the City. The growth of the Japanese is remarkable, but notice also that the group of 'others' has held its share well. European banks are presenting increasing competition both inside the City and elsewhere. The UK's share of European banking business fell by 2 per cent in the first half of 1989.

The full impact of European deregulation is still to be felt. The prospect of a single market in financial services in 1992 has led various national banking authorities to relax and reform the systems under which their banks operate. The German and Italian central banks for example, have taken steps to reduce the proportions of bank assets that they insist are held in liquid reserves. The effect of such moves must be to increase competition within Europe. This

FIGURE 4.2
The Major Bank Groups' Shares of London's International Banking Business 1978–88 (percentages)

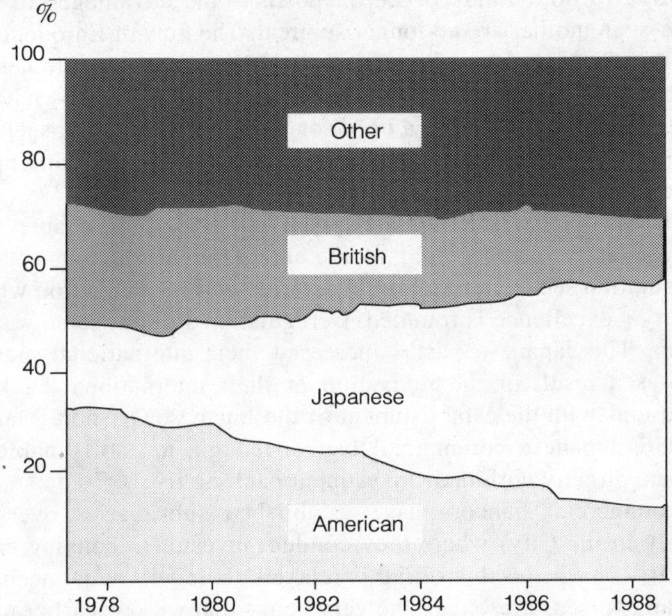

SOURCE *Bank of England Quarterly Bulletin*, May 1989.

will, of course, enable UK banks to vie for business that is currently hard to reach. The Spanish market is already beckoning. The Royal Bank of Scotland has formed a link with the local Banco Santander, and NatWest is establishing branches in Spain under its own name. At the same time, though, European business will no longer necessarily be attracted to London. European financial conglomerates may well develop that can rival any service which the UK can currently offer. As if that were not enough, the huge open market offered by the EC will be an even greater attraction to the vast conglomerates of Japan and the USA. This argument suggests that, the further international deregulation has to run, the more that UK banks stand to lose.

The City still leads the world in genuine cross-border banking (much of the Japanese and European growth is in foreign currency business for domestic clients) but this may be a dying market. The Euromarkets are getting smaller. Liberalisation within Europe will make them smaller still. Progressive deregulation removes the incentive to hold funds in Eurodeposits – the advantages of one centre over another are no longer so great. The flow of Eurodeposits into the City has dwindled to a trickle. Increasing volumes of banking business can now be handled within a customer's own home country. There will still be a need for foreign currency transactions and so on, but the market for traditional international banking is bound to be cut away.

It begins to look as though the apocalyptic title of this chapter was no overstatement if applied to the international banking sphere. Deregulation seems to be about to destroy the very market on which the City's excellence is founded. Deregulation still has some way to go too. The Japanese vastly increased their international market share as a result of the relaxation of their international banking regulations with the establishment of the Japanese Offshore Market in 1986. Japanese commercial banks, though, are still unable to compete directly with their investment banking rivals. To do so, the big commercial bankers have established subsidiaries overseas (mainly in the City) where they conduct investment banking business. If – or when – this ruling is relaxed, there will be no need for such an overseas presence. The very banks that we saw earlier to be responsible for the lion's share of the City's international bond dealing may then leave the City for good. What price London's international pre-eminence then?

Flash in Japan?

We must not be too apocalyptic, though. International and domestic developments may conspire to show that the Japanese surge of the late 1980s is unsustainable. A natural extension of the deregulation that has dominated the decade has been the attempt to draw up an international rule book under which all banks, from whatever country, will agree to operate. In 1988, the world's bankers met in Switzerland to agree the Basle Capital Convergence Accord. The detail is complicated but it boils down to a requirement for all banks to hold capital equivalent to at least 8 per cent of the value of their assets (which is calculated to take into account their degree of risk). This will have little effect on UK banks who are fairly well-capitalised anyway. But the Japanese are in a rather different position.

During the 1980s, the newly deregulated banks of Japan, the USA and continental Europe pursued policies of reckless international growth rather than capital accumulation. As the world economy slowed, much of the lending proved riskier than expected. American banks were the first to suffer, finding themselves charged higher rates of interest as doubts spread about their profitability. Japanese banks face similar humiliation in the early 1990s. They need to increase their profits quickly in order to generate capital in time for 1993 when the Basle Accord becomes binding. This is sure to lead to changes in the way in which they do business. They are bound to become far more selective in their lending. They may have to charge higher rates of interest. And they are likely to become more interested in fee-income business such as traditional corporate finance.

There is a further cloud on their horizon. 1990 saw a dramatic, extended and unprecedented fall on the Japanese stock market. Japanese banks hold a good deal of capital in the form of equities. These are now worth considerably less, making the search for new sources of capital all the more acute. It also, of course, reduces the value of the banks' own equity capital. At the same time there are fears of a collapse in the sky-high Japanese property market. Many outstanding loans from Japanese banks are secured on property. If the UK's property market collapse of 1973 is anything to go by, this could cause worrying tremors within the banking sector. In the UK one bank collapsed (London County) and others were saved by a 'lifeboat' arranged by the Bank of England and funded (very reluctantly) by the large commercial banks.

No one is predicting a collapse of the Japanese banking sector. Such a suggestion is absurd. Nonetheless, the world of international banking is being squeezed. It was described in a late-1990 Warburg Securities research document as 'among the most bombed-out sectors of the global market'. It seems that it will be the Japanese and Americans who will be the first to control their expansion, raise their interest rates, reduce the rate of growth of their international lending and concentrate on consolidating capital.

The competition for UK banks and for the City of London is real enough, but it would surely be premature to build too gloomy a view on the rather unusual developments of the later 1980s.

The Challenge at Home

It is ironic that the lack of regulation that sparked the City's success in international markets should contrast so sharply with the way in which domestic banking was managed until the 1980s. All banks required authorisation from the Bank of England (no great surprise there) and were then subjected to rules stipulating cash and liquidity ratios. 12.5 per cent of assets had to be held in liquid form; 1.5 per cent in deposits at the Bank of England. Further to this, direct penalties on lending banks (the supplementary special deposits scheme or 'corset') were used by the Bank of England in an effort to restrict bank lending. The justification for this (and it is not altogether a weak one) was that an efficient financial system must be based upon complete confidence. This required thorough protection of depositors through a sensible and prudent system of regulation. A more cynical interpretation might be that, in return for the Bank of England's generous restriction of competition through its authorisation policy, banks were then pawns of Government so far as the scale and direction of bank lending were concerned. Whichever way you see it, the system was not working. The controls only applied to UK clearing banks. The effect was to divert lending away from them to an uncontrolled 'fringe' banking sector whose greatest talent was always to be one step ahead of the regulatory authorities.

The Government decided that the only solution was to abandon all but the most basic controls. There had been earlier attempts to deregulate British banking – most prominently in the Competition and Credit Control package of 1971 – but none had really had the courage of its convictions. Between 1979 and 1981 virtually the entire system beyond the basic authorisation requirements was swept away. By 1985 banks simply had to hold 0.45 per cent of their assets at the Bank of England. The Bank is still responsible for authorisation, the rules for which were readjusted in the 1987 Banking Act after the Johnson Matthey banking collapse of 1984. The Act specifies the regularity with which the Bank of England will monitor the balance-sheets of banks in order to check the prudence of their behaviour. It also establishes a fund from which depositors can seek partial reimbursement in the event of a banking collapse.

Deregulation, along with the abolition of exchange controls in 1979, had a number of effects on UK banking. By removing the distinction between the 'official' and 'fringe' banking sectors, it effectively increased the scale of UK banking. Between 1980 and 1990, the assets of authorised UK banks increased from £279 billion to £1257 billion – an average increase of 16 per cent per year. This, of course, means that it generated a vast increase in bank lending (a bank's assets are mainly its loans). Table 4.1 shows trends in bank lending. Many of the increases recorded are immense. Most remarkable are the rates of rise of commercial bank lending to the service sector, particularly the financial sector itself, and the increase in personal-sector lending. These contrast with more modest increases in lending to the manufacturing and primary sectors. Critics claim that this proves deregulation of bank lending to have encouraged irresponsibility: banks, they say, are (if left to themselves) too readily geared to short-term, non-productive lending and fail to give necessary support to the long-term investment requirements of the manufacturing sector.

We cannot be surprised if a deregulated banking industry behaves in such a way as to maximise its own profits. That is its aim. It would be a remarkable private bank that genuinely put the interests of others ahead of the interests of its own shareholders. Nonetheless, the government itself seems to accept that the benefits of bank deregulation are less certain than in other areas. In the early 1980s, in the depth of the recession – and in the wake of major attempts to reduce government interference in the banking sector – the Bank of England asked commercial banks to look generously on customers in the manufacturing sector who were finding financial difficulty. Loans were to be extended and rescheduled. Foreclosure was to be avoided if possible. A similar suggestion was made in 1990 when recession once again loomed. Injury was added to insult when a windfall tax on commercial banks' profits was levied in the early 1980s. This can look uncannily like a government trying to have it both ways: deregulating an industry and then reimposing capricious regulations when it suits them to do so. Perhaps the truth is that banking is too important as a protector of savings and a source of funds for industry ever to be entirely free of the protection or regulation of government.

By removing distinctions within the banking sector (and by

TABLE 4.1
Lending by Major UK Clearing Banks, 1983–9

Borrower	*1983*	*1984*	*1985*	*1986*	*1987*	*1988*	*1989*
Agriculture, forestry etc	4 785	5 058	5 611	5 778	5 317	5 731	6 076
Manufacturing	11 165	12 221	12 932	14 396	15 244	20 106	23 772
Construction	2 944	3 335	3 893	4 332	4 975	7 383	10 091
Distribution, catering etc	9 400	10 232	11 483	12 663	14 621	17 352	21 813
Transport	2 186	2 041	2 062	1 947	1 989	2 417	3 047
Financial services	6 960	7 688	10 395	13 247	17 423	21 892	29 096
Other services	7 968	9 721	11 921	14 639	18 342	26 915	37 049
Persons	22 915	26 016	31 039	40 735	51 189	64 668	72 373

SOURCE Banking Information Service, *Abstract of Banking Statistics*, May 1990.

abolishing exchange controls) deregulation has, of course, increased the competition faced by UK banks. Where the banking market was once neatly fenced off, it is now open to all. Competition from abroad has been important, particularly in lending to the corporate sector. High interest rates in the UK between 1988 and the early 1990s certainly diverted some borrowing to overseas sources and attracted foreign bankers to the UK market. The single European market of 1992 is bound to confirm these trends. More intense competition, though, has come from other domestic institutions – particularly the building societies. They were traditionally in a different line of business to banks. They collected savings and lent for property purchase. Building societies had a virtual monopoly of this lucrative mortgage market. Deregulation in the early 1980s found banks keen to increase lending in a period when the corporate sector was severely depressed. They needed customers who were happy to borrow more. The domestic mortgage market beckoned

FIGURE 4.3
Lending by Banks and Building Societies for House Purchase, 1979–89

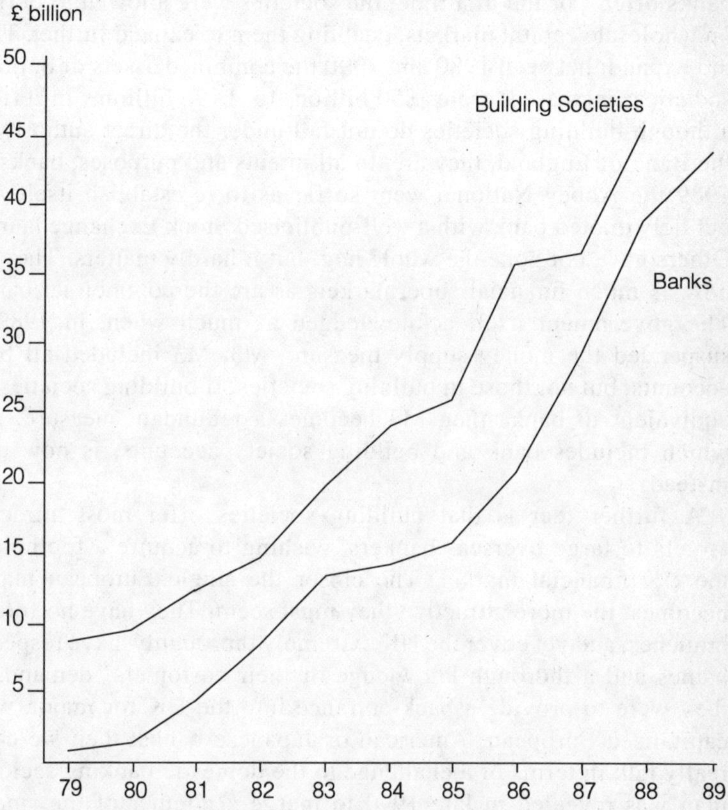

SOURCE Banking Information Service, *Abstract of Banking Statistics,* May 1990.

seductively. Figure 4.3 shows how successful banks have been in increasing their share of this lending over the decade.

With banks muscling in on their traditional sphere of activity, it was only a matter of time before building societies would seek some retribution. The Building Societies Act of 1986 gave the societies the right to compete directly with banks. They now offer cheque accounts, they have joined the new clearing house arrangements, they can lend for reasons other than house purchase, offer insurance and investment services, they can issue credit cards and have the same range of savings accounts and easy-access cash facilities that banks offer. For the first time, the societies were allowed to borrow on wholesale capital markets, enabling them to expand further. They did expand: between 1980 and 1990 the combined assets of building societies increased from £50 billion to £196 billion. In effect, although building societies do not fall under the direct authority of the Bank of England, they are, to all intents and purposes, banks. In 1989 the Abbey National went so far as to re-establish itself as a publicly quoted bank with a well-publicised Stock Exchange launch. Others have not gone the whole hog, but it hardly matters. They are now as much financial supermarkets as are the commercial banks. The government itself acknowledged as much when, in 1989, it suspended the money supply measure, M3. M3 included all bank accounts, but not those in building societies. If building societies are equivalent to banks then M3 becomes a redundant measure. M4, which includes bank and building society accounts, is now used instead.

A further fear is that building societies offer most attractive targets to large overseas bankers, wishing to acquire a foothold in the UK financial market. The closer the single European market becomes, the more attractive they must seem. They have no foreign branches, and yet cover the UK extremely thoroughly, have respected names and a thorough knowledge of their customers' demands. If they were to provide a back entrance into the UK for major, well-capitalised European, American or Japanese banks, then we could really talk in terms of a challenge to the domestic banking sector. A plan was revealed in late 1990 to merge a number of the smaller societies (under the name of Bank of Edinburgh) in the hope of protecting them from predators. It will probably come to nothing; they are likely to remain as vulnerable as ever.

Competition does not just come from building societies and foreign banks. Even high-street stores have joined the lending business. For many years, they acted as agents for other lenders when they encouraged customers to buy goods on credit. Increasingly, they are providing the service themselves. Marks & Spencer are the trail-blazers with a separate financial services division and, since 1988, a unit trust scheme as well as a store card. Tesco have pioneered a cash withdrawal scheme. If banks have become financial supermarkets, supermarkets now appear to be returning the compliment.

Bankers No More

Of all the changes we have identified, it is surely this exposure to competition that has been most responsible for the astonishing changes that the British banking industry has undergone in the past ten years. It has encouraged a degree of creativity and innovation that were previously unknown within the domestic banking market. Banks used to offer current accounts and deposit accounts – not what you could call a wide choice. Now there is a range of interest-bearing cheque and savings accounts, with or without charges, with fixed or variable rates on overdrafts, that beggars description. Competition has certainly succeeded in improving product range. It has also improved service in other ways: EFTPOS (Electronic Funds Transfer At Point Of Sale) schemes, such as 'Switch' and 'Connect', allow customers to transfer money without the need for cheques; Midland has set up a branch-free subsidiary (First Direct) that offers banking by telephone, and higher interest on deposits; the Royal Bank of Scotland has pioneered home and office banking by computer.

Competition has also attracted banks into new areas of activity in the desperate search for profit. One aspect of this is simply the movement of one type of bank into the world more usually frequented by another. There are other sides to it too.

Banks have diversified into areas that were previously far outside the realm of bankers. Lloyds owns the largest chain of estate agents in the UK. All the major clearers except National Westminster (NatWest) have developed their own insurance, investment and pension products which they actively promote to their customers. NatWest decided to stick with a broking function. It is too early to tell how successful these ventures will be, though Lloyds may have regretted their investment during the property slump of 1989–90.

The European challenge of the 1990s is seen by some as offering a further spur to conglomeration and diversification. The wholesale inter-bank markets will probably change little. They have been multinational in character for a long time and, as we have seen, are already dominated by vast international organisations. It is in the retail markets – dealing with personal customers and smaller companies – that the scale of the newly opening European market may attract further merger activity, in an attempt to build pan-European financial conglomerates. If so, UK banks are bound to be heavily involved. This may turn out to be a mistake. It will take time for the retail market to be genuinely unified. Local preferences for particular types of financial product will persist for some time. Perhaps specialist niche operators actually have the most to gain. It would be a pity if banks were to repeat the mistakes of Big Bang and to rush headlong into a new and overcrowded market.

Be that as it may, it is clear that even before the European adventure British banks are no longer simple bankers. The industry began the decade as a well-ordered, conveniently protected and rather disparate group of specialist operators. Commercial banks were specialists at attracting private deposits. Merchant banks concentrated on the arcane field of corporate finance. Building societies were mortgage lenders. By 1990 such distinctions no longer apply. Nearly everybody is now able to do nearly everything. Quite a lot do. The process is not over yet. Commercial banks still stand out because of their huge branch networks. But development in communications technology is making the branch network less important than once it was. Economising on branches would represent a vast saving for the banks. We have already referred to the experiments of Midland and Royal Bank of Scotland in this field. If branches disappear then it really will be hard to spot the difference between one type of bank and another.

Has It All Been Worth It?

Finally, what effects have all these changes had on the service offered to banks' customers? The product range has been hugely increased, which is presumably a benefit. There has also been a vast increase in lending to private customers. It is not hard to see the inflationary implications of this, particularly in the period from 1987–8. The reckless dash into mortgage lending in the early and middle 1980s helped to cause a fierce surge in house prices which itself fuelled inflation and, when recession finally set in, meant hardship for those who had over-borrowed. The dramatic increase in merger and takeover activity was surely in part prompted by ambitious banks keen to generate the huge fee incomes that could be earned by helping to achieve or to resist acquisition.

More serious than all of this, perhaps, are the changes that have occurred in the relationship between bankers and their corporate customers. Bankers used to pride themselves on how well they knew the needs and special circumstances of corporate clients. Such relationships were based upon many years of shared business. The highly competitive world of today gives little reward for such good banking practice. The collapse of the Polly Peck Corporation in October 1990 was seen by some as an avoidable disaster. The company could boast 100 bankers, falling over themselves to lend. Much of that lending turned out to be ill-advised simply because the bankers knew too little about the company in question. Only 8 per cent of the company's loans were specifically secured. The collapse of Johnson Matthey, the mistakes made by County NatWest in the Blue Arrow affair, the problems of Morgan Grenfell are all attributable to much the same phenomena. In a deregulated system it seems that there will always be someone who will be prepared to do business. Competition is so fierce that activities that are not directly profitable – such as building a long-term relationship with clients – become considerably less attractive. The domestic banking market of the UK has come increasingly to mirror the behaviour of the international market where lending has been cavalier and, occasionally, reckless. International banking has faced and is, as we have seen, still facing a crisis that results ultimately from careless lending. Talking of the problems facing Japanese banks in late 1990, Mr Taizo Hashida, chairman and President of Fuji Bank, said: 'I'm afraid that...supervision at some banks became a little soft. Now we are tightening. We must keep public trust.' It would be a pity if the untidy conlgomerates of the new domestic banking market of the UK were to make the same mistakes.

1990 saw references in the financial press to a 'new' practice in corporate banking; it is called 'relationship banking'. The 'extraordinary' notion is that bankers should build stable long-term relationships with their clients, should offer detailed corporate advice and should no longer stand prepared to lend to any fly-by-night outfit that happens to come by. Large companies have supported the idea. ICI has gone from some sixty bankers down to twelve. Charges may be higher, but the service will be better; and you will be able to trust your bank when times get hard. It is the attraction of marriage over the one-night stand. What is so remarkable, of course, is that this is no more than traditional – pre-new City – banking practice. It is being presented as the height of sophistication. It is probably no more than a reaction to the bad lending experiences of the late 1980s. With the 'new' system, banks can levy charges without lending money. When the market picks up again, 'relationship banking' will once more be treated as the boring and expensive old has-been that it appeared in early 1980s.

The death of banking may extend beyond the disappearance of the traditional British niche banking house; beyond even the decimation of the international banking sector through deregulation and over-expansion. It may extend as far as the decline of the qualities of prudence and foresight in the execution of banking business. It would be heresy to say that deregulation has been a mistake. It is equally short-sighted to think that a simple increase in competition can be relied upon to allocate funds in the most desirable way. Traditional banking may be dead but it is to be hoped that we have not heard the last of some of its practices.

5 Free-for-All on the Foreign Exchanges

The Roller-Coaster

If you had been travelling to the USA in 1979, you would have been offered round about $1.80 for every pound that you hoped to exchange. If you were able, you would have been well-advised to postpone your trip until 1980 or 1981, when you could have received as much as $2.40 for each of your pounds. You would have been very disappointed if you had waited much longer. By early 1985 your pounds would have fallen in value to little more than $1.05. In the headier days of the later 1980s, their value rose again. By 1987 you could have got $1.50 for your pound. If you had hung on to the end of the decade you could have done even better. By late 1990 the pound was almost back to $2.00 again. These changes may not sound especially large, but they actually represent price fluctuations of as much as 100 per cent in little more than five years. You would be surprised to encounter many other products whose price doubled and halved with such regularity.

Of course, this fairground ride may have as much to do with the circumstances in the USA as in the UK. The pound's experience against the Deutschmark and the yen are not so different, though. All three exchange rates are given in Figure 5.1. In the early 1970s, British travellers to West Germany received a monstrous eight Deutschmarks for each solitary pound. By 1979, they would have got less than four. In 1981, it was back up to five. The remainder of the decade showed a more or less steady decline in the value of the

FIGURE 5.1
Sterling Exchange Rates, 1979–90

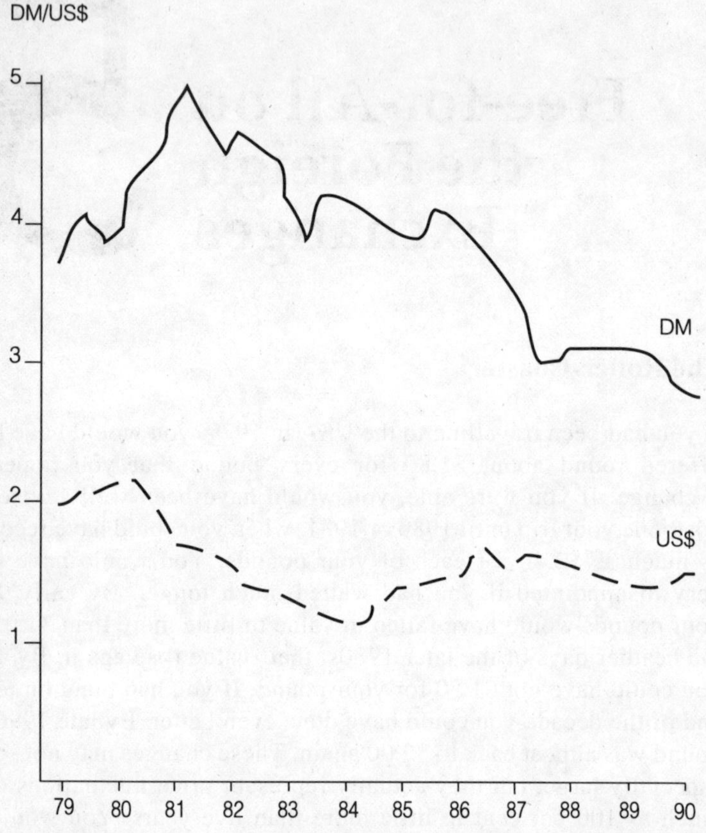

SOURCE *Barclays Economic Review,* various issues.

pound against the Deutschmark. The UK entered the Exchange Rate Mechanism of the EC in October 1990 at a central rate of DM2.95. Fluctuations against the yen are similar.

It comes as no surprise that the 1980s should have been a period of frenzied activity in the foreign exchange market. This mirrors the developments we have already recorded in other financial markets.

The central issue here, though, is the question of what actually accounts for the extra activity.

Do changes in the exchange rate accurately reflect changes in the underlying strength of the economy? Or does the increased volatility of the market over the past ten years tell us more about the market itself than it does about the genuine values of the currencies traded?

The question is neatly illustrated by the debate that followed the decision to join the ERM in October 1990. How were we best to explain the Chancellor's timing? Was this a hard-headed political ruse to steal the thunder from the final day of the Labour Party Conference? Or was it the straightforward result of economic circumstance?

There was a third option which, in the end, found the greatest favour. The timing was determined by the market, not by the Chancellor at all. The foreign exchange market was sure that joining the system was in the interests of the UK economy. The market was beginning to doubt the government's resolve. Every further week in which we did not join the mechanism led to greater disappointment. A disappointed market sells pounds. The Chancellor had either to support the pound with higher interest rates or do what it wanted and join the ERM. Higher interest rates were out of the question with a recession already looming. So, join the ERM it was.

Such a scenario is bound to be too one-sided to be completely accurate. Whether it is the full story or not, it suggests an important view: that the psychology of the foreign exchange market is itself a major factor in influencing exchange rates. Rather than being an innocent means through which outside forces bring about changes in currency value, perhaps the market has become a major force in its own right. If so, what does it think it is doing?

These huge questions will form the theme of this chapter. We must also consider the future. Our rather belated entry into the ERM is important in other ways. It returns us (along with our major trading partners) to the pre-1972 days of fixed exchange rates. What implications does this have for the foreign exchange market of the new City? Beyond even that, if the movement towards a single currency for Europe continues to gather pace, will there be a need for a foreign exchange market at all? Are the roller-coaster rides of the 1980s destined to be transformed finally into a tranquil rural railway journey?

The Foreign Exchange Market at Work

Most of the business in the foreign exchange markets of the City and other financial centres is done by banks. Each has a dealing-room which, for the major part of each working day, appears to be utter chaos. Young men and women bawl ferociously at one another and into two or three telephones at the same time. At the other end of the telephone lines are other young men and women in similar dealing-rooms in similar banks in similar financial centres.

The market is, of course, international. It is said to 'open' at 1am (Greenwich Mean Time) when the Tokyo market begins dealing. By about 9am, dealing switches to Europe – mainly to London, though Frankfurt and Zurich are significant centres too. New York opens at about 2p.m. It will dominate the market until it closes at 10p.m. There is a lull until Tokyo opens, though smaller markets operate in Los Angeles and San Francisco. Once again, London is ideally placed to bridge the time gap; it can deal with Tokyo in the morning and New York in the afternoon.

If a company needs, say, dollars, it will contact a dealer and explain how many it wants to buy. The dealer (who is likely to be a banker) may be able to satisfy the demand at once from the holdings of his own bank. If this is not possible, he will either phone other dealers to buy the dollars, or contact a broker who will undertake to find a seller in return for a commission. If the company wants the currency at once, then the deal will be conducted at the 'spot' rate – the going market rate at the time the deal is struck. Dealers, of course, buy currency at a lower price than they sell it, so the spot rate actually consists of two prices (the difference being called the 'spread'). The market also allows buying and selling of currencies for delivery in the future at 'forward' rates. Thus a client is able to buy dollars for delivery in, say, three months' time at a price agreed today. We shall look into these forward markets in the next chapter.

In 1989 the foreign exchange market of the City was estimated by the Bank of England to be conducting some $187 billion worth of business per day. This figure is more than twice the 1986 level, and means that London still retains its position as the busiest foreign exchange centre in the world. Of course, the concentration of international banks in the City (noted in Chapter 4) is bound to give it a lead in markets dominated by bankers. Foreign banks account for about 80 per cent of the City's daily dealing. Americans are the major players, with about 40 per cent of the City's total business. UK banks themselves are responsible for 20 per cent. Japanese banks have increased their volume of London business considerably but are still some way behind at 11 per cent of daily dealing (up from 7 per cent in 1986). The Bank for International Settlements estimated the global foreign exchange market to be worth about $650 billion per day in 1989, so London has a respectable 30 per cent of the market.

As well as the banks (referred to as 'principals' in foreign exchange dealing), a great part of market business involves the services of foreign exchange brokers. These are companies (or individuals) who arrange deals rather than dealing themselves. Around 38 per cent of currency deals are arranged through brokers. The proportion is falling slightly but is still a lot higher than the 15 per cent (up from 11 per cent in 1986) of deals that are conducted directly between principals (probably banks) and their customers (presumably corporations). This, of course, still leaves a large proportion – around 47 per cent – of foreign exchange transactions that are actually conducted between principals. So, over $87 billion of the $187 billion worth of business that takes place daily in the City, involves bankers in the UK and overseas exchanging currencies with one another.

It is tempting to conclude from all this that about half of the work of the foreign exchange market is somehow unnecessary or frivolous since it does not seem to involve a final customer either directly or indirectly (through a broker). Such a conclusion is premature. In order to conduct business on behalf of customers, banks must buy currencies from other dealers. Inevitably, then, a good deal of the market's activity must involve this sort of transaction. It is only the same as a retailer purchasing goods from a wholesaler before selling them on to the customer who ordered them. This sort of activity helps to make a market efficient.

It may also be that transactions between two currencies use the intermediary of a third. This would help to bump up the proportion of inter-dealer trading in a manner that is really fairly innocent. The vast majority of deals in the currency markets of the City and elsewhere involve US dollars. The proportion is actually staggering. In 1989 only 9 per cent of all currency trading in London did not involve dollars. In 1986 it had been only 3 per cent. 27 per cent of the City's deals are between dollars and sterling. This still leaves some 64 per cent of all deals taking place in London (about $120 billion worth) that involve exchanges between dollars and other non-sterling currencies. The City is actually the largest centre in the world for this sort of transaction involving non-local currencies (presumably because of the concentration of international banks). Figure 5.2 shows the actual breakdown.

The supremacy of the dollar is largely explained by its importance in international trade. It is widely used by all traders, especially when one or more of the partners to a transaction is from a country whose currency is non-convertible – not able to be bought and sold

FIGURE 5.2
Analysis of Currency Transactions in London, 1986 and 1989

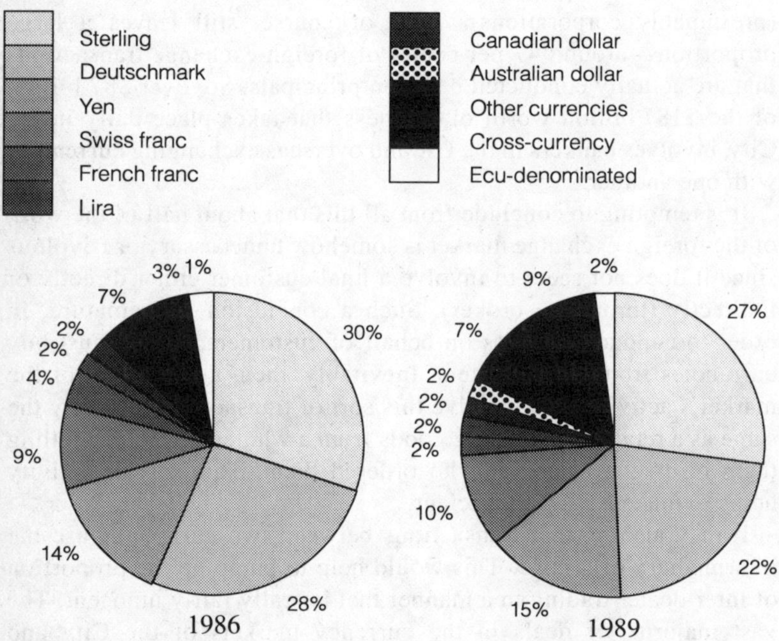

In all except 'cross-currency' transactions, US dollars are exchanged for the currency named

SOURCE *Bank of England Quarterly Bulletin*, November 1989.

in international markets. The dollar is frequently acceptable to both sides of such a deal. As a result, dealing in dollars is far more active than in other currencies. So dealers take advantage of the easy availability of dollars to use them as a form of proxy in deals that directly involve other currencies. Commissioned to exchange, say, sterling for yen, they may choose to go through the medium of dollars. If so, the number of inter-bank deals will have increased misleadingly. The extra deals are still relating to the needs of the outside customer.

It is anyway becoming increasingly difficult to distinguish between the activities of banks and some of their customers. An increasing number of large companies operate in foreign exchange markets as if they were banks. They hold large balances of foreign currency and may well be approached by banks and brokers exactly as if they were a principal in the market. All this makes it very hard to draw many safe conclusions from the direction of currency dealing in the modern market.

One simple point is blindingly obvious even from this analysis of the foreign exchange market. It has grown remarkably, both in London and elsewhere. What is more, it has grown a great deal faster than the international trade that it is supposed to be financing. The Bank for International Settlements concluded its 1989 survey of the global foreign exchange market with the observation that 'the expansion of turnover since 1986 is considerably greater than can be accounted for by the growth in the value of world trade; financially driven transactions appear to have become increasingly important'. That last phrase about 'financially driven transactions' has a dark signficance which must be investigated

What Changes Exchange Rates?

The Old, Old Story

Generations of economics students have cheerfully accepted the proposition that exchange rates are determined by trade flows. The reasoning is well-known: an exchange rate is simply a price – the price of one currency expressed in terms of another. Like any other price, it reflects the purchasing power of money. If a standard basket of goods costs £100 in the UK and DM300 in Germany, then the purchasing power of £1 is equivalent to that of DM3.0. The exchange rate will reflect this. If prices rise faster in the UK than in Germany, then the purchasing power of sterling falls relative to the Deutschmark – so the value of the pound will fall below DM3.0. The actual mechanism that brings about this exchange rate – or 'purchasing power parity' as it is called – is simple market forces. If British inflation is higher than that in Germany, but the exchange rate is still at £1:DM3.0, then the British would be far better off buying their goods from Germany – taking advantage of lower relative prices. The British will, therefore, be falling over themselves to exchange their pounds for Deutschmarks in an effort to buy German imports. Supply of pounds in foreign exchange markets has risen. So has demand for Deutschmarks. As in any other market, the price of the pound will fall, and that of the Deutschmark will rise. This means the exchange rate will change from £1:DM3.0 to, perhaps, £1:DM2.75. The 'purchasing power parity' is restored – you now need only DM2.75 in Germany to buy what £1 will purchase in the UK. Once this parity is reached, the rush to exchange currencies diminishes and we are, once again, in equilibrium.

It all seems engagingly neat. Fluctuations in exchange rates are caused by trading flows, which themselves result from divergences in the purchasing power of particular currencies. The exchange rate fluctuations serve to eliminate the differences in purchasing power. What could be simpler?

If only it were true. The principle is sound enough but, as generations of economics students have almost certainly thought quietly to themselves, there must be more to it than that. A good deal of evidence shows that there is. As you will have noticed, the theory suggests that exchange rates are determined by flows of trade, which are themselves directed by movements in international prices. Well, the Germans and the Japanese are known to have been net exporters and to have experienced lower inflation than most other countries for many years. Why, then, do the Deutschmark and the yen not continually rise in value against all other currencies? For they do not. The USA has totted up some of the most alarming trade deficits during the later 1980s. Admittedly, the dollar has fallen (sometimes dramatically) at various times, but it has risen too. How come? More to the point, perhaps, we are daily informed on news broadcasts that the value of the pound has risen or fallen or that it has 'come under pressure' during a day's trading. Are these excitements entirely explained by daily fluctuations in the relative prices of Scotch whisky and German sausage? Prices are hardly that volatile. Nor, for that matter, is trade. And how are we able to join an exchange rate system whilst at the same time running a higher rate of inflation than our main partners and a trade deficit of some £10 billion per year? Should not all this make our currency fall in value?

The Bank for International Settlements (BIS) gives the game away. The volume of currency traded is vastly greater than can be accounted for simply by trade flows. If exporting and importing were the only reasons for changing currencies, the foreign exchange markets would be very drab places. As the BIS says, 'financially driven transactions' are the cause of the increase in activity on foreign exchange markets. These are the real reasons for the bulk of currency exchange; so they are the main cause of changes in exchange rates.

It should, by now, come as no surprise to learn that the 1980s have witnessed an enormous increase in the volume of such international transactions. Progressive deregulation and, especially, the abolition of exchange controls have removed the barriers to free flows of capital between nations. Investors have a virtually free choice when it comes to deciding which securities to buy and where to buy them. This, of course, leads to increased currency exchange. It also causes the prices of the securities themselves to be increasingly volatile, which gives greater reason to buy and sell them. This, in turn, leads to a further boom in the 'financially driven' transactions referred to by the BIS. The foreign exchange market, then, is no longer driven by markets for traded goods where international money flows are comparatively small and where price changes are laboriously slow, but rather by markets for financial assets where flows of investment capital are huge and where prices can change by the second (thanks to the electronic systems employed) and give rise to more and more movements of money.

The markets involved here are for the same bonds and securities that we encountered earlier. The main motive for buying and selling such assets lies with the rate of interest. The simple argument goes that if British interest rates are higher than those in Germany, then a German with money to lend would rather lend it to a British borrower. So he will buy British securities, and change his Deutschmarks into pounds in order to do so. This will help to push up the exchange rate of the pound against the Deutschmark. This certainly goes some way to explaining why Chancellor Lawson raised UK interest rates in January 1985 when the pound appeared to be sinking without trace against the dollar, and again in October 1989 when the German Bundesbank raised its rates. In each case, Lawson was

FIGURE 5.3
The Exchange Rate and the Interest Rate, 1983–90

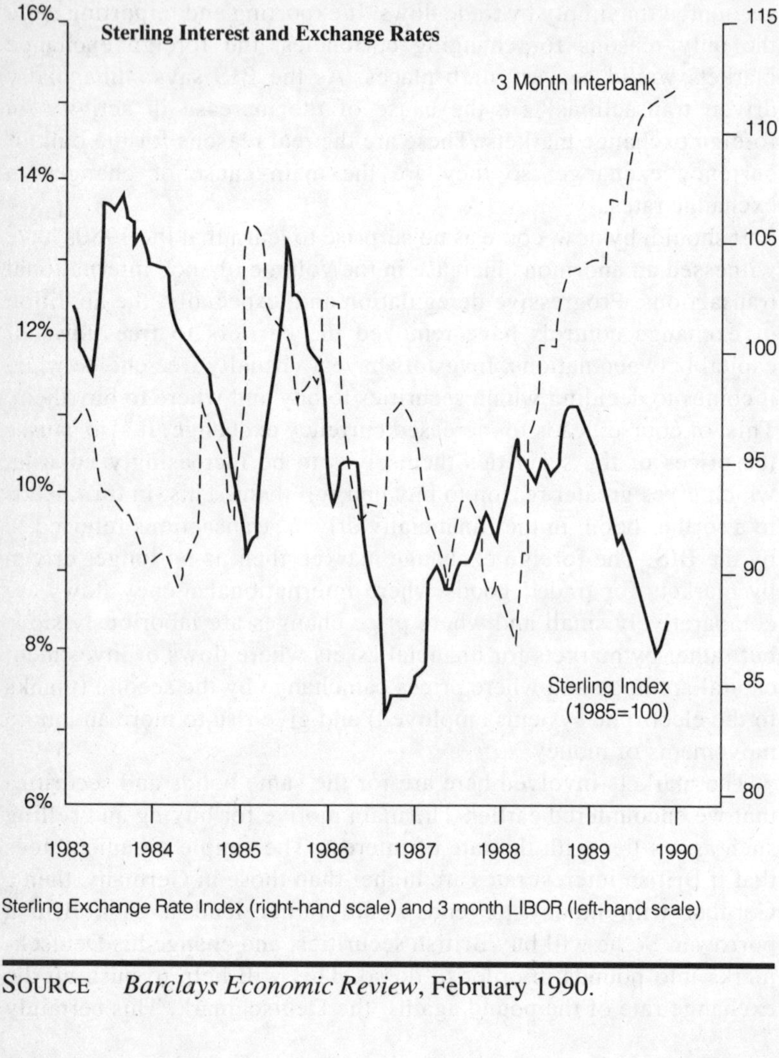

Sterling Exchange Rate Index (right-hand scale) and 3 month LIBOR (left-hand scale)

SOURCE *Barclays Economic Review*, February 1990.

hoping to attract money into the UK, or, at least, to prevent it from leaving. So he was protecting the exchange rate.

Sadly, these simple interest rate changes alone are not going to be enough to explain exchange rate fluctuations. Figure 5.3 relates changes in UK interest rates (represented by LIBOR) to the average exchange rate between sterling and all other currencies (known as the sterling index). It certainly shows periods where changes in interest rates seem to have caused the pound to rise or fall. 1985 offers a particularly clear example. But there are rather more occasions where the relationship is strained to say the least. Further analysis raises more doubts. Figure 5.4 compares short-term interest rates in the UK and in Germany. Rates in the UK were at least 5 per cent higher than those in Germany for almost every year betwen 1981 and 1991. The margin was usually greater than that. Why has this not drained the Federal Republic of all spare cash? Why is the pound not up to DM8 again, or even more? Speaking of Germany and the UK, the events of October 1989 require a little more analysis too. Chancellor Lawson's decision to raise UK interest rates to 15 per cent came just twenty minutes after the Bundesbank's new rate was announced. The situation was so severe that $2.8 billion of UK reserves were spent in that twenty minutes to support the value of the pound before the changing of British interest rates helped to stem the haemorrhage. Can this flight from sterling be entirely the result of the opportunity to earn an extra fraction of a per cent on German bonds?

The New Pantomime

Investors are affected not only by the nominal rate of interest but also by the real rate. This is the rate of interest minus the rate of inflation. High rates of inflation are likely to depress the value of a currency since they are sure to harm a nation's trade. Investing in a country with high interest rates and high inflation could prove foolhardy. By the time you have earned your year's interest, the value of the currency could have declined so far as a result of inflation that all your return is wiped out when you come to convert back into your own currency. This helps to explain the attraction of the currencies of low inflation countries (like Germany) even when their interest rates are comparatively low. The low inflation is likely to make them appreciate anyway. Interest payments will be a bonus.

FIGURE 5.4
Short-term Interest Rates in the UK and Germany, 1979–90

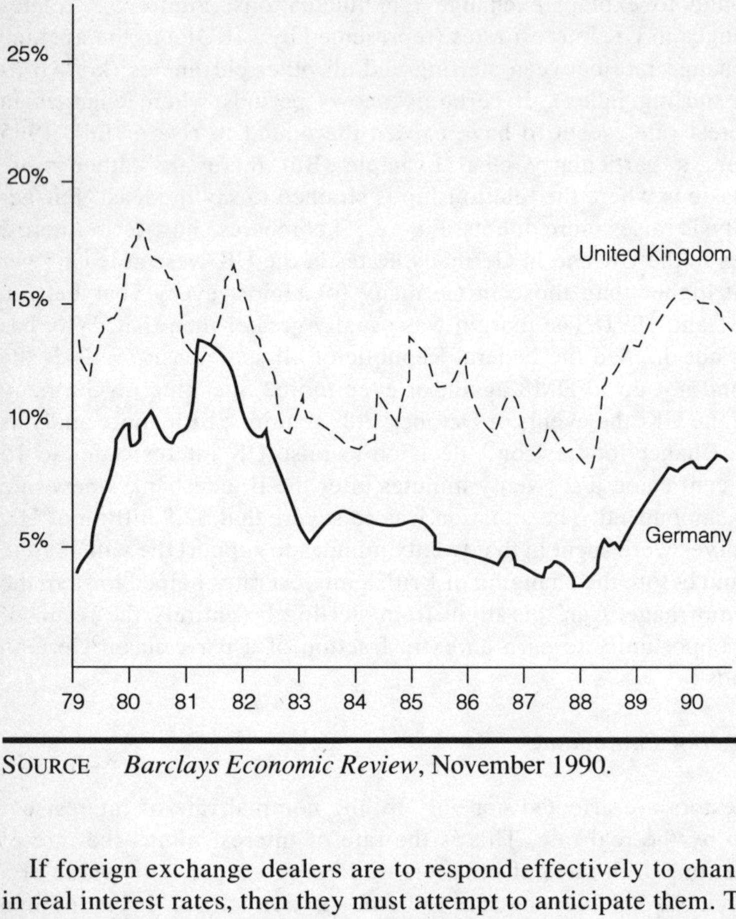

SOURCE *Barclays Economic Review*, November 1990.

If foreign exchange dealers are to respond effectively to changes in real interest rates, then they must attempt to anticipate them. This means that they try to predict national inflation rates. Dealing departments therefore rely today upon the services of armies of economists who monitor the complex statistical information about various national economies. By analysis of trends in inflation, output, employment and so on, they hope to be able to estimate future trends in inflation and interest rates. They hope that this will give an accurate idea of whether assets purchased in that country will, in time, offer a good rate of return when earnings are finally reconverted into the home currency. The market tries to anticipate likely developments within each national economy. If it anticipates them correctly, then the announcement of changes in inflation, interest rates and so on will have no effect on the exchange rate. Dealers will already have absorbed the implications of the news, before it was announced. It sounds crazy, but it is true; the market is working in advance of itself and so only reacts strongly to unexpected data. At its most ludicrous, this means that changes in the exchange rate are caused by the failure of analysts to predict correctly. It can make life hard for governments; in late 1990, for example, Chancellor Lamont had trouble deciding whether the fall in sterling was in anticipation of a reduction in interest rates (in which case an actual cut in rates would have no further ill-effects) or whether such a policy would make sterling fall even further.

At its most perfect theory suggests that exchange rates are ultimately determined by the principle of 'portfolio balance'. Exchange rates are affected by the decisions of investors who are shifting their portfolios from one country to another – purchasing securities, for example, in the UK rather than Germany. This means that exchange rate changes actually come to represent changes in the perceived real rate of return on portfolio investments. So, in answer to our earlier question, changes in exchange rate come about because investors constantly respond to previous changes in exchange rates by adjusting their portfolios in accordance with their changed perceptions.

This sounds unduly complicated but is reasonably convincing. It seems to imply that the level of the exchange rate depends not upon trade flows but upon the activities of investors in buying securities. You would presume that this behaviour is based to some extent on the analysis that professional economists have made of the economic circumstances prevailing in the particular countries that they study and in their estimates of those countries' future prospects. The 'portfolio balance' principle does not actually require this specialist advice, though. If exchange rate fluctuations reflect the perceived rates of return on assets, then changes in exchange rates are themselves enough to determine how portfolios should be rearranged. The exchange rate becomes a sort of shorthand expression of all the other factors that the economists are sweating away to analyse. Why not just respond to the exchange rate itself?

Taken to this extreme, the main explanation of the foreign

exchange market's behaviour appears to be the market itself. Exchange rates change as funds are moved on the foreign exchange market. The major movements of funds are brought about by shifts in investments. The signals that lead to these shifts in investments are changes in exchange rates. So, exchange rate changes are caused by changes in exchange rates. This may seem a disturbing conclusion. It should be remembered, too, that it is a comparatively new phenomenon for it can only operate in a market where movements of portfolio funds are sufficiently large as to be the major (or only) cause of exchange rate fluctuations. This can only occur when international deregulation allows funds to move freely from country to country.

The new City, then, is the home of a foreign exchange market from the realms of pantomime – a market that can interpret its own behaviour as the basis for blind panic or ludicrous optimism. Of course, it is not quite as silly as it sounds. The new gurus of the market are a group of technical analysts who have come to be known as 'chartists'.

The Magic of the Chartists

It is comforting to believe that fluctuations in exchange rates reflect underlying strengths and weaknesses in national economies. Beyond simple trade flows, they respond to a range of genuine economic influences such as inflation and the success of government policy. If this is the case, then the exchange rate could be seen as a valuable single indicator of a country's economic standing, distilled through the convenient efficiency of the foreign exchange market.

The existence of chartists could undermine such a notion. We have referred already to the specialist economists who advise foreign exchange dealers. They are not alone. Almost all dealers today rely also upon the services of technical analysts (chartists) whose study is not of the economies whose currencies are being traded, but of the market itself. Chart analysis aims to identify patterns in exchange rates over time, in the hope that these patterns might repeat themselves and that, by recognising them, dealers will know what to do next. For example, 'reversal patterns' indicate that a particular trend is due to be reversed. By studying past patterns, chartists can advise dealers of the best time to buy or sell a currency

FIGURE 5.5
An Example of the 'Head and Shoulders' Chart Used by Chartists

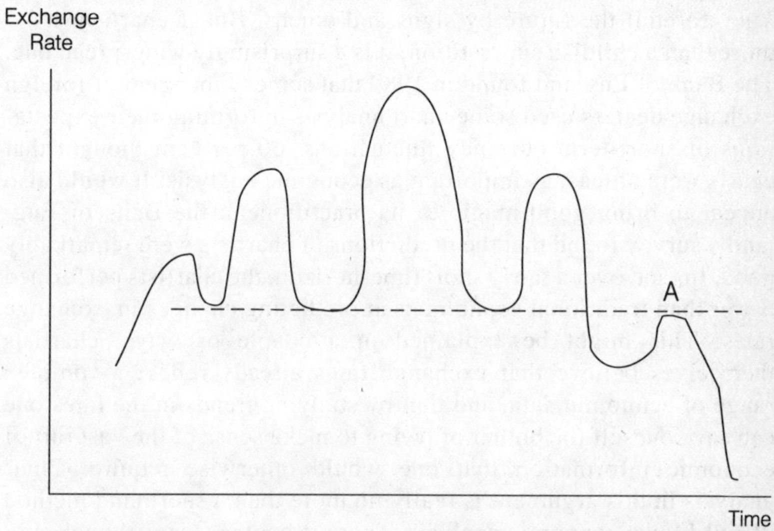

If the exchange rate does not rise to pass the level shown at point *A*, then chartists anticipate a reversal of the pattern shown.

SOURCE *Bank of England Quarterly Bulletin*, November 1989.

in order to anticipate a change in value that is predicted by the patterns. The patterns from which they work are highly specific. Some are generally known: the 'head and shoulders reversal', for example, is shown in Figure 5.5. It predicts that a small increase in value (the left-hand 'shoulder') will be followed by a far larger one (the 'head') and that there will a further small price increase (the right-hand 'shoulder') before the price falls away. By expecting the 'head', dealers have a clearer idea of when they should buy and when sell. Other patterns – the 'broadening top' which predicts a series of price rises followed by a deep fall, and the 'double bottom' which shows two price falls separated by a significant rise – are widely accepted. Individual analysts, though, are constantly searching for patterns that they alone recognise in the hope of gaining an advantage over the rest of the market. As well as looking for patterns, they also study rates of change of currency prices to build 'momentum' models which predict future fluctuations on the basis of the speed with which observed changes have occurred.

Chartists seem to be the financial equivalent of witch-doctors. They foretell the future by signs and omens. But if chartism is no more than a childish superstition, it is a surprisingly widespread one. The Bank of England found in 1989 that some 90 per cent of foreign exchange dealers used some chart analysis in forming their expectations of short-term currency fluctuations. 60 per cent thought that charts were at least as important as economic analysis. It would also appear to bring good magic to its practitioners: the Bank of England's survey found that the predictions of chartists were remarkably good. In fact, over a fairly short time-horizon, the chartists performed better than traditional economists at predicting changes in exchange rates. This might be explained in a couple of ways: chartists themselves believe that exchange rates already reflect a complex range of economic data, and that by studying trends in the rates one can save oneself the bother of trying to make sense of the vast raft of economic information that one would otherwise require. Chart analysis in this argument is really no more than a shorthand method of full-blown economic analysis. There is another view, though. If a large proportion of the market is working on this sort of technical prediction, then it will become self-fulfilling. If charts imply that rates are about to rise, then dealers will be advised to buy and so rates will rise. This, of course, will reinforce faith in the chartists' predictions and so the process will recur.

The good magic may not end with the simple success of chartists' predictions. It is reckoned that the use of chart analysis should help to stabilise the foreign exchange market. If dealers are seeking to repeat patterns in price movements, then currencies should conform to these patterns rather than lurching wildly up or down. The Bank of England also found sufficient difference in individual chartists' predictions to mean that the market was not being reduced to a series of graph-copying exercises.

Nonetheless, a few concerns remain. As chartism becomes more widespread and more sophisticated, the chances are that predictions might converge and cause wider fluctuations in exchange rates than were either predicted or desirable. There is an impact upon government policy, too. The Bank of England itself in one of its excellent educational presentations describes a situation in which the Bank watches sterling fall in value to $1.626 and then knows that it must act to support the pound, since it is nearing a value which will trigger selling in the market. This implies that government policy is being dictated by a market which regards its own whimsical rules of thumb as more significant than actual economic data. Only 8 per cent of foreign exchange dealers admit to believing that chartism and economic analysis do not mix. Problems might nonetheless arise if too many of the remaining 92 per cent prefer the chart to the analysis at the same time. There is a further concern too. It is widely believed that, while markets may respond to capricious influences in the short term, their long-term behaviour nonetheless manages to reflect genuine economic factors. In effect, the long-term rate represents a real equilibrium even though there may be short-term fluctuations around it. Might there be a danger that over-dependence upon chart analysis can deflect the exchange rate from its current long-term trend and leave us with a rate that reflects no more than the market's own analysis of past trends? At the moment the market believes that the long-term trend will always come through. But it can only come through via the behaviour of dealers themselves.

Exchange Rate Systems and Cartels

It comes increasingly to look as though the foreign exchange market is riddled with imperfections. We have not seen the last of them. It was revealed in autumn 1990 that ten of the major banks dealing in the market had attempted to form a cartel to influence the setting of prices. They were not aiming to control exchange rates, but rather to increase the spread between buying and selling prices in the currency market in order to increase the profit margins of dealers. The agreement, apparently, was that large deals would only be conducted with dealers offering a spread of at least 0.1 cent in the dollar. This is twice as large as the spreads then being offered elsewhere in the market. The agreement (which lacked the support of three market leaders: NatWest, Citibank and Chase Manhattan) was an attempt to improve cash flow within the market. It appears to have failed as members of the cartel found themselves isolated. It is further evidence, though, of the ways in which this market seems to find that market forces alone are not enough.

Governments are the worst offenders. The major reason for the increase in foreign exchange market activity over the past fifteen years has been the breakdown of fixed exchange rate systems. From 1946 until the early 1970s, exchange rates were fixed in the Bretton Woods system. The value of individual currencies was set in terms of US dollars. governments agreed to intervene in currency markets as necessary to maintain their currency's fixed value. The existence of exchange controls, of course, meant that international capital flows were vastly reduced and so currencies came under less pressure. The system worked reasonably well until the late 1960s when large American trade deficits inevitably pushed the dollar down in value. Attempts were made to hold the system together, but it crumbled during the early 1970s. It ushered in a period of free-for-all which became even more frantic with the abolition of exchange controls in various centres in the 1980s. When there is nothing to stop money moving between countries, the business of money-changers (which is all that the foreign exchange market really is) increases accordingly.

Governments did not like the free-for-all. It is one thing to believe in market forces. This becomes harder when one doubts the good sense and validity of the market itself. There were a number of occasions during the 1980s when governments formed cartels a great deal more effective than that of the banks. The most obvious, of course, is the Exchange Rate Mechanism (ERM) of the European Community but there were others. In 1985, in what became known as the Plaza Agreement, the group of five leading industrial nations (including the UK) agreed to encourage a 10 per cent fall in the value of the US dollar by telling the market that they regarded it as overvalued. A fund was allocated to provide hard backing for the words. By 1987 the problem was reversed. In the Louvre Accord of that year, an agreement was made (by the G7 countries this time) to support the dollar if it fell more than 5 per cent below specified rates against the Deutschmark and yen.

It is tempting to conclude that these cartels – for that is what they are – reflect a basic lack of faith on the part of national governments in the reliability of the foreign exchange market. Perhaps they fear the reliance upon chartists. They know that short-term market fluctuations can temporarily destabilise a currency value for reasons that have as much to do with the psychology of the market itself as with the economy concerned. Perhaps they trust the market in the long run, but their short-run fears are sufficient to make them intervene. Margaret Thatcher famously scorned attempts to reduce the surging pound in 1988, insisting that 'you cannot buck the market'. Yet she was fully prepared to allow sterling to join the ERM in 1990 which, if not actually bucking the market, can hardly be interpreted as an avowal of faith in it.

The free play of market forces has probably never been a genuine reality in foreign exchange markets. Nonetheless, the 1970s and 1980s have seen a greater measure of freedom than most periods. How long can even that degree of freedom last?

Europe and the Future

Current developments within the European Community make the Louvre and Plaza Accords seem very insignificant attempts to interfere with the freedom of the foreign exchange market. The ERM was established in 1979 and, by the end of 1990, involved all EC currencies save the Portuguese escudo and the Greek drachma. Member- governments agree to limit the fluctuation of their currency value to within 2.25 per cent (6 per cent for the peseta and sterling) of an agreed central value. This central value may be expressed in terms of each of the other member-currencies (including Europe's own currency, the ECU), but it is the Deutschmark rate that provides the benchmark of the system.

The breakdown of the Bretton Woods system in the early 1970s is sometimes said to have split the world into three exchange-rate blocs. We have already seen the phenomenal importance of the US dollar in currency markets and it will come as no surprise that the dollar bloc is particularly influential, covering North, South and Central America, much of the Middle East (since oil trade is so dependent upon the dollar) as well as a good proportion of the developing worlds of Africa and the Far East. Much of the remainder of the Far East depends upon the yen, though its influence is limited by the Japanese government's reluctance to allow their currency to take the international position that their country's economic strength might dictate. The Japanese are still keen to control their currency in order to direct trade. The third bloc covers Europe and is based on the Deutschmark. Germany is the largest and most successful of the European economies and is a major trading influence both within Europe and elsewhere. It is inevitable that the ERM, for all its supposed dependence upon the ECU, becomes in effect a Deutschmark system.

Arguments elsewhere have given full consideration to the effect of ERM membership upon trade and inflation, upon employment and interest rates. We are concerned here with its effects upon foreign exchange markets. Clearly, an agreement of this kind must limit the extent to which exchange rates fluctuate. This is its purpose. Whilst this may seem to impose a constraint upon the market, it is really no more than an added piece of information to be absorbed. If the pound is nearing its upper limit against the Deutschmark, then the market has good reason to anticipate a fall in its value. This may be precipitated by a fall in UK interest rates as the authorities hope to encourage selling of pounds. It may simply involve limited selling by the Bank of England. It may not require either of these. If the pound is nearing its upper limit, then the market can make the decision to sell pounds without any external cajoling from the UK, since they are already anticipating a fall. One might describe membership of the ERM as no more than a system of chartism where the authorities have designed the chart. In this sense there is no reason to expect the market to be significantly affected. Fluctuations will be smaller, but risks will be reduced and so the volumes of currency traded are unlikely to stabilise. Membership of the ERM may bring a discipline to the market, but not a dampening effect.

This, of course, is especially true when it is remembered how few deals are directly between EC currencies. The dollar is outside the ERM and so margins of fluctuation remain wide. We should probably expect to see a further increase in the proportion of deals that do not involve dollars, especially those involving Deutschmarks, but the proportion will remain small for many years to come.

The development of a common currency may have rather more significant effects. Clearly, it must cause a simple reduction in dealing. All the deals that are currently needed for the exchange of one EC currency for another will be redundant. It is hard to tell exactly how large such business is since so much of it is channelled through the medium of dollars. We can be sure, though, that it is large, for we know the volumes of trade taking place between member-countries. As well as this there are currency flows caused by interest rate differentials. These will no longer require the services of the foreign exchange market. It is likely, then, that the market will be affected by such a development. It would be wrong to exaggerate the likely effects. Business in dollars and yen will still be enormously important and it is to be expected that any single European currency will attract a great deal of business in itself, for it will be an extremely important trading currency. It would not be absurd to suggest that, in the very long run, such a currency might come to threaten the dollar's domination of the foreign exchange market.

Important for London is the question of the European Central Bank that would be necessary to administer and control such a currency. This bank's influence on European interest rates would be very great. The location of the bank might generate a more specific area of influence too. It is in Chapter 8 that we consider central banking in detail. For now, it is enough to know that the major role of such a bank is to act as 'guardian' of the currency. Today this is bound to entail the control of interest rates – both as a means of affecting currency value in foreign exchange markets, and in order to control domestic inflation, and thus the value of the currency measured against goods. A European Central Bank will therefore have significant power over interest rates throughout the EC. Will this make the city of its location an important financial centre in itself? Perhaps banks, whose business is to anticipate and react to interest rate changes, will feel the need to be physically near the seat of such decision-making. There are those who attribute Frankfurt's rise as an international banking centre to the location within it of the Bundesbank, widely recognised as one of the world's most influential central banks. The same reasoning could lead the European end of the foreign exchange market to desert London for some more central location.

Logically, there is no particular reason why it should. Communications are now so good that physical location is far less important than once it was. Indeed, if banks are going to desert London they would seem better advised to do so on the basis of cost, and to find a site where property values are lower and transport systems more efficient. If foreign exchange dealers are seeking to be close to anything, it is probably other foreign exchange dealers. The past success of London as a dollar-trading centre also proves that proximity to the source of a currency is fairly unimportant in developing the knack of dealing in it. The Bundesbank's siting may have helped Frankfurt's development as a banking centre, but it was already important. That is why it was chosen. So, even if European

Monetary Union does become firmly established, it would be premature to predict a quick end to the City's dominance in the European foreign exchange market.

Europe and the Future of Futures

Chapter 6 is devoted to a full analysis of the City's markets in financial and commodity futures, forwards and options. A large proportion of these contracts involve currencies and they may be more affected by developments within the EC than the 'spot' market that we have so far considered.

Whilst the majority (64 per cent in 1989) of foreign exchange dealing is still for immediate delivery (the 'spot' market), markets in forward currencies have grown rapidly over the 1970s and 1980s. It is tempting to regard such deals as a sophisticated form of gambling and to see the market as no more than a respectable version of the dog-track. The judgement is unfair. The main use of forward markets is for the hedging of risks to avoid loss rather than to make profit.

An exporter selling goods to the USA in mid-1990 would have faced an exchange rate of about $1.75 to the pound. If he priced his goods at £1000, then he would have agreed on dollar revenues of $1750. By the end of the year, the pound had risen to $1.95. When the exporter now receives his dollars, he finds them worth under £900. This has clearly reduced his profit on the deal and may even have caused a loss. Uncertainty like this can discourage trade altogether. The forward market removes the uncertainty. At the time of the original deal, our exporter also arranges (for a fee, of course) to sell $1750 in six months' time for £1000 (effectively locking himself into the going exchange rate). In this way, he receives the £1000 he needs, for the cost of the contract. It is a form of insurance. Of course, he also sacrifices any further profit he might have made if the pound had fallen to, say, $1.50. He has agreed to sell his dollars for £1000, though they would now be worth almost £1200 (as the seller of the contract, of course, hopes that they will be). The exporter can try to have things both ways by using an option contract rather than a forward contract. This gives him the right to swap his dollars for £1000, though he does not have to exercise the option. If the exchange rate is $1.95, he will do so. If it is $1.50, he will not. He has covered his loss without endangering the possibility of profit.

Options, unsurprisingly, are more expensive than forward contracts.

A major aim of the European exchange rate system and of the move towards a single currency is that, by eliminating or reducing exchange rate fluctuations, trade will be promoted. A side-effect must surely be that the need for forward markets will be reduced. If international trade is less risky, then firms will not need the insurance offered by these markets. In 1989, the Bank of England estimated that forward currency dealing in London was worth around $50 billion a day. Of course, much of this will involve non-European currencies and will be unaffected. Nonetheless, there is bound to be a fall in demand for these contracts. This could turn out to be the most significant immediate effect, as far as the City is concerned, of our participation in the ERM and of the move towards a single currency. Between 1986 and 1989 the volume of dealing in ECU on the London foreign exchange market rose faster than that in any other single currency. It still represents only around 2 per cent of daily business, but the increase implies that there is an attraction in a currency that is increasingly acceptable throughout Europe. Altogether, trends seem firmly towards the use of controlled currencies and a consequent decline in demand for the services of forward currency markets in London and elsewhere.

Whatever Happened to Speculators?

There may be those who are surprised to have come across no reference in this chapter to the activities of currency speculators. Back in the 1960s it was widely believed that exchange rates were being controlled by rich and unscrupulous men who spent their days swapping their fortunes from currency to currency, callously watching governments fall as they did so. It was never really like that. The prime movers in currency markets are international banks and multinational corporations. As we have seen, the Bank for International Settlements describes the bulk of foreign currency transactions as being 'financially driven'. This is not the same as speculation.

Corporations and banks can frequently find themselves holding large sums of money. They know that these sums will soon be spent, in the meantime they wish to achieve a return on their cash. The way to do this is to buy some sort of asset, probably a security or bond, that can be readily sold when the need arises. Inevitably, they will search for the securities that offer the best rate of return. This will entail moving their cash from country to country as real rates of return are estimated to change with international events and with expectations of the future. There is no doubt that the scale of this sort of activity increased dramatically with the abandonment of fixed exchange rates, with deregulation and, particularly, with the removal of exchange controls. International capital flows are now very sensitive to changes in interest rates and to international economic news of all kinds. This increased sensitivity has caused greater volatility in exchange rates and has led governments to re-establish some forms of control over this important market (through agreements, accords and full-blown exchange rate systems).

It would be unfair, however, to regard these banks and corporations as the reincarnation of the pantomime-villain speculators of the 1960s. They are doing no more than you or I do when we move some our savings from the bank to the building society or from shares to an endowment policy. They are innocently seeking the best return on their assets. If their activities are damaging, then one should not blame them but rather attempt to direct their actions so that the damage is minimised. That has begun in the 1980s and we shall see more of it in the 1990s.

6 Looking to the Futures

Origins

Markets in futures and options contracts are generally regarded as part of the more modern and sophisticated side of the City's business. There is, as somebody once said, nothing new under the sun. In 1694 a City financier is recorded as having enquired of brokers 'how many guineas a share' he might receive for 'the liberty to accept or refuse such shares at such a price at any time within six months, or other time they shall agree for'. He was offering brokers the option to buy or sell shares in the future at a price agreed now. Exactly the same deal can be conducted today on the London Traded Options Market (merged in 1990 with the London International Financial Futures Exchange – LIFFE). He was actually offering what is called an 'American option', since it can be exercised at any time before its date of expiry ('at any time within six months'). There are also 'European options' which can only be exercised on their date of expiry.

Options do not only exist in shares. In fact, despite this promising start in the seventeenth century, the current market in share options in the City dates only from 1958. The market was not permitted on the floor of the Stock Exchange until 1978. It caught on quickly enough. In 1978 around 9000 contracts were traded each month. By 1987 the figure passed one million per month. The reason, interestingly, for the delay in the formal establishment of a traded options market was the fear that such dealing would expose the Exchange to criticism on the grounds of excessive and destabilising speculation. It is easy to see how such criticism might arise. On the face of it, markets in options and futures would seem simply to provide the opportunity for making rich men richer – perhaps at the expense of prices in the underlying market. This question of the purpose and value of such markets, and of their effects upon others, will provide a theme for this chapter.

It is not in the area of shares or other financial securities that we find the true origin of futures and options contracts. It is, as we saw in Chapter 2, in markets for agricultural commodities. The great agricultural states of the American mid-West take their products to the commodity markets of Chicago for exchange. Prices in agricultural markets are subject to wide fluctuation as harvests and growing conditions vary. Futures contracts developed in Chicago as a means of guaranteeing prices. Chicago remains the acknowledged centre of global trading in futures and options contracts. Until comparatively recently, commodity futures were still the most actively traded contracts of this kind. Markets in various minerals and specific agricultural products flourish in London today. Their development has been tame, though, when compared with the recent growth of financial futures.

Markets in financial futures have developed all over the world since the late 1970s. Toronto, New York, Tokyo, Paris, Singapore and many others now compete with Chicago. London joined the market in 1982 when LIFFE was established. Figure 6.1 shows the growth of global trading in interest rate futures. From 20 000 contracts in 1975, all of which were arranged in Chicago, the market had swollen by 1988 to over 156 million per year. Chicago's share of this business fell from 100 per cent to 64 per cent. It is clearly still the centre of the market. LIFFE dominates the European end, of which it can boast around 50 per cent. Globally, though, this is an area where London does not dominate. It has about 8.5 per cent of the world market, behind Tokyo and ahead of Paris, but no threat as far as North America is concerned.

The growth of financial futures in the 1980s has been astonishing. They take the form of contracts to lend or borrow money, or to exchange currencies, on specific future dates at interest or exchange rates set in the contract. We accounted earlier for the growth of futures contracts in commodities by describing the volatility of prices in the underlying markets. If you are producing wheat for

FIGURE 6.1
The Growing Trade in Interest-rate Futures Contracts, 1975–88

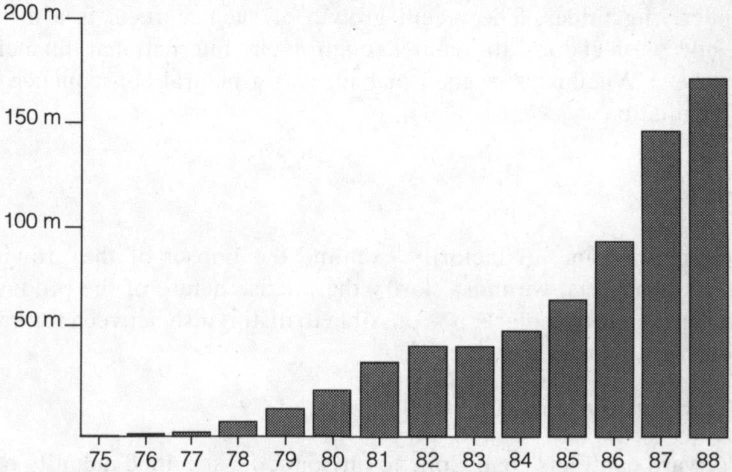

SOURCE *Bank of England Quarterly Bulletin*, August 1989

delivery in six months' time, then the prospect of a significant fall in the price of wheat is a worrying one. A contract that allows you to fix the price today may well be very attractive. The same reasoning applies to financial futures. Their growth can be explained in terms of the volatility of underlying prices.

The breakdown of the Bretton Woods fixed exchange rate system in the early 1970s led to a period of considerably increased currency fluctuation. The uncertainty that this created prompted a demand for contracts in foreign exchange futures in the same way that our wheat farmer was encouraged to use the futures market to reduce the risk that price fluctuations presented to him.

International deregulation, accompanied by the abandonment of exchange controls, has encouraged far greater international capital movements in the 1980s than occurred previously. This, in its turn, has led to wider fluctuations in interest rates. Interest rates are the price of borrowing. Large movements of available funds into and out of a borrowing market are bound to alter the market price (the rate of interest). As before, this volatility increases the uncertainty of those who know that they will need to borrow in the future. So there is likely to be an increase in demand for futures contracts that allow one to reduce this uncertainty and to plan ahead.

Markets in futures and options, then, flourish on uncertainty about underlying prices. The recent growth of such markets is a direct result of decisions to remove controls in international financial markets. Whether it is good or bad, it is a natural consequence of deregulation.

Products

Before we can satisfactorily examine the impact of the growing futures markets, we must clarify the precise nature of the products traded. In the first place, it is possible to distinguish between forward contracts, futures and options.

Forward Contracts

Forward contracts enable one to buy or sell a specified quantity of a given item on a stated future date, at a price agreed today. Each forward contract is drawn up specially to serve the purposes of a given trader. As we have already seen, such a contract might be for a physical product such as cocoa or sugar, or, perhaps, for currency. A forward contract will have been drawn up by a banker on behalf of a specific client. It is sure to have been designed with the aim of limiting the risk of a price change. So forward contracts in sugar are likely to be used by companies who produce sugar or who need to buy it; the users of forward contracts in Deutschmarks will be firms who import from or export to Germany. Since the contracts are drawn up in order to cover a specific future transaction, they are not easily tradeable. Indeed, it is unlikely that the company using the contract would wish to trade it, since their belief is that holding the contract will enable them to reduce a given risk. Most forward contracts are not bought or sold after they have been drawn up. They are held until their due date, and are then used to fix the price of a given transaction. This is an important way in which they differ from futures and options contracts, which very rarely culminate in the genuine transaction that they describe. The forward market offers a distinct service to traders in the underlying products. Others are unlikely to use it. The same cannot be said of the markets we consider next.

Futures contracts

Future contracts follow precisely the same principle as forwards, except that they are standardised. Thus, each cocoa future traded on the London Futures and Options Exchange (LFOX) represents 10 tonnes of cocoa, it will be priced in pounds sterling and will be for delivery in either March, May, July, September or December. The minimum length of a contract, therefore, is two months, and the maximum (since the market can only quote seven trading months in advance) is somewhere around fourteen months. So, if in March you wished to cover a deal involving 50 tonnes of cocoa for delivery in six months time, you could buy five contracts due to expire in September. Of course, since the contracts are standardised, they will not match every dealer's need precisely. If your deal involves 43 tonnes of cocoa for October delivery, then you cannot cover your risk exactly. The advantage, though, is that the costs of drawing up a specific contract are avoided and, most importantly, these standardised contracts are readily tradeable. Since everyone knows what the contract represents, it is easy to price it, and to find a buyer or seller. Futures contracts are actively dealt in organised markets. Contracts in cocoa, coffee and sugar are available at LFOX. The London Metal Exchange quotes futures contracts in lead, zinc, nickel, aluminium, silver and so on. The Baltic Exchange has a market in potato futures.

Financial futures, traded at LIFFE, extend precisely the same principle to financial products. Dollar futures, for example, are for $1 million and must expire in March, June, September or December. There are various forms of interest rate future. One possibility is a £500 000 contract that, again, matures in March, June, September or December. Others involve specific financial instruments such as gilt-edged stock, Japanese Government Bonds and US Treasury Bonds. In all these cases, the contract will specify a rate of interest, and so the market is trying to gauge likely movements in future rates. We shall look at these products and their users in greater detail later in the chapter. For now, it is enough to recognise that where forward contracts are the equivalent of clothes made-to-measure for a specific client, futures are off-the-peg and are, therefore, cheaper to use and attract a far larger market. This is important. As we shall see, part of the function of a futures market is that it should be active. Dealers need to know that they can buy and sell easily. It is essential, then, that the products can appeal to as many potential customers as possible.

Options Contracts

Options contracts are exactly what their name suggests. They offer the right to buy or to sell a specific quantity of a specific item at a specific price on a given future date. They are exactly the same as futures contracts, except that the buyer of the contract does not have to exercise it. The advantage is easy to grasp. Suppose that you are dealing with Americans and agree a bargain that will bring you $1000 in three months' time. You are worried that the pound will rise against the dollar in the interim. If so, your $1000 will be worth fewer pounds. A futures contract would allow you to lock in to the current exchange rate so that you know in advance what your $1000 will be worth in three months. But suppose the pound fell against the dollar. That would allow you to earn more from your $1000 than you currently expect. A futures contract would insure you against losing but would also prevent you from gaining. It would fix the exchange rate at a given level. An options contract leaves you with the right to decide whether to deal at the exchange rate specified in the contract or at the going rate in three months' time. If the pound has risen you will exercise your option. If it has fallen you will not. The contract insures you against loss but does not restrict your ability to profit. It seems ideal. Unsurprisingly, an option will cost you more than a futures contract.

It is possible to buy options in commodities or in financial instruments. LFOX deals options in cocoa, coffee and sugar. LIFFE deals currency and interest rate futures as well as a comparatively new product based upon the *Financial Times*–Stock Exchange Ordinary Share Index (the FT–SE Index). These are explained thoroughly in the next section. It is also possible to buy and sell share options in the City. The market has moved from the Stock Exchange to LIFFE. The principle, again, is simple. Instead of buying actual shares, one may buy the right to buy the shares at a set price on a given future date. If the price turns out to be higher, then one exercises the option and profits. If it is lower, the option remains unexercised and one chalks it up to experience. The option could, of course, be to sell rather than to buy. The impact of this market on conventional equity dealing bears investigation. Options are far cheaper than shares, so the margin for profit is considerably increased, while the scope for loss remains limited by one's right not to exercise the option. This might boost the urge to speculate and help to precipitate wider fluctuations in prices on the underlying market. We will consider this issue towards the end of the chapter.

An option to buy (be it shares, currency, a commodity or a financial instrument) is known as a 'call' option, whereas an option to sell is a 'put' option. As we saw earlier, 'American' options may be exercised at any time before their date of expiry. 'European' options may only be exercised on their expiry date. The vast majority of options traded in the City, and all the financial options traded at LIFFE, are American.

It is important to realise that most of the deals in futures and options contracts in London and elsewhere, lead to no actual, physical, transactions. Most buyers of three-month sugar futures would be shocked to see a bulk sugar transporter draw up outside the office. The dealing is either used as a form of insurance or as a speculative venture. The contracts are usually 'closed out' at or before expiry by buying an exactly opposite contract. For example, the holder of a contract to buy three-month sugar can close out by purchasing another contract to sell the same commodity on the same day. The two contracts cancel one another out. No sugar is involved.

In a broad sense, the contracts traded in commodity markets do not differ from the financial contracts traded on the floor of LIFFE and elsewhere. It is this financial market, though, that is the fastest growing and, therefore, currently the most significant. We must examine it further.

Currency Contracts

In Chapter 5 it was explained that a futures contract in currency is a promise to exchange a specified sum on a given future date at an exchange rate agreed at the time of the contract. Until April 1990, these contracts were traded at LIFFE. They are now left to the foreign exchange market. Like all futures and options contracts, they are standardised. Most future currency contracts are based on the dollar. There are dollar/sterling dollar/Deutschmark and dollar/yen contracts available. They are for specified, standard sums. The price at which each contract is traded on any particular day will depend upon expectations of future exchange rates and, more importantly, upon differences and expected differences between national interest rates. This is not just due to the fact that such differences will affect exchange rates. It is mainly because dealers are seeking to anticipate the gain or loss that one could experience by investing cash overseas for (usually) three months and covering the risk with a future currency contract. This seems complicated. An example may help to make it clearer.

• *The Pricing of Currency Futures*

Suppose interest rates in the UK are currently 10 per cent while in the USA they are 15 per cent. Financiers with an eye to profit are bound to change sterling into dollars and invest it at the higher interest rate. They can then insure their risk with a futures contract that allows them to lock into the current exchange rate. In this way, they can be sure to make a profit in sterling when they convert their cash in three months' time.

In fact, the profit they make will depend upon the cost of the futures contract. The interest differential in this example would be so attractive and demand for three month dollar futures so great that dealers would push up their price. The price of the contracts, then, can be seen to depend upon the differences between national interest rates. The larger they are, the greater the upward pressure upon futures prices.

One of the functions of the market is to provide a reliable means of pricing these complex contracts, as well as a means of buying and selling them.

The pricing of options is even more complicated. The difference between futures and options (as we have already seen) is that the holder does not have to exercise his right to buy (or sell) the underlying currency. This is good news for the holder of the option since it allows him to cover the risk of loss without endangering the possibility of profit. It must, however, be bad news for the seller of the contract. If the buyer has a high chance of profit and little possibility of loss, then the seller must have a high chance of loss and a slim opportunity for profit. The price should reflect this. The seller's gain should arise from the price he receives from the contract itself. Arcane mathematical formulae exist that express options prices as a function of the price of the currency concerned, the level of interest rates, the time-span of the option and the expected volatility of the exchange rate.

LIFFE's Work

Financial Futures

Futures markets offer a means of risk management. The more risks there are, the greater the demand for such contracts. LIFFE owes its birth in 1982 to the increased volatility of both interest rates and exchange rates that resulted first from the breakdown of the fixed exchange rate system in the early 1970s and then from the increase in international capital mobility that was caused by deregulation in the 1980s.

London probably seems rather slow in developing a foothold in this market. In fact, LIFFE was the second major exchange to be set up outside North America (the Sydney Futures Exchange was earlier in 1979). The Tokyo exchange did not follow until 1985. The market is, nonetheless, still dominated by Chicago. Part of London's strength, as in so many other financial markets, results from its convenient position within international time zones. It can straddle the gap between the Far East and the USA, trading with Tokyo in the morning and Chicago in the afternoon. As Figure 6.1 shows, the market is growing rapidly. Growth has continued since 1988 – LIFFE boasted a 60 per cent increase in its business in 1990. It does, however, face growing competition from within Europe – most significantly from the French exchange (MATIF: *Marche à Terme d'Instruments Financiers*) which dates only from 1986 but which already rivals LIFFE in terms of the turnover in interest-rate contracts. The fight is on to be the central financial futures exchange of the single European market. It seems to be between the British and the French; the German exchange only opened in November 1990. LIFFE looks favourite for the top position, but MATIF boasted 24 million deals in the first ten months of 1990, only one million behind LIFFE. Like ordinary retailers, much will depend on their ability to offer the products that the customers want. LIFFE's contracts in German government bonds are very successful

– though some of this business may be lost to the infant German exchange. It is believed that a contract based on a pan-European share index will be the key. It will be complicated to devise, but popular with fund managers who invest in Europe, Japan and the USA. Both LIFFE and MATIF are working on it.

LIFFE is a market (or exchange) not unlike the old pre-Big Bang Stock Exchange. It provides a centre for trade in specific financial instruments. The vast majority of instruments traded are contracts in financial instruments and in interest rates. In addition to these, there is now a futures contract based on the FT–SE Index. Customers in these markets must first contact (probably through a bank or broker) a member of LIFFE. Their order will then be phoned through to the floor of the exchange where traders deal through a hectic combination of 'open outcry' (shouting at one another) and hand signals. The advantage of this chaotic system is said to be that all bids and offers are made openly and competition is thus ensured. Members must (theoretically) deal with the first trader to signal acceptance. All deals are recorded on clearing slips and are technically between the customer and the exchange itself. LIFFE therefore is the buyer or seller in every deal that takes place. In this way, the exchange bears all the risk of customers who might fail to honour a deal. This must help to boost business. An experimental electronic trading system has been in operation since December 1989. It seems successful; it managed to cope with 2000 deals a minute soon after the UK joined the ERM. At the moment it is only in use when the floor traders have gone home. For a market dealing in such sophisticated contracts, they are surprisingly attached to the old-fashioned chaos of open outcry.

Interest Rate Contracts

Most of the dealing conducted at LIFFE is in interest-rate contracts. The principle behind an interest-rate future (or option) is that it offers the opportunity to borrow or lend a specific sum at a specified rate of interest for a given period in the future. The market arises because many companies and many banks find themselves committed to future borrowing or lending and worried by the possibility that interest-rate fluctuations could disturb their finances. If you are committed to borrowing £1 million, then an increase of just half of 1 per cent in the rate of interest will cost you £5000 a year. An interest-rate futures contract can help to cover this risk.

There are ten different interest-rate futures traded at LIFFE. Four of them are of the reasonably straightforward type outlined above. These are the three-month contracts in sterling, Eurodollars, Euro-deutschmark, and ECU. In each case the contract is based on a specific, notional sum of money (the sterling contract is for £500 000; the Eurodollar contract for $1 million and so on). The contracts will mature in March, June, September or December. The price of the contract is calculated by deducting the rate of interest that it offers from 100. So, if it offers 12 per cent, the price is 88. This is something of a simplification, however. The money value of the contract actually depends upon the difference between the interest rate that it offers and the going market rate. The minimum difference that a contract can offer is one hundredth of 1 per cent (called a 'tick'). Each sterling contract is for interest on a sum of £500 000 invested for three months. So, each tick is worth 0.01 per cent of £500 000, divided by 4 (since the contract is for a quarter of a year). This comes to £12.50. This means that every single point by which the price changes represents 100 ticks, or £1250. Once again, the system probably seems unduly complicated. Perhaps an example will help.

- *Interest Rate Futures*

Suppose a borrower knows that his £500 000 loan is due to be renegotiated in three months time. Current interest rates are 10 per cent. He is worried that they are set to rise as high as 13 per cent over the next three months. The borrower can sell a contract at LIFFE by which he notionally promises to lend £500 000 at whatever the going interest rate is in three months time. The price of this contract is 90 (100 – 10), since the current interest rate is 10 per cent.

In the meantime the interest rate goes up to 13 per cent. This reduces the price of the interest rate contract from the 90 for which our borrower sold it, to 87 (100 – 13). He can now close out his deal by buying an exactly similar contract (by which he notionally agrees to borrow £500 000). These contracts cancel one another completely, but since he sold the first for 90 and bought the second for 87, he has made a profit of 300 ticks – or £3750. This will exactly compensate for the additional 3 per cent interest that he has to pay on his genuine three-month loan.

The use of futures contracts is unlikely to work out as conveniently in reality as it does for the borrower in our example. Nonetheless, this shows the appeal of such contracts. The three-month sterling contract is one of the most popular of LIFFE's products. Over three and a half million of them were traded in 1988. As well as this sort of contract, though, (available in dollars, Deutschmarks and ECU as well as sterling) there is another form of interest rate contract available. These contracts are not expressed as sums of money, but rather in terms of underlying securities.

Contracts in Money Market Instruments

LIFFE offers six such contracts. Three are for UK government gilt-edged securities – there are 'short gilt', 'medium gilt' and 'long gilt' contracts which differ according to the life to maturity of the underlying stock. In addition, LIFFE deals contracts in US Treasury Bonds, Japanese Government Bonds and German Government Bonds. The 'long gilt' and US Treasury Bond contracts are the most popular. Options are available in these and in the German Government Bond contract.

Money-market futures sound complicated but are actually rather simpler than the interest rate contracts considered above. They specify a given value of stock. For example, the 'long gilt' contract (the most popular of all at LIFFE) is for £50 000 worth of 20-year, 12 per cent, gilt-edged stock. Gilt-edged stock is explained in Chapter 7. For now, it is enough to know that the stock referred to here would offer the holder 12 per cent of £50 000 (£6000) every year for twenty years. It would offer this same sum regardless of what happened to interest rates elsewhere in the economy. The value of the stock might rise above or fall below £50 000, then, if interest rates were to change from 12 per cent. So, the price for which you might buy such stock in the future depends upon your estimate of future-interest rate movements. LIFFE offers people the chance to gamble on their hunches of future interest-rate trends. If you think the rate will be way below 12 per cent in three months time, then you will be prepared to pay a good deal more than £50 000 for the stock, for it will still offer you £6000 per year. With interest rates lower than 12 per cent, a return of £6000 per year represents an investment of more than £50 000.

The contracts dealt at LIFFE are not gilt-edged securities themselves but promises to buy or sell gilt-edged stock at a given price in the future. In fact, gilt-edged stock very rarely changes hands as a result of such contracts. They are simply bought and sold in much the same way as shares, in the hope of a trading profit. Profit or loss depends upon the price of each contract. The price of these contracts (as with the interest-rate futures considered earlier) depends upon the difference between the going interest rate and the one expected in the future. The price of the contract traded at LIFFE is, once again, expressed as a number based upon 100. This represents the £50 000 face value of the stock. The price can change by a minimum of one thirty-second of a point at a time (again, this minimum move is called a 'tick'). Another example will serve to illustrate how such a contract can be used.

•*Gilts Futures*

You are fairly sure that long-term gilt-edged securities are currently undervalued. You feel sure that interest rates will fall in the next three months, and that this will push the price of gilts up. The current price of the futures contract might be 103–25 (103 and 25 ticks). Since it is more than 100, the market already thinks that the stock is worth more than £50 000. You think it will rise further. If you are right, then you will be able to sell the contract in three months time for more – perhaps 105–14. You have made a profit of 53 ticks, which actually represents £828.12, since each tick is worth £15.625 (one thirty-second of 1 per cent of £50 000).

Each financial futures exchange designs its own products, for which it then provides a market. The contracts in Japanese and German Government bonds are a comparatively new addition to LIFFE's range. They lag some way behind the gilts and US Treasury Bond contracts in terms of popularity. In designing a new product, the exchange not only has to decide the underlying instrument (in the case of contracts like these) but also the nominal value and the coupon value (the fixed interest rate). The aim is to find products that suit the needs of the market. The value, therefore, is crucial. Too high and dealers will be scared. Too low and it is not worth dealing. LIFFE has found that the ideal value is related to the time-span of the underlying instrument. Thus, the 20-year gilt contract considered above has a nominal value of only £50 000, while the three-month currency contract was for £500 000. Three-month Eurodeutschmark contracts are for DM1 million, but the contract in 10-year German government Bonds is for only DM250 000. The longer the maturity of the instrument, the wider is the possibility of price fluctuation. Therefore, dealers are better able to control their exposure to risk (and happier to buy the contracts) if the individual contract sizes are smaller. The most recent addition to LIFFE's product range has been a contract based upon the FT–SE 100 Index.

The FT–SE Index Contract

The appeal of futures contracts seems always to depend upon the volatility of underlying prices. Unpredictable prices generate risk. Futures contracts can be used to limit this risk. The prices of shares change a lot. A contract based on share prices was a natural development. It was originally designed to appeal in particular to fund managers, who are more exposed than most to fluctuations in share prices. The contract does not specify individual shares (it is possible to buy options in individual shares, which are explained later in the chapter) but is based upon the FT–SE Index itself. The Index on any day is divided by 10 to give the price of the contract. Each contract notionally represents a portfolio of 'average' shares for delivery (or purchase) in March, June, September or December. If the Index rises in the intervening months, then the price of the contract will rise too, and so it can be sold for a profit. Once again, an example will help.

•*FT–SE Index Futures*

A fund manager is expecting to receive £1million in three months' time. He will invest this in shares. In the meantime, he is concerned that prices are set to rise. He may not get such good value for his £1 million when he is able to spend it. The FT–SE Index stands at 1500. This means that the price of a futures contract is 150. A 'tick' for this contract is one twentieth of a point and costs £12.50. So, each of today's contracts represents £37 500 (there are 3000 ticks in the price of the current Index and each tick costs £12.50). To cover £1 million worth of risk, our manager will need about 26 contracts.

If share prices rise by 10 per cent in the next three months, then the Index will rise to 1650. The price of the contract has risen to 165. Our fund manager is able to sell his 26 contracts at a profit of 300 ticks each. This means a total profit of £97 500.

The shares he wishes to buy with the £1 million will cost (on average) 10 per cent more than they did when he bought the FT–SE futures. Fortunately, he has earned almost exactly that from the contracts.

As you can see, no shares ever change hands. In fact, there is really no need for an intention or even a desire to buy shares. The futures contract is really just a way of gambling on changes in the FT–SE Index. Most of the trade in this contract, as far as we can tell, comes not from fund managers but from speculators. Seen in that light, it may appear that LIFFE is not so different from a High Street betting shop. Perhaps we should look into this.

Punters

It is widely agreed that there are three classes of customer in futures and options markets. The first and most innocent is the *hedger*. The hedger is legitimately involved in the market for the product underlying the contract and is, therefore, exposed to direct risk by the prospect of future price fluctuations. In the market for cocoa futures, he might be a chocolate manufacturer. Any corporation can hedge by using interest-rate futures, for any corporation borrows. Banks, as lenders, are exposed to interest-rate risk too, so they can hedge in the same market. Futures based on money market instruments or the FT–SE Index can help fund managers to cover the risks to which they are exposed, for their business is the purchase and sale of gilts and shares in the hope of the best return for their investors. None of these customers trades in futures markets simply in order to make a profit on the deal. Their motivation is to use futures trading as a way of avoiding or reducing a loss to which they are exposed anyway.

Hedgers, of course, do not need to use the services of an organised exchange like LIFFE or LFOX. They may prefer to have a particular forward or option contract drawn up to cover their special risk. This is done by bankers and is referred to as the OTC (over-the-counter) market. It has distinct advantages, especially in the area of currency options and futures. The contract can specify the exact sum, in the actual currency, over the precise length of time that is necessary for the risk involved. The Bank of England records a fall in the number of exchange-traded currency options after 1987. It attributes this to the growing appeal of the OTC market. The other two classes of customer on exchanges like LIFFE and LFOX are less attracted by the OTC market, however. They are *speculators* and *arbitrageurs*.

Speculators deal in futures and options contracts with the simple hope of being able to buy them for a lower price than they receive when they sell them. They are concerned about the underlying products only in so far as they affect the price of the futures or option contracts. Arbitrageurs hope to profit by exploiting anomalies between the prices of futures and option contracts, and the prices of the underlying products. If the price of, say, coffee futures seems low relative to the expected price of coffee, then the arbritrageur will buy up the futures expecting to profit when the coffee price rises.

It is easy to deride speculators and arbitrageurs as no more than gamblers, hoping to profit from a market intended for the legitimate use of others. The exchanges are keen to stress that such traders do serve a useful purpose. First, they provide liquidity for the market. A market restricted to hedgers would be small and would not be able to offer a reliable flow of buyers and sellers. The market would fail. The existence of speculators and arbitrageurs provides a constant supply of contracts for purchase and sale, and so actually creates the market for hedgers to use. In addition, it is pointed out that, by acting on the price anomalies that they find, arbitrageurs should quickly eliminate such anomalies. So they are actually helping to move prices to equilibrium. The diagrams in Figure 6.2 illustrate the argument. Above is the expected state of the coffee market in three months' time. Below, the current state of the market in three months' coffee futures. At first, coffee futures appear to offer a very good deal. The contracts effectively give the right to buy coffee at price P_2 in three months' time, and sell it at once at the higher price P_1. Arbitrageurs will rush to buy coffee futures. This raises the demand for the contracts to D_1, pushing up their price until it more

FIGURE 6.2
The Possible Effects of Arbitrage in the Coffee Market

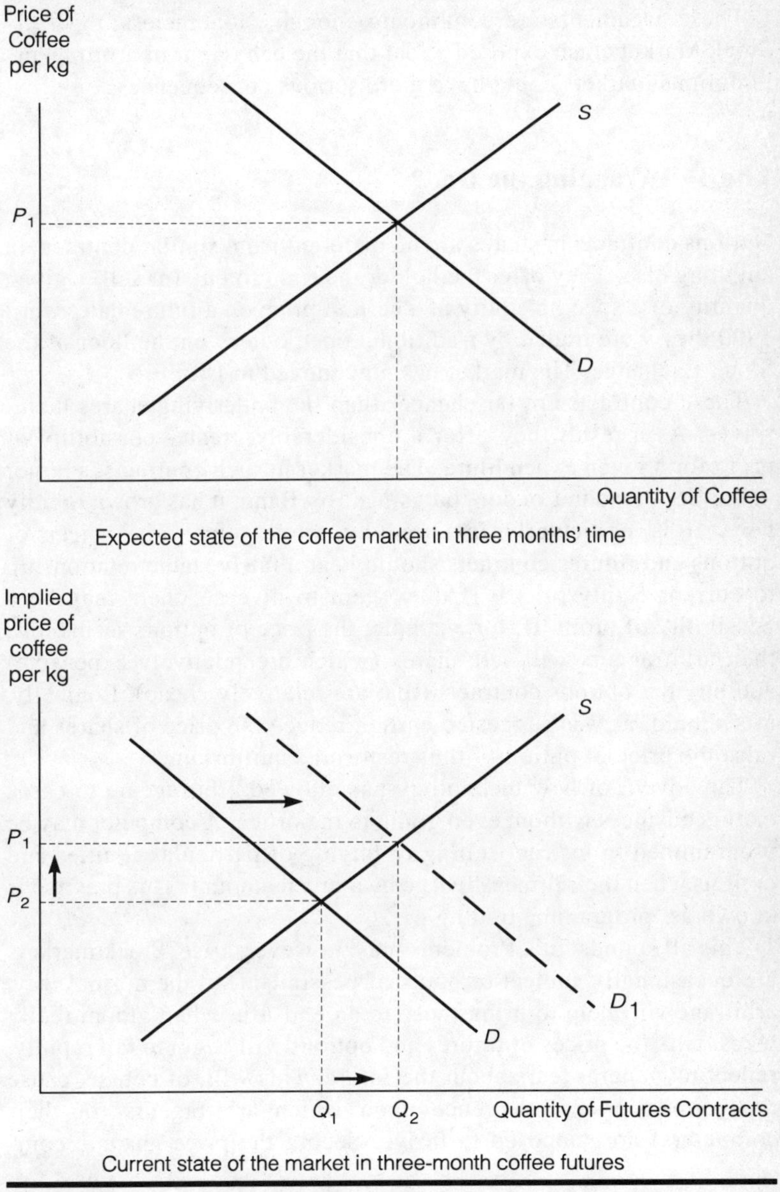

Current state of the market in three-month coffee futures

accurately reflects the expected state of the underlying market – by which time, of course, demand will stabilise. It seems, then, that arbitrageurs are actually hastening the move towards market equilibrium.

These arguments are convincing enough. Nonetheless, the 1987 Stock Market crash exposed a fear that the behaviour of arbitrageurs in options markets could have more serious consequences.

The Tail Wagging the Dog?

Options contracts in shares are no different from similar contracts in anything else. They offer the holder the right to buy (or sell) a given quantity of a specific equity at a certain price on a future date. Until 1990 they were traded by traditional open outcry on the floor of the Stock Exchange. The market has now moved to LIFFE.

These contracts are far cheaper than the underlying shares themselves. As a result they offer a considerably greater possibility of profit for a given expenditure. The market in such contracts is larger in the USA than in London, but, since Big Bang, it has grown rapidly here. It is particularly favoured by arbitrageurs. The prices of options and futures contracts should bear a fairly stable relationship to current equity prices. If they seem to diverge, there may be a possibility of profit. If, for example, the price of options seems low, then arbitrageurs will sell shares (which are relatively expensive) and buy the options contracts (that are relatively cheap). Logically, this should, as was suggested earlier, reduce the price of shares and raise the price of options – thus restoring equilibrium.

The advent of new technology has allowed arbitrageurs to carry on this business without even going to the office. A computer may be programmed to instruct selling or buying of particular equities and options when their prices diverge by a given amount. This practice is known as 'programme trading'.

This all sounds fine. Problems may, however, arise. Stock markets are occasionally subject to bouts of pessimism. In the normal way, arbitrage will help to bring these to an end. But when gloom really takes hold, the prices of futures and options will begin to fall rapidly, reflecting general fears about the future. This will, of course, cause the sort of price divergence upon which arbitrageurs (or their computers) are supposed to thrive. Seeing the price change, computers throughout the City (or, more likely, throughout New York) trigger selling of equities, with the intention of buying options contracts. If this selling is on a sufficiently large scale, though, it may be hard to find buyers. Faced with more and more selling orders, dealers must mark share prices down further and further. This spreads greater pessimism which depresses futures and options prices even more. So, the computer programmes try to sell more stock and so the spiral continues.

Something like this happened on Wall Street in October 1987. The City suffered rather less because futures and options markets are not so popular here. It did have some effect, though. Since options are still traded face-to-face, the market carried on even when a number of equity market-makers had stopped answering their phones. Panic was therefore expressed in falling options prices. This, of course, triggered the computers to try to dump more shares.

It is impossible to tell how significant this sort of effect really is. There have always been periods of stampede in equity markets. It would be wrong to blame them now on the development of futures and options.

Nonetheless, it has led some to fear for the future. Greater use of such instruments may expose markets – in currencies and other securities as well as shares – to periods of wild volatility when expectations of the future become particularly uncertain. Ultimately this means that behaviour in futures markets can come to determine the level of underlying prices, rather than the other way around. In the USA in 1987 this came to be known as the 'futures tail wagging the equities dog'.

Believers in market efficiency like to claim that prices in futures markets must in the long run reflect conditions in the markets for the underlying products. It is easy to see that they should, since a futures contract is no more than a claim to supply or demand that same commodity. Nonetheless, the experience of equity markets in 1987 might suggest that short-run price movements are based on something less than purely rational expectations. We saw a similar phenomenon in the market for foreign exchange in Chapter 5. The trouble with speculative markets is that dealers do not work on what they privately believe should happen, but rather on what they think other dealers will expect. It seems that it is possible for such markets to generate wild price changes simply out of a fear of wild price changes. When this happens, the supposed relationship to the market in the underlying product has broken down. In fact, if we are to believe the version of the 1987 crash outlined above, panic in the futures market can cause price fluctuations in the underlying market that are quite unwarranted. Futures prices come to determine current prices. The tail wags the dog. It is easy to sensationalise such a possibility. It should be distinctly rare. It may still occur. With the rapid growth of futures markets it may even become more common.

Swaps

There is, surprisingly, more than a scenic boat trip to connect the London borough of Hammersmith and Fulham with the City. In 1990 the borough hit the headlines of the financial pages as well as the television news because of its extraordinary activities in the interest-rate swap market.

Contracts in futures and options may have been around for hundreds of years, but these markets are still the scene of some of the most rapid and radical innovation in the financial services industry. The swap markets (in currencies and commodities as well as interest rates) are one of the newest markets of the new City. In an industry that prides itself on its adaptability, these products are 'state of the art'.

The deals are a variation of futures and options contracts. In principle, an interest-rate swap simply enables two different borrowers to pay one another's interest charges. It may be hard to see why they should want to do this. The situation will normally be that one of the borrowers is committed to a fixed interest rate while the other is paying a floating rate. The swap is another way of gambling on expectations of future interest-rate movements. If you swap a fixed for a floating rate and rates fall, then you will gain. If they rise, you will lose. The effect is similar to buying a futures contract.

Swaps are arranged by banks, who earn fat fees from the business. They themselves will frequently be the other party to a swap deal arranged for a corporate client. The knack as far as the bank is concerned lies in fixing strings of such deals that effectively cancel one another out. In this way the bank's own risk is covered by its clients – provided that none of them default on their payments. The busiest banks will run 'swaps books' that record the complex sequences of deals. The market originated in the simple fact that companies were able to raise funds more easily in some markets than in others. Thus, one might be able to borrow dollars cheaply whereas another might have a good credit rating in Japan. If the first needs yen and the second dollars, then they can swap loans, and each will get a better deal than it can manage on its own. The bank, of course, simply acts as a broker for the deal. Banks quickly realised that they could extend this market themselves. It started, then, as an exercise in borrowing another company's credit-worthiness. It has now developed into a speculative market in which not all of the players are themselves creditworthy. The borough of Hammersmith and Fulham engaged in this market in a big way. At one point the council had 0.5 per cent of the world's market in interest-rate swaps. They put together almost 600 deals, worth around £6 billion. Sadly, they were unable to continue meeting their payments. The gambles had not worked out. This was saddest for the seventy or so banks involved who, between them, lost well over £166 million as a result of the council's speculations (which had been the work of council officers, incidentally, operating without the approval of elected councillors). The Law Lords have since ruled that it is illegal for local authorities to enter into swap deals.

The swaps market grew dramatically over the 1980s. In 1983 it was estimated to do about $3 billion worth of business. By 1987 this had risen to over $300 billion worth. Like the other markets considered in this chapter, it thrives on uncertainty. Volatility in interest and exchange rates creates risk, as well as generating opportunities for speculative profit. Corporate treasurers and finance directors are eager to find ways of limiting the risk and maximising the profit. Deals that offer the choice between fixed and floating interest rates are just one method. Increasingly common are swaps that involve both currencies and interest rates. A floating-rate sterling loan might be swapped for a fixed-rate loan in dollars. This combines speculation on changes in interest rates and exchange rates. It is a risky deal.

Inevitably, there is now a secondary market in swaps. Deals can be sold to third parties. The price of the swap will depend upon how well the gamble is turning out. If you have swapped a fixed- for a floating-rate loan and rates fall, then the swap itself becomes more valuable and may be sold. The market has become further complicated by reverse swap contracts and swap options.

All this is further evidence of the manner in which the deregulated markets of the 1980s have created opportunities for borrowers. No longer restricted to their own currency or their domestic interest rates, borrowers are able to set up the cheapest deal that they can manage, and then to swap it for the deal that they wanted in the first place. It increases liquidity immensely. It could also, of course, be said to increase even further the unnecessary risks to which bankers expose themselves. We referred in Chapter 4 to the danger that deregulation within the banking sector has encouraged bankers to take risks that would previously not have been contemplated. It has, to some extent, undermined the traditional relationship between banker and client. The astonishing development of the interest-rate swap market must have hastened this. The market cannot take as much account of creditworthiness as was once customary. Presumably, the unfortunate banks who were involved in the Hammersmith and Fulham fiasco discovered this to their cost. As has so often been the case in our investigation of the markets of the new City, it seems that deregulation has increased liquidity, competition, innovation and efficiency – but at a certain cost.

7 Money and Interest

Wholesale Money

If nothing else has so far emerged from this account of the City of London, it is surely clear that a lot changed in the 1980s. The particular causes of this may be discussed for years to come, but international deregulation (or liberalisation, as it has also come to be known) has to be the most prominent factor. Financial markets have grown extravagantly and competition within them is vigorous, if not cut-throat. The advantages are obvious – a free and efficient flow of cash is essential if producers of goods and services are to respond quickly and effectively to developments within their own markets. The financial services provided by the City and similar centres offer necessary lubrication to the wheels of industry. The better the quality of the lubricant, the faster the wheels can turn.

It is easy to overlook the fact that the financial services industry will itself need lubrication. If banks and building societies and investing institutions and foreign-currency dealers and futures and options exchanges are to fulfil their function of allocating funds to the corporate customers who can make the best use of them, then there must exist some system for the allocation of funds between these financial players. It will need to be a fairly complex system. The more direct and efficient the lubrication of industry is to be, the more sophisticated and flexible must be the system that serves the lubricators. The network of arrangements that directs funds within the financial services industry is collectively known as 'the money markets'. There is another, perhaps more straightforward, way of looking at them. Financial dealers make profits by borrowing money more cheaply than they lend it on to companies or to individuals. The money markets are the means through which they borrow it.

These markets are wholesale. The borrowers and lenders are mostly financial institutions of some kind. What Billingsgate is to fish, Smithfield is to meat, and Nine Elms is to fruit and vegetables, the money markets of the City are to cash. They are where the money-men get their money and the financiers get their finance. You will also have guessed that these markets have undergone something of a transformation in the past ten years. They are the engine-room of the City. The ability of the financial services industry to respond to the challenge of deregulation depends upon the increasing efficiency of these money markets.

The Money Markets

Traditional textbook accounts of this area usually distinguish a complex raft of different markets. One effect of the development of the new City has been to make these distinctions a good deal harder to pin down.

The Euromarket (that we touched on in Chapter 4) should be easy to isolate, since it arranges deals in currencies held outside their country of origin. The wholesale markets that most interest us would seem to be the so-called 'sterling money markets'. Loans here are all in pounds, but there is, apparently, more than one such market. You may find references to an 'interbank' market (where banks lend to one another) that is seemingly quite different from the 'local authority market' (where local councils can raise funds), both of which are separate from the 'discount market'. This is the one that usually gets most attention, for it is the means by which the Bank of England (occasionally) influences short-term interest rates on behalf of the government. In addition to this there is the 'gilt-edged market', where long- and medium-term government securities are bought and sold. The Bank can actually use this market to influence the structure of long-term interest rates. It is even possible to find references to 'the parallel money markets' – a term which simply combines the interbank and local authority markets.

All these do exist but they are no longer as distinct as the traditional descriptions imply. They differ only in that they deal in different sorts of securities. The lenders and borrowers are much the same. Most of them are banks. The purpose of the markets is the same too. They all give financial institutions (among others) easy access to funds. Eurocurrency and sterling markets sound easily distinguishable, since they are markets in different types of money. In the days before deregulation and especially before the abolition of exchange controls, the distinction was pretty straighforward. We can, however, no longer assume that the loans arranged by British banks for their corporate customers will inevitably be in sterling. In so far as banks need access to foreign currency in order to pursue their business, the Euromarkets may be crucial to the lubrication of international financial markets. They have been as important a source of wholesale funds for the City's financial dealers as the sterling money markets. An important part of the job of today's bank treasurers and finance directors is to find the cheapest means of borrowing and the best opportunities for lending. With the use of swaps and options, they can switch between currencies and interest rates with ease. In a manner of speaking, then, deregulation means that the Euro- and sterling markets are no longer distinct. The markets of today are so fluid that one might think of them as a single vast international exchange with a number of local branches.

The confusion does not end with the overlap between Euromarkets and the sterling money markets. The different elements of the sterling market are not quite as easy to isolate as their names suggest. They have no physical market-place. They simply describe the buying and selling of particular securities (or financial instruments) through international computer, telephone and telex connections. The dealers in each market are frequently the same. Most of them are banks. It is only the functions of the markets, and the instruments traded, that differ.

The interbank market serves a distinct purpose. Banks need a reliable flow of short-term funds. Inevitably, some will have a plentiful supply while others may need to borrow. They lend to one another. The loans are arranged over the telephone and are normally for sums of £1 million or so. Sometimes they will be very short term (perhaps overnight), sometimes for a matter of months. They will never be long term and are always in sterling.

Local authorities borrow money to cover time-lags between necessary expenditure and the receipt of income from taxes, grants, rents and so on. They issue fixed-interest securities which guarantee their holders a set payment each year. Like shares, they are bought and sold many times after they are issued. Anyone may buy such securities. The original buyers are usually banks or institutional investors, who may sell them on to members of the public or to corporations. The local authority market certainly exists but is not really distinct from markets in other securities.

Discount markets customarily form the core of accounts of the sterling money markets. It is right that they should. They serve much the same function as the interbank market (which is effectively a part of the discount market) but extend further. They are used by operators other than just banks and involve the dealing of short-term securities. Descriptions of the discount markets usually centre on the role of the Bank of England within them. We look at the markets, and at the role of the Bank, later in the chapter. The markets are genuinely important as the main means through which banks and similar institutions raise the short-term funds that they need to balance their books. The mechanism is trade in Treasury bills, commercial bills, gilt-edged stock nearing its maturity and Certificates of Deposit (CDs). All these are explained later. Banks which are short of cash raise it by selling these securities. The markets are also distinguished by the existence of a special sort of institution – the discount houses – which operate, effectively, as market-makers in the securities traded. Discount houses are always available to buy or sell the bills and CDs, though they will adjust prices according to market conditions in order to be sure of a profit. Discount houses make the market as liquid and efficient as possible. They also make it extremely sensitive. They play an important part in the determination of short-term interest rates by responding to market conditions.

The gilt-edged market is very similar to the local authority market. It describes the buying and selling of securities that are issued by central government to cover expenditure. It has changed a lot over the 1980s. We examine the changes and their implications towards the end of the chapter.

Despite all the complexities involved, the Euromarkets and the discount market do genuinely provide the lubrication that was described earlier. This chapter will concentrate upon them. Accounts of these markets tend to look most intently at their mechanics. They are complicated and certainly require explanation. It should be remembered, though, that the markets serve an important function.

Their efficiency determines the efficiency of the financial system itself. The markets have developed a good deal in recent years. One major administrative reform can be considered at once. The efficiency of markets depends not only upon systems of dealing, but also upon systems of settlement. Traders may become disenchanted with a market that takes unduly long to record and settle transactions. Just as the Bank of England introduced a computerised register of gilts holders in 1986 (called the Central Gilts Office), so it proudly opened a Central Moneymarkets Office in October 1990. This not only has the advantage of speeding settlement in these markets, but also of discouraging theft. Many of the instruments traded in moneymarkets are 'bearer bonds'. This means that no register of them is kept and the holder of the bond is automatically entitled to the returns upon it. In early 1990 an unfortunate City messenger was robbed of £292 million worth of such instruments. The crime was virtually undetectable. Whether or not the Central Moneymarkets Office succeeds in making City money-markets more attractive to dealers, it should at least make them less attractive to muggers.

It is in these money markets that the government hopes to affect and even determine the interest rates that have become an increasingly important element of economic policy. Later in the chapter we investigate precisely how rates are determined. Does the government really set them? Or are they fixed by the market? The answer is crucial if we are to understand the limits of government policy-making.

The Nature of Euromarkets

This is not the first time that we have come across the Euromarkets. As early as Chapter 1, it was suggested that they have a special importance in the recent development of the City. They came up again in Chapter 4 as a major sphere of international banking activity. There are one or two details to add here. We shall be most concerned, though, with the use to which the markets are put – and by the question of whether or not their time has passed.

The growth of Euromarkets has been described as the single most important development in the post-war financial world. It enabled an increase in borrowing and lending that would otherwise have been impossible. Their development in the early 1960s can be seen as a dress rehearsal for the full deregulation of international markets that finally took place twenty years later. Euromarkets allowed bankers to operate beyond the reach of national regulations. It was that pressure that brought them into existence. It is, of course, less strong now. Most of the rules are in the process of being abolished, or at least relaxed. The Euromarkets may turn out to be no more than the flared trousers or platform shoes of the financial markets – a bizarre fad of the 1960s and 1970s.

The basis of the Euromarket is the deposit of currency at banks in another country. It began, as we saw in Chapter 4, when the Soviet government deposited dollars at a bank in France rather than in the USA. Dollars were, for a long time, the major Eurocurrency. The Soviet government's motive for holding dollars outside the USA was pressing but unusual (they feared that hostile Americans might freeze their assets). The growth of the market was based on a more universal desire for increased profit by bankers. In the 1960s the American government imposed quite severe exchange controls which hindered domestic banks from lending dollars overseas. An offshore source of dollars (often held in the overseas branches of US banks) was necessary to satisfy the demand for dollar loans. At the same time, successive American governments sought to prevent interest rates from rising too high. It was thus far more appealing to American bankers to move their dollar deposits to Europe, where interest rates were more attractive. The Euromarket was genuinely international. American bankers were not moving their deposits to, say, Britain but rather to a general, offshore financial market that came under no-one's regulation and where interest rates were determined by flows of funds rather than by governments. The Euromarket of the 1960s and 1970s seemed at the time to be the only authentically free financial market in the world. This was its great attraction. In their domestic markets at this time all banks were subject to some degree of control. This usually involved a requirement to hold a given proportion of highly liquid assets at little or no interest. Operating in Euromarkets required no such obligation. Since the banks were not having to sacrifice interest by holding these reserve assets, they could afford to lend more cheaply than in their domestic markets. Euromarkets managed, therefore, to offer lower interest to lenders and, at the same time, higher interest to depositors (since rates were not suppressed by government interference). It must have seemed a financial paradise. It is no surprise that the markets were successful. London became their centre, but it should be stressed that this was not because of high or low interest rates in the UK. The market was not physically in London. It was not physically anywhere. It was simply a group of international financiers with telephone and telex connections to one another. The market was wherever they were. The telephones happened to ring in London more often than elsewhere because there were so many international bankers there already and because the Bank of England (realising, one assumes, that London was on to a good thing) chose not to interfere. It was a supranational market. It existed above and beyond national boundaries. Interest rates in Euromarkets were not national rates but international rates.

Euromoney and Eurocapital

The majority of simple Euroloans were, and still are, short term. They may be overnight, or can range up to a week, a month, three months and even a year. Longer-term loans normally involve the Eurobond market. We might say, then, that there are two different sorts of Euromarket. There is a 'Euromoney' market where Eurocurrencies are borrowed and lent for short periods. Whilst multinational companies and institutional investors are involved here, it is largely an interbank market. It enables banks to settle temporary shortages and surpluses of funds with ease. The sums involved are large, around $1 million at a time, and interest rates are based upon LIBOR. This, then, is a money-market like the sterling money-markets. It offers wholesale currency. These markets are immensely liquid. Interest rates can change by a minimum of one-sixteenth of 1 per cent. Such changes are eagerly anticipated and can lead to the movement of many millions of dollars from one bank to another.

As well as this 'Euromoney' market, there is a 'Eurocapital' market where Eurocurrencies are used by banks to form the basis of large loans to corporations, to other banks and to governments. Very large loans (such as those made to developing countries in the 1970s) are normally put together by a syndicate of international banks. Syndicated lending of this kind was described in Chapter 4. Its attractiveness to banks has been severely reduced by the problems of international debt. Far more common is the issue of Eurobonds. These are securities with a life of some years. They are sold by a bank on behalf of a customer and are bought by other banks or large corporations or by wealthy individuals with Eurocurrency deposits.

The growth of the Eurobond market has been extraordinary. In the twenty years following 1963 it increased around two-thousandfold. By the middle 1980s the market was reckoned to be worth about $200 billion a year. In 1986, the UK government was able to raise $4.5 billion in a single issue.

Originally, such bonds carried a fixed rate of interest. The bonds have coupons attached to them. The holder claims the annual interest payment by tearing off these coupons and presenting them to the issuing company. They are 'bearer bonds', and so interest may be claimed by whoever is currently holding the bond. No central register of holders is maintained. This can make them an especially attractive investment for people who are reluctant to share their earnings with the taxman. They are, apparently, particularly popular with high earners in countries with high tax rates, such as Belgium and Holland.

The increased volatility of interest rates in the 1980s led to the development of Floating Rate Notes (FRNs). These are no more than Eurobonds with a floating rate of interest. They became popular at a time when rates were high. Borrowers were reluctant to accept fixed interest, fearing the prospect of excessive payments in the future. Simple bank lending is mostly at floating interest rates, so the banks were also happy to borrow in Euromarkets at floating rates. The rates on FRNs are normally linked to six-month LIBOR (the rate at which banks lend money to one another for six months in London). The market boomed dramatically in the middle 1980s with up to $45 billion worth of FRNs issued in a single year. It has fallen back since then. There are, today, many other variations on the traditional fixed-interest Eurobond. 'Zero-coupon' bonds offer no interest but may be bought for a discount. With 'debt-convertible' bonds the holder can choose to convert from a floating to a fixed rate of interest if rates fall especially low. 'Equity-convertible' bonds may be exchanged for shares in the company that issued them. The range of bonds available is vast.

Boom and Bust in the Euromarkets

Tales of the growth of the Euromarkets in the 1960s and 1970s are legendary. Precise information is hard to pin down, nonetheless we are told that the volume of Eurodeposits was increasing over this period at the rate of about 20 per cent each year. It apparently stood at some $2 trillion in the middle 1980s. We saw earlier that the Eurobond market grew even more dramatically – two thousandfold in twenty years. Turnover of Eurobonds was estimated to reach some $358 billion in the first six months of 1989. The scale of the market is virtually incomprehensible. So is its growth. It would seem appropriate to illustrate this section with tables of extravagant statistics or with elaborately steep graphs that would show the drama even more clearly. Sadly this cannot be done. The reason is instructive.

Euromarkets do not have a physical existence of their own. The banks that accept Eurodeposits also accept all other forms of deposit. The same banks that arrange Eurobond issues also issue other forms of bond. The companies that borrow by issuing Eurobonds, borrow by issuing various other types of bond as well. The financiers and institutions who buy Eurobonds also buy all the other securities available. The companies depositing Eurocurrencies deposit every other form of currency too. The activities of Euromarkets – accepting deposits, making loans, drawing up financial instruments and making markets in them – are the standard activities of any financial centre. All that separates these markets from others doing the same thing, is that they do not fall directly under any national regulations. The international nature of the business makes it hard to monitor. What makes it hardest of all, though, is the problem of deciding when an activity falls within the Euromarket rather than some other national (or international) market. The Bank of England, in an article about sterling bond issues in 1988, wrote: 'The...sterling bond market...may be regarded as comprising two overlapping sectors – the domestic and sterling Eurobond sectors. *The distinction is rather artificial* since issues in both market sectors are launched in London and largely embrace the same borrowers and financial intermediaries' [author's italics].

In the 1960s and 1970s it was rather easier to work out where the

Euromarkets began and where they ended. It was at least fairly simple to assert that a dollar bond issue launched in London was part of the Eurobond market whilst one launched in New York was not. The huge growth of Euromarkets at this time should be carefully interpreted. It does not really represent a new form of financial activity, but rather traditional borrowing and lending being conducted in a new 'free' environment. The growth shows the pent-up demand for financial activity that was discouraged by domestic regulations. In a sense, then, it was all simply a curtain-raiser for deregulation in the 1980s. Measuring the Euromarkets in the 1980s is, as the Bank of England suggests, an arbitrary procedure. If currency can move freely between centres, then the decision to launch a bond issue in London rather than New York should not be seen as an attempt to tap a completely different market.

Just as the Euromarket was born out of regulations, so deregulation must threaten its existence. The flow of Eurodeposits has dwindled to a trickle. By 1985 the market that had been growing at over 20 per cent per year had slowed to under 4 per cent. It was falling in the later 1980s. It would be wrong to treat this development in too apocalyptic a manner, though. It is not that the activity that used to occur on Euromarkets is no longer occurring. It is rather that we can no longer distinguish Euromarket activity from any other; the Euromarket has been merged into the huge international financial market that was born in the 1980s. Perhaps this is the wrong way round – the Euromarket could be said to have absorbed the national markets. After all, it is the separate regulated and restricted markets that have ceased to exist. The relatively unregulated international market has grown. Whichever way one chooses to see it, the fact is that Euromarket activity can no longer be distinguished from any other. In the words of the Bank of England: 'The distinction is rather artificial.' In this sense the Euromarkets are dying. The real implications of this are for the City of London itself. The City was the centre of these markets; the business will be far more evenly spread in future.

The Discount Market

At the core of London's short-term money-markets, lies the discount market. City mythology has it that this is the most efficient money-market in the world. Generations of commentators have asserted with confidence that it is quite unlike any other of the world's such markets. That may not be accurate for very much longer.

The role of the market is to provide short-term liquidity to the banking system. This means that it offers banks easy access to short-term loans. The main lenders are other banks. The peculiarity of the market lies in the middle-men. Just as market-makers on the Stock Exchange keep the equity market buoyant by buying from those who want to sell and selling to those who want to buy, and just as speculators on futures and options exchanges help the market to function by increasing the availability of buyers and sellers, so it is discount houses that create the liquidity in the discount market. They are widely treated as one of the City's most rare and exotic species. In fact they are not much different from the market-makers and the speculators. They help their market to function by being ready to buy from banks who wish to sell and to sell to banks who want to buy.

The instruments being bought and sold in the discount market are short-term Treasury and commercial bills and Certificates of Deposit (CDs).

Treasury Bills

Treasury bills are issued by the Bank of England on behalf of the government. Their main function will be explained later – it is not to raise funds for government spending (gilt-edged stock is used for that). The bills have a fixed face value and a set date on which they mature (normally three or six months from the day of issue). The holder on that date is entitled to the face value. They are sold by auction on Fridays. The buyers will only offer prices below the bills' face value, or they will be unable to earn a return. Thus they are said to be buying the bills 'at a discount', or even 'discounting' the bills. The percentage that they offer below the bills' face value is called the 'discount rate'. This is why the market in which these instruments are traded is called the 'discount market' and the institutions at its heart are the discount houses. Table 7.1 shows the Treasury bill issues for August 1990. The first column records the total value of bills for which bids were received. Anyone may bid (though for a minimum of £50 000 worth) and the Bank will allocate the bills however it wishes. As you can see, the issues were all oversubscribed and the Bank allotted £500 million worth of bills each week regardless of the bids received. The basis upon which the Bank will decide how many bills to allocate is explained in the next section. Base rates at this time stood at around 15 per cent. Bidders, therefore, were only prepared to offer prices that gave them a discount rate of over 14 per cent.

TABLE 7.1
The Treasury Bill Issue in August 1990

Date	*Amount applied for £ million*	*Amount allotted £ million*	*Discount rate % per annum*
3 August	1725	500	14.34
10 August	2318	500	14.34
17 August	2042	500	14.35
24 August	2715	500	14.26
31 August	2883	500	14.29

SOURCE *Bank of England Quarterly Bulletin*, November 1990.

Commercial Bills

Commercial bills (sometimes referred to as 'commercial paper') operate in precisely the same way as Treasury bills except that they are issued by corporations rather than by the government. Such bills are normally issued through banks and, if the company is reputable, the bank will authorise the bill. This indicates that the bank guarantees payment at maturity. If a commercial bill is accepted in this way, it can be known as a 'bank bill', and becomes a good deal more saleable. Commercial bills are bought for prices below their face value (discounted) in exactly the same manner as Treasury bills.

Certificates of Deposit (CDs)

CDs have become an increasingly important instrument in the discount market. They emerge from lenders rather than borrowers. A loan is made for a given period. Interest will be paid when the loan expires. If the lender wishes to recover the funds, he can sell the loan (which is no more than a claim to a sum of money – or a deposit – on a given future date). CDs are pieces of paper that state that the holder has lent money to a bank or building society and is entitled to a specific sum on a given date. The pieces of paper can be bought and sold just like the bills outlined above. Again, the buying prices will be lower than the face value of the CDs. They, too, are discounted.

On any day, when customers' transactions are calculated, some banks will find themselves temporarily short of cash. Others will have a surplus. The discount market offers the first group the opportunity to raise cash quickly by selling Treasury bills, commercial bills or CDs. The buyers may well be the other banks, who find themselves with cash on their hands. It is perfectly possible and, indeed, common for banks to deal with one another in this way. Discount houses, though, are always available to make a market in the instruments traded. It is, therefore, the discount houses that generate liquidity in the market and enable it to fulfil its function. Their speciality is the Treasury bill. They are responsible for a lot of the Friday bidding. They actually underwrite each issue, promising to buy any unsold bills. As you can tell, they have a particularly close relationship with the Bank of England. It is the influence of the Bank of England in the discount market that makes the market more than just a technical adjunct to the banking industry. It is here that the Bank carries out the government's instructions with regard to short-term interest-rate policy.

The Bank's Work

The daily movement of funds in the discount market is very large. It is measured in hundreds or thousands of millions of pounds. The market is, in essence, like any other. There is a supply of bills and CDs (offered by banks and discount houses who wish to borrow), and there is a demand for them (representing the willingness of other banks and discount houses to lend). As in any other market, if the supply is greater than the demand then the price of the bills will fall. If demand outstrips supply, the price will rise. The price of bills will fluctuate on a daily basis as circumstances within the discount market alter.

The difference between this market and others is that the price that it determines is a great deal more influential. The prices at which bills and CDs are traded in the discount market affects short-term interest rates in the economy. As we saw above, bills are bought at a discount below their face value. The bigger the discount (that is, the lower the price at which they are bought), the higher is the discount rate, and, therefore, the higher is the effective rate of interest that they offer. A simple example should make this clear.

• *The Short-Term Interest Rate and the Discount Rate*
A three-month bill might have a face value of £100 000. Suppose that it is bought for £96 500. This represents a discount of £3500 on the bill's face value – or a discount rate over three months of 3.5 per cent. The simple annual discount rate would therefore be 14 per cent (since three months is a quarter of a year).

The rate of interest earned is slightly higher than the discount rate, since the buyer is making £3500 on an investment of £96 500 (not £100 000). The short-term rate of interest is, in fact, 14.5 per cent per annum.

By affecting the price of bills, therefore, changes in demand and supply in the discount market actually affect discount rates and the short-term rate of interest. If, in our example, the supply of bills had been higher, then the price might have been even lower (£95 000, perhaps). So the discount rate would have been higher (20 per cent) and so would the short-term rate of interest (21 per cent in this example).

What this tiresome mathematics shows is that demand and supply in the discount market can have very wide effects. Changes in short-term interest rates have implications for demand throughout the economy as well as affecting the exchange rate in the manner explained in Chapter 5. In very simple terms what happens is that if banks have to pay a higher rate for the funds that they borrow in the discount market, then they will also have to charge a higher rate to customers who are borrowing from them.

Left to itself, if demand for and supply of bills were to fluctuate from day to day (which it is bound to do), then the discount market would generate volatility in short-term interest rates that might be destabilising for the entire economy. This is where the Bank of England comes in. The Bank monitors the market on a daily, or even hourly, basis with the intention of smoothing out fluctuations in the flow of funds and keeping interest rates more or less stable.

Until very recently, discount houses were the conduit for the Bank's money-market operations. The system works something like this:

• *Bank of England Money-Market Operations*

The largest movements of short-term funds in the economy are between the banking sector and the government. These involve payments of tax, most government spending, interest payments on gilt-edged stock and so on. The daily flow of funds is very large. The Bank of England acts as banker both to the government and to the banking sector. It is, therefore, uniquely placed to estimate the daily flow. At 9.00a.m. each morning, a meeting is held at the Bank at which the likely net flow is estimated. The Bank announces its conclusion – to the nearest £50 million.

If it reckons that the market is likely to be short of funds (which is the most common occurrence) then the Bank is prepared to make cash available in order to prevent a sharp rise in short-term interest rates. The Bank announces its willingness to buy bills from discount houses – thus injecting liquidity into the market. In market terms, it is increasing demand for bills and thus stopping their price from falling and the interest rate from rising. If the Bank underestimates the shortage, then it is prepared to lend directly to discount houses in the afternoon. This is known as 'late assistance'.

There will be days when the Bank estimates that there will be surplus funds in the market. It prepares to absorb them by selling bills to discount houses. Treasury bills may be issued specifically for this purpose. Since discount houses underwrite each Treasury bill issue, the Bank can be sure that the surplus funds will be absorbed. This, of course, is why the underwriting agreement has been made. It is essential that the bills be bought if interest rates are not to fall. A new issue may not be required. The job may be done by selling bills that the Bank bought on an earlier occasion when the market was under-funded.

You will notice that the Bank's function is merely to smooth the operation of the market. It is not seeking to direct it, but rather to help market forces to work effectively. The Bank is not setting interest rates. It is preventing unnecessary fluctuations that would otherwise occur.

It is also worth pointing out that the main use of Treasury bills is to enable the Bank to manage these money-market operations. They provide a source of liquidity within the discount market. There were periods in the 1980s when they hardly featured. The Bank is prepared to use bank bills (commercial bills accepted by a bank) or certain local authority bills to support the money-market. For a period, bank bills were for a period, used far more regularly than Treasury bills. The key to these operations is the need to ensure an efficient and liquid market. If there is a plentiful supply of bank bills then there is no need to introduce other instruments. More recently, the Bank has returned to more traditional habits and the Treasury bill issue has grown. The weekly issue was back up to £650 million worth in autumn 1990, having fallen as low as £100 million worth in 1986 and 1987. Table 7.2 shows the details of the Bank's money-market support over a few days in 1990. Bank bills were most commonly used at that time. The use of local authority bills was very rare. This is typical of the later 1980s, but the scene could easily change.

Developments in the discount market have been less dramatic than in many other City markets over the 1980s. We cannot justifiably describe a new discount market for the new City. The Bank of England however, has tried to eliminate the discount houses' monopoly of market-making activities. It has invited applications from any other firms who would like to enjoy the 'special dealing relationships' that were once the prerogative of the discount houses. The nature of the relationship is the same as ever – the new entrants must deal with banks, make markets in bills and must deal directly with the Bank of England and underwrite the weekly Treasury bill issue. There is, therefore, no planned change in the operation of the market, merely in the personnel and the vocabulary (newcomers will not necessarily be known as discount houses). Motives for this were probably mixed. In part it reflects the new liberalising zeal which wishes to dismantle monopolies and restrictive practices wherever they might lurk. This only goes so far, though. The actual system of operation in the markets will become no less restrictive. The new

TABLE 7.2

Bank of England Operations in the Money Market in October 1990 (£ million)

Date	*Band**	*Treasury bills*		*Local Authority bills*		*Bank bills*		*Late assistance*
		Amount	*Rate (%)*	*Amount*	*Rate (%)*	*Amount*	*Rate (%)*	
1 October	1					26	14.87	60
	2	4	14.75	2	14.75	308	14.75	
2 October	1					26	14.87	10
	2					636	14.75	
3 October	2					767	14.75	
4 October	1	386	14.87			29	14.87	165
	2	106	14.75			118	14.75	
5 October	2	1	14.75			267	14.75	230
8 October	1					156	13.87	325
	2					233	13.75	
9 October								180
10 October	1					127	13.87	120
	2					121	13.75	
11 October	1					74	13.87	
	2	13	13.75			248	13.75	

* Band 1 bills have 1–14 days left to maturity. Band 2 have 15–33 days left.

SOURCE *Bank of England Quarterly Bulletin*, November 1990.

'discount houses' will all need Bank of England approval. The market is not being genuinely opened.

At least as important as missionary zeal was a recognition that there were not enough discount houses left. The number had fallen to eight by 1988. Several had been involved in the monster mergers that had been encouraged by Big Bang. The day of tiny specialist dealers of this kind was passing. The Bank had to extend eligibility simply in order to ensure that the job was done. The plan was announced in 1988. The Bank has not been embarrassed by a rush of applicants. By 1990, two new firms had been recruited. This may not be enough.

Who Really Sets Interest Rates?

There are those who will regard the previous section as hopelessly naive. Its suggestion that the Bank of England simply guides interest rates towards stability at the market's given level – no more than a visible version of Adam Smith's 'invisible hand' – may be treated with scorn. Perhaps it should be.

There is no doubt that the vast majority of the Bank's activities in the money-markets are innocently directed towards achieving stability. The Bank is not trying to force the market to set a different interest rate, but is hoping to avoid a sudden, temporary, rise or fall.

There are days when its operations are less innocent. The government may wish to change the level of interest rates as a matter of policy. The manner in which this is done involves the Bank's money-market activities. The Bank will simply alter the price at which it is prepared to buy bills from, or sell them to the market. In this way, short-term interest rates are forced up or down in the discount market. Banks that are having to pay higher rates for their own short-term funds, will pass the increase on to their borrowers and so on. This only affects short-term interest rates, since only short-term loans are involved. Nonetheless, it appears to indicate direct government intervention. Table 7.2 shows the detail of Bank of England operations in the money market over a period of a few days in October 1990. The discount rates on Treasury bills and bank bills are also given. All this activity involved the Bank in buying bills from the market. The discount rates show the price level at which the Bank was buying. At first, all the rates were around 14.75 per cent. Suddenly, on 8 October, they fell to around 13.75 per cent. What happened? Had the market suddenly changed its mind? How did the Bank know that the magic level for stability was now a full percentage point lower than before?

It was not intuition or clairvoyance. The government had decided that it was time for sterling to join the EC's Exchange Rate Mechanism (ERM). Predicting a surge in demand for pounds, they hoped to offset this to a degree by lowering UK interest rates. On

Friday 5 October, it was announced that the rate at which the Bank would support the money market on Monday was to be 1 per cent lower than the rate on Friday. Since the new rate was formally announced in advance, this episode technically represents a return to the Bank of England's Minimum Lending Rate (MLR) that was supposed to have been abandoned in the early 1980s. Whatever the technique used, though, the conclusion seems inescapable. The Bank of England had actually raised short-term interest rates when the market, left to itself, would not have done so. The same can be seen in October 1989, when rates were raised from 14 to 15 per cent. MLR was not employed this time. The Bank simply reduced the price at which it was prepared to buy bills. So perhaps the last section was hopelessly naive. If the Bank can change rates when it wants to, then it is not innocently smoothing the market. It is being actively interventionist. Such intervention may not be restricted to days when rates change. There may be many more occasions when the Bank's efforts to 'stabilise' the interest rate actually fix it at a level with which pure market forces are not satisfied.

We must be careful again. Conclusions like this are seductive but overstate the case. The examples of October 1989 and 1990 reveal more. On both occasions the interest-rate changes were precipitated by international events. In 1989, German interest rates were increased. British rates followed a mere twenty minutes later. The pressure on sterling during those twenty minutes had been immense. British rates had to rise. Market forces would have raised them anyway. The Bank of England was simply short-cutting market forces, and giving an important sign to foreign exchange dealers that the UK government was willing to support the currency. The Bank would insist that this was not tampering with market forces. It was making the market more efficient by reducing the time that it took to respond to changed circumstances. Similarly, the fall in 1990 occurred because the government was sure that buying of sterling when the markets opened on Monday might raise it too near to its ERM limit. Market forces would have brought about a fall in the interest rate. The government was simply predicting this and thus avoiding the temporary destabilisation that might have resulted. Again, the Bank was making the market respond more efficiently.

These are strong examples of the Bank's case, but any interest-rate change could be interpreted in the same way. The Bank does not tamper with market forces but hurries them along. The furthest that the Bank will go in this is to say that, while increases in interest rates are forced on them by the market, the timing of interest-rate reductions is a matter of greater freedom for the government and the Bank. The market forces rates up; the Bank eases them down. The Bank, then, is everybody's friend. Perhaps this lets them off rather lightly.

The truth must be that it is impossible to tell exactly what accounts for an interest rate change, because it is not clear where pure market forces begin and end. The ERM makes this problem all the more complicated. If sterling is falling towards its lower limit, the Bank may be instructed to raise interest-rates. Is this a response to market forces? Perhaps so. After all, the change is forced upon the government by the foreign exchange market. But the agreement to fix sterling in this way was not made by the market. It was deliberate government policy. The interest-rate change results inevitably from this policy decision. In that sense, it is pure interventionism. The argument is fairly sterile. The simple fact is that the government's ability to control interest rates is certainly limited by the attitudes of the short-term money and foreign exchange markets. The government can only get away with movements that can be, at least in part, explained as 'natural' in view of market developments.

Gilts

Before leaving markets for money and the determination of interest rates, it is time to look at the market for long-term government securities – gilt-edged stock. These securities are issued by the government in order to raise money with which to fund spending programmes. In principle, the issue of stock will only be necessary if tax revenues are insufficient to cover planned expenditures (if the government is operating a Public Sector Borrowing Requirement – a PSBR). If taxes are bringing in enough, then we might expect no stock to be issued. The reality is slightly more complicated, in that some borrowing may still be needed to cover cash-flow problems. The government may also have other motives for issuing the securities. Nonetheless, Figure 7.1 shows that the stock of gilt-edged securities in the market did go up when the government was having to borrow in the early 1980s, and fell rapidly towards the end of the decade when tax revenues grew with the expanding economy (this

FIGURE 7.1
Changes in the Stock of Gilt-edged Securities, 1981-90

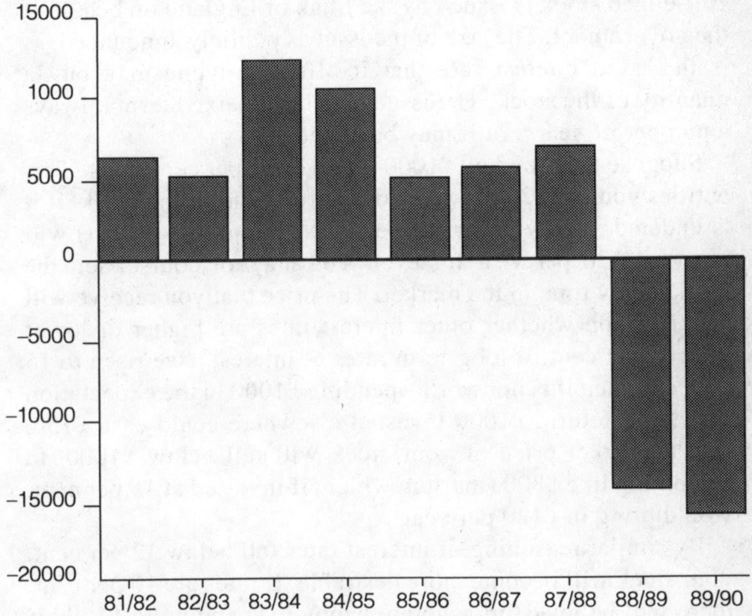

SOURCE *Bank of England Quarterly Bulletin.*

came to be known as a period of Public Sector Debt Repayment – PSDR).

This decline in the availability of stock is one of the stories of the 1980s as far as the gilt-edged market is concerned. The other relates to changes in dealing arrangements in the market that were brought about at the time of Big Bang. Before examining these developments, it would be a good idea to explain how such securities work. Perhaps an example is called for (see overleaf).

Gilts are issued by the Bank of England on behalf of the government. Issues are advertised and, usually, made available 'on tap' through the Stock Exchange. This means that the securities are available from the date of issue but do not all have to be sold on that day. More recently the Bank has experimented with auctions of gilt-edged stock, where bids are invited and the issue divided between

• *Gilt-Edged Securities*

Gilt-edged stock is issued by the Bank of England on behalf of the government. The size of the issue is publicly announced, as is the fixed interest rate that it offers. Anyone may buy a quantity of the stock. The issue may have a fixed term (always a number of years) or it may be undated.

Suppose that you buy £1000 worth of 12 per cent stock. This entitles you to £120 per year for the full term of the stock. If it is undated, then you (or the person to whom you pass it) will receive £120 per year for ever. You may, of course, sell the stock at any time in the market. The price that you receive will depend upon whether other interest rates are higher or lower than 12 per cent. If long-term rates of interest have risen to 15 per cent, then it is not worth spending £1000 in the expectation of a £120 return. £1000 invested elsewhere could earn £150. So the market price of your stock will fall below £1000, to something like £800 (the sum which, if invested at 15 per cent, would bring in £120 per year).

By similar reasoning, if interest rates fall below 12 per cent, your stock will become more desirable. If rates are 10 per cent, there will be investors who are happy to spend up to £1200 if they can be sure of an annual return of £120.

So the market price of gilt-edged securities will vary inversely with the current long-term interest rate.

those offering the best prices. Three auctions were held in 1987 and 1988 and were regarded as fairly successful (each was over-subscribed at least one and a half times). They were suspended only as a result of the decision not to issue new stock. In late 1988 the Bank introduced 'reverse auctions'. It offered to buy in specified stocks from the market and invited sellers to suggest prices. Only the lowest, of course, were accepted. The aim was to bring about a modest reduction in the stock of outstanding debt. Neither the Bank nor the government (for reasons explained in the next section) has an interest in decimating the gilts market. Changing government finances are, in any case, likely to spell a temporary end to reverse auctions in the early 1990s.

The New Gilt-Edged Market

The manner in which gilt-edged securities are traded has always resembled the market in shares. They are mostly bought and sold on the Stock Exchange. In fact, trade in gilts is responsible for some 65 per cent of the Exchange's total turnover. The old pre-Big Bang dealing system was virtually the same as for shares – except that it was even more tightly concentrated. Two jobbers (Wedd Durlacher and Akroyd & Smithers) dominated the market. There were about a dozen brokers who, between them, accounted for over 90 per cent of transactions. The customers were mainly banks (who preferred stocks that were nearing maturity) and investment institutions (who were happy to buy securities with some time to run). Private non-corporate clients accounted for only about 7 per cent of the market. With only two serious jobbers, there was hardly any intramarket dealing. If one had tried to sell to the other, it would immediately have revealed its position to its only major competitor. Needless to say, commissions were fixed.

All this had to change with Big Bang. The new rules for membership and the new Stock Exchange dealing arrangements were inevitably extended to the gilts market. The aim was to generate competition and liquidity by increasing the number of market-makers. Intramarket dealing was to be encouraged by the introduction of a new species – the inter-dealer broker (IDB). IDBs do not buy and sell themselves, but act as intermediaries between market-makers who wish to adjust their positions. This is designed to generate further liquidity without threatening competition. The Bank of England took responsibility for overseeing the new market.

The new arrangements attracted entrants from overseas as well as from elsewhere in the City. Twenty-seven market-makers registered in 1986. All were, of course, divisions of the huge conglomerates that were put together in anticipation of Big Bang. Wedd Durlacher became part of Barclays de Zoete Wedd, while Akroyd & Smithers joined the Mercury Securities conglomerate put together by S. G. Warburg. These were probably the two most prestigious groupings to emerge from the pre-Big Bang jockeying. Altogether, the changes represented something like a sixfold increase in the capitalisation of the market. Turnover increased accordingly. It doubled within months of Big Bang. The huge surge was, predictably, in intramarket activity. The drop in commission also encouraged a burst of trade from banks and institutions. Large deals are usually executed without any commission at all. As a result the average bargain in this part of the market has risen to about £2 million. The share of the retail customer – the private non-corporate buyer – has fallen accordingly to little more than 5 per cent of the market.

The picture is not all rosy. It soon became clear that there was not enough business for twenty-seven market-makers. The prospect of a PSDR which encouraged the government to stop issuing new stock, and to buy up existing securities could only make the overcrowding worse. By 1990 the number of market-makers had shrunk to nineteen. It is surprising that it had not fallen lower. Casualties include such prominent names as Chase Manhattan, Merrill Lynch, Hill Samuel, Citicorp, Morgan Grenfell, Prudential Bache and Crédit Lyonnais. The reasons are simple. They were losing money hand over fist. Market losses in the first year of the new system were estimated at £50 million. One of the retiring chairmen described the situation in a piece of beguiling double-talk as 'not losing money but failing to cover costs'. The distinction is a narrow one. The Bank of England seemed anxious to sound as optimistic as possible in 1989, describing 'significant improvement' as market-makers were 'close to break-even'. Indeed, it was partly in an attempt to revive the spirits of disillusioned gilts traders that the Bank relaxed the discount houses' market-making monopoly in the short-term money-market in 1988. It offered them what it thought would be seen as an opportunity for profit to offset gilt-edged losses. Market-makers were not easily convinced. Perhaps they had reason not to trust the hand that purported to feed them. As we shall see in a moment, the government needs a gilt-edged market for more than just borrowing, and yet grumpy market-makers in the late 1980s could have been forgiven for thinking that they had been seduced into the market under false pretences. Soon after they arrived the government seemed to close the market down by ceasing to issue securities.

Whether the new system has succeeded or failed, then, depends upon your point of view. It has led to large losses. But the market is busier and more liquid. The innovation of IDBs appears to have been a success. It has certainly helped to boost intramarket business. The problem, predictably, is that there are too many of them. Six have been authorised while there is probably only sufficient business for three. The enthusiasm of the two major Japanese houses, Nomura and Daiwa, to be registered as market-makers in 1988 may make us more optimistic about the future. Certainly, the period of PSDR is drawing gradually to a close. An economic slow-down has quickly reduced tax revenues and caused a clear change in government finances.

There can be no doubt that the government and the Bank wish to see a successful gilts market. The government's interest in the market goes way beyond a concern with its own finances. Just as it can influence short-term interest rates through the discount market, so long-term rates are affected by activity in the gilts market. Gilts are by far the most actively traded medium- and long-term securities. By controlling the supply of these stocks, the government (via the Bank of England) has an effect on their prices and thus on rates of interest. Once again, this is not a matter of heavy-handed fixing of rates, but rather of discreet influence. It is, nonetheless, real. Both the Bank and the government want a healthy and buoyant market. It has been a more direct agent of government monetary control in the past, as extra gilts have been issued in an attempt to soak up idle bank deposits within the economy – a practice known as 'overfunding' and officially suspended in 1985. It might easily be revived. The market also serves the City itself. A ready supply of gilts helps professional investors to maintain a balanced portfolio. Gilts are long-term, low-risk investments and are widely sought after as a means of offsetting the higher risk of short-term securities issued by companies. In this sense too, the gilts market is important to the functioning of efficient capital markets. It accounts for a staggering £4000 billion worth of business per day. Whatever the peculiar problems of the late 1980s, we can be sure that such an important market will settle and will continue to play a major role in the City's financial services industry well into the next century.

8 The New Old Lady

Centrepiece of the City

The Bank of England has already cropped up a number of times in this account of the City of London. In the previous chapter we considered its key role in ensuring the liquidity of the short-term money markets, and its influence over both long- and short-term interest rates. Earlier, there were oblique references to the Bank's role in the supervision of City markets as well as to its advice to government regarding the control of them. It has appeared so far as a stately amalgamation of spy, nanny and friend to the other financial operators of the City. Perhaps this is not so wide of the mark.

The Bank seems to lie at the very heart of the City. In the first place, it stands pretty near the geographical centre – opposite Mansion House (the home of the Lord Mayor) and the Royal Exchange (now home of LIFFE), only a few yards' walk from the Stock Exchange in one direction and Guildhall in the other. The position is apt. Turn right and you encounter symbols of the old City – the quaintly historical features of Mansion House and Guildhall. To the left, in the form of LIFFE and the Stock Exchange, are the hectic, frenzied markets of the new City. The Bank stands statuesque at the crossroads, looking not unlike the National Trust's version of a maximum security prison, and doing its best to fuse the two aspects of the City's split personality.

The contradictions, or at least ambiguities, of its role are more than simply geographical. It is, as we have seen, an active player within a number of City markets (especially for money and foreign exchange) yet it is also their supervisor. It is a bank with the normal responsibilities that any banker accepts, yet it also charged with the direct operation of various aspects of government economic policy. Is it really a bank? Or is it an arm of the Treasury? Is it simply a political agent in disguise? Or is it above the shady world of politics?

These are the issues that we shall address in this chapter, culminating in the controversial question of the Bank's proposed independence. Before we can analyse the full implications of the Bank's role, though, we need a clearer idea of what it actually does.

It is easily forgotten that the Bank of England is, genuinely, a bank. True, its customers are not quite the same as those of a typical High Street bank and it does not have much of a branch network. It does have branches (called regional offices) in Birmingham, Bristol, Leeds, Manchester and Newcastle, whose main role is to manage the issue of banknotes in their region. But the Bank of England falls some way short of Barclays or the National Westminster in this respect. Nonetheless, it carries out traditional banking responsibilities for two major types of client: government departments, each of which has its own account at the Bank; and commercial banks, which also each have an account. There are one or two private customers as well – mostly the Bank's own employees – but they need not worry us too much.

Any bank performs particular services for its customers. The main examples are:

- holding deposits;
- offering facilities for easy settlement of debts;
- arranging loans;
- providing general financial advice.

The Bank of England fulfils these same functions for the government and for the banking sector.

Banker to the Government

Obviously, the financial needs of the government are rather broader than those of the typical private customer, but the principle is identical. The government receives considerable bodies of revenue from taxation, privatisation, occasional commercial ventures and so on. It needs this money stored in a manner that is safe and accessible. The Inland Revenue has accounts at the Bank of England into which much of this money is paid. It will be transferred to accounts held by individual government departments according to the government's agreed expenditure programme. When the time comes for these departments to spend their allotted sums, the accounts are run down – normally by means of direct transfers into the accounts of other banks (which are also held at the Bank of England). Payments of social security, for example, might find their way into circulation through money being transferred from the Department of Social Security's accounts at the Bank of England to the accounts of the National Giro Bank. From there they are passed to their recipients.

This covers the first two of the banking functions listed earlier. The Bank of England provides the government with a large number of traditional bank accounts in which money is stored. It also offers an easy means for this money to be spent – normally by direct transfer to other banks. The deposits could be spent by cheque if the government wished.

The Bank also arranges loans on the government's behalf. The job here is a good deal more complicated than it would be for the average private customer, but it is still a traditional banking function. The government may borrow for a variety of reasons and in a number of ways. The Bank of England will always manage the arrangements. The most obvious reason for government borrowing is to finance spending. For this purpose, a sterling loan will be required for a number of years. Such needs are met by the issue of gilt-edged stock. The nature of these securities and the manner of their issue were explained in Chapter 7. Responsibility lies entirely with the Bank of England. The Bank advises on how much stock to issue, at what fixed rate of interest and for what period of time. The decisions are influenced both by the Bank's view of what the market will be most keen to buy, and by its concern to balance the stock of outstanding securities. It will, for example, wish to avoid a situation where large volumes of securities mature at the same time. This might strain the government's finances, since large expenditures would be needed to redeem the stock. So, the Bank plans to issue varieties of medium- and long-term securities to avoid such crises. It will also buy securities in the market and replace them with others in an attempt to maintain a continuing balance in the government's outstanding debt. This is known as the Bank's 'funding' policy. Table 8.1 gives an example of it in operation over the late 1980s. At first, the Bank seems to have wanted to boost the proportion of stock in the medium-term (5–15 year) bracket. In the first two financial years shown more of this stock is issued than the others. After the first year, it also appears keen to reduce the proportion of long-term stock. Less of this is issued in 1987/8, and more is repurchased in 1988/9. It seems happy to leave the shortest term (1–5 years) in the market. By 1989/90, policy has changed slightly. The Bank is still buying in long-term securities but seems eager now to remove some of the medium-term stock that it had issued a few years previously. The process is one of continually adjusting the Bank's own sales and purchases in order to maintain the the most appropriate balance between the proportions of short- , medium- and long-term debt outstanding. The practice of 'overfunding' – where the Bank issues more securities than are needed in an effort to absorb bank deposits in the economy – was described in the last chapter.

The Bank will advise the government on the appropriate method for a new issue of gilt-edged stock – an auction, perhaps, or the use of the 'tap'. In the case of auctions, the Bank is responsible for the allocation of the stock. During the later 1980s when the government had no need of new issues of securities, the Bank advised on the volumes of stock to buy back from the market. It will have decided

TABLE 8.1
Sales and Purchases of Government Stock, 1986–90 (in £ million)*

Financial year	*Total*	*1–5 year stocks*	*5–15 year stocks*	*15-year and undated stocks*
1986–87	+12 132	+2 558	+5 124	+4 450
1987–88	+12 462	+3 879	+4 917	+3 666
1988–89	−5 757	−655	−1 691	−3 411
1989–90	−5 824	−669	−3 626	−1 529

* Sales are signified by a + sign, purchases by a − sign
SOURCE *Bank of England Quarterly Bulletin*, November 1990.

which particular stocks it was wisest to acquire (an extension of its funding policy) and was, of course, directly responsible for entering the market to acquire them. Similarly, it was the Bank that organised and operated the 'reverse auctions' of 1988 and 1989.

The Bank maintains a record of all transactions in gilt-edged stock and a list of all stock-holders. This is needed for annual interest payments and for the redemption of stock as it matures. It is an immense job, now handled by the Central Gilts Office which was set up by the Bank in 1986.

All this represents a huge and, in one sense, very specific responsibility. In another, though, it should be seen as no more than the traditional work of a bank in organising the borrowing requirements of a customer. It is some steps beyond an overdraft facility, but only its scale distinguishes it from the organisation of bond issues for large corporate clients.

The government's sterling borrowing does not end with gilt-edged stock. It also issues Treasury bills. These too were explained in Chapter 7. Although their primary purpose is to ease short-term cash flows in the money market, they are nevertheless a form of borrowing. We saw in the last chapter that the issue of these securities is entirely a matter for the Bank's decision and execution. Government interest-rate policy may affect it, but the Bank manages the procedure. It is also, of course, responsible for redeeming the bills as they fall due. It was instrumental in the establishment of a Central Moneymarkets Office in 1990 which looks after the administration and settlement of these and other short-term securities.

The government's borrowing needs do not stop at sterling. Foreign exchange may be required if balance-of-payments difficulties are draining the official reserves, as well as to enable the Bank to support sterling in the foreign exchange market (particularly now that we are returning to semi-fixed exchange rates). Once again, the Bank will arrange any such loans. In the past it has exploited the syndicated Euroloan market. Alternatively, the International Monetary Fund or other overseas sources might be approached.

Altogether, then, the Bank's role in managing government borrowing is vast. It also has wider implications. We know already that interest-rate policy is transacted by means of the markets in Treasury bills and gilt-edged securities. Nonetheless, in the first place, the Bank's role is that of banker.

The final banking responsibility listed earlier was the provision of financial advice. The Bank of England offers advice to the government regarding its financial position. The Bank will discuss matters such as the issue of gilt-edged securities and Treasury bills with government representatives, and will offer technical advice based upon its own experience. The process does not stop here, though.

Advice inevitably ranges to matters beyond the narrow realm of normal banking practice. This highlights the ambiguous nature of the Bank's position. Simply by virtue of being the government's specialist banker, it becomes directly involved in political decisions. The Bank can – and does – influence policy. In the first place, its advice will be enlisted over matters relating to the actual operation of the banking system and the financial markets. It is a specialist in this area. In recent years the Bank's input into decisions regarding deregulation, Big Bang, supervision arrangements and so on, has been critical. To describe it as influential is to underrate it. The Bank has been instrumental in these changes. Its advice goes beyond the technical operations of the financial system, though. It has a key part to play in the detail and even the timing and technique of monetary policies. The most important examples (considered fully in earlier chapters) are the control of interest rates and exchange rates. The Bank is not merely the executant of these policies. Its advice is crucial. This is not to say that the government has to listen, nor that the Bank (at the moment) has any power of veto over the policy finally laid down. If you take your car to the garage, you do not have to take advice from the mechanic although he is likely to have a far greater input into 'car repair policy' than anyone else. The Bank of England is a highly respected and experienced financial mechanic.

Bankers' Bank

Banks themselves form the other main group of the Bank of England's customers. Once again, the basic services offered are no different from those provided by any bank to any client.

Each authorised bank has an account at the Bank of England. These accounts are not only a convenient way of holding liquid funds. They are also the means by which banks acquire cash for distribution to their own customers. The banks order cash from the Bank of England and pay for it either by selling worn notes back to the Bank or, if this is insufficient to cover their order, by running down their Bank of England accounts. The accounts serve another key function. Major clearing banks (and now building societies too) are members of the Clearing House Automated Payment System (CHAPS) which calculates the net payments necessary between member-banks in order to settle each day's business. These payments are actually made through adjustments in each bank's holding at the Bank of England. The Bank, therefore, fulfils the first two banking functions with some panache – it holds deposits and offers efficient means of settling debts.

We have already seen that the Bank of England helps its bank customers to borrow. Its behaviour in the short-term money markets, although technically directed towards discount houses (and their new colleagues), is in fact a method of making funds available to the banking system itself. By controlling the liquidity of the market, the Bank is standing prepared to offer funds whenever they are required. This is how it gets its nickname of 'lender of last resort'.

The Bank's willingness to support the banking system goes beyond lending in the short-term money markets. It takes responsibility for the banking system itself and has, on more than one occasion, organised rescue operations (known as 'lifeboats') for troubled banks. These normally involve the provision of funds – often from other banks, as well as from the Bank of England – on condition that improvements are made in the running of the bank concerned. In 1984 the Bank actually bought one such bank – Johnson Matthey – for the sum of £1. It sounds a bargain. As we shall see later in the chapter it actually represents the biggest blot on what had otherwise been a fairly good decade for the Bank of England. For the time being it serves as an extreme example of the Bank's willingness to lend to its banking customers.

Predictably, the Bank is not short of advice for these customers. At one level this is no more than the customary specialist advice that a banker might offer to a client. The particular requirements of banks as clients will be different from those of other customers, even corporations. Nonetheless, the Bank has much expertise in this area and its advice will be sought and valued. It is true, though, that the Bank is probably more generous with its advice than most. After all, it is not just banker to the commercial banks, it is supervisor of the system – it monitors the balance sheets of all of them and keeps a close eye on the business that they conduct. It meets regularly with senior managers in an effort to ensure that the banks are prudently run. You might argue that this is no more than the sensible, cautious behaviour of any banker who regularly lends to particular customers. It does go further. The Bank can, in desperate situations, actually deny a bank the authorisation to operate. This is quite a few steps beyond the authority of the average bank manager. It raises once again the ambiguity of the Bank's role as banker and much, much more.

More than Just a Bank

It is palpably clear that the Bank of England is more than just a bank. The manner in which its traditional banking activities spill over into other, more controversial and more interesting areas – control of interest and exchange rates, supervision and direction of banks, agent of monetary policy and so on – is already apparent.

Many people have attempted over the years to sum up in a well-turned phrase the extra responsibilities of a central bank. The Bank of England currently favours something along the lines of 'guardian of the currency'. It may sound a bit melodramatic, but it does the job rather well.

There are two aspects to the value of a currency. First, and probably most obvious, there is its international value. This refers to the rates at which it may be exchanged for other currencies. A major part of the Bank's job is to monitor and, perhaps, to influence these exchange rates. We have touched on this already. The Bank is at pains to describe its role (just as in the short-term money markets) as one of smoothing the market in order to achieve stability. Exchange rates have an important impact upon trade flows. Unnecessary volatility can discourage trade altogether. Inevitably, there will be international capital flows occurring on any one day which (left to themselves) might cause such volatility. The role of the Bank is to monitor the market and to enter it as buyer or seller whenever it is thought that the rate is moving too far from the Bank's own estimate of sterling's trend. The Bank has a typical foreign-exchange dealing-room for the purpose. It adds to or runs down the government's official currency reserves as it deals, and the transactions are recorded in the Bank's Exchange Equalisation Account. All this, of course, raises exactly the same problem that we faced in the earlier section about interest-rate determination. Is the Bank actually fixing

FIGURE 8.1
UK Official Reserves in 1990 ($ million)

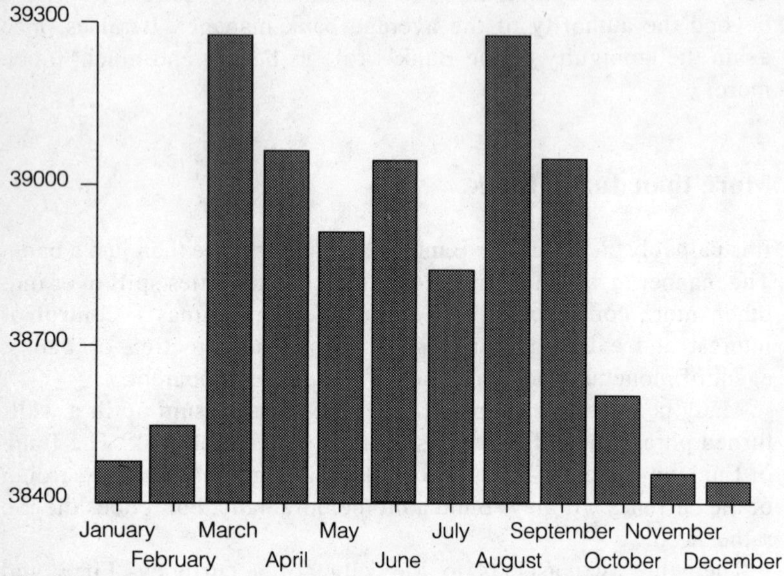

SOURCE *Bank of England Quarterly Bulletin*, February 1991.

the exchange rate? Or is it innocently helping the market to function more effectively than it otherwise might?

The changes in foreign currency reserves recorded in Figure 8.1 are certainly large enough to suggest that more is at work than mere trade flows. The Bank is surely using the reserves to intervene in the foreign exchange market. But is it actually trying to distort market forces?

The experience of the 1980s gives us conflicting clues. The incoming Conservative government of 1979 was in no doubt that exchange rates were best left to market forces. This helps to explain why exchange controls were abolished. The Bank's job was simply to be one of recognising the trend in sterling's value, and offsetting any wild fluctuations around that trend. Thus, the pound was able to reach $2.40 in 1981 and to fall to almost $1.00 in 1985. She did not say it until 1988, but the Thatcher dictum 'You cannot buck the market', describes the prevailing attitude very well.

How different is all this from the period from around 1985 onwards, when the exchange rate against the Deutschmark was being used as an overt standard against which to measure the success of anti-inflation policy. Chancellor Lawson went so far as to voice his belief that sterling should be worth around DM3.00. The role of the Bank of England at this period must have been to turn the Chancellor's view into actuality by its intervention in the market – even, on occasions by altering interest rates in the discount market. Whether or not this qualifies as attempting to 'buck the market', it surely gives the Bank a more direct role in the determination of exchange rates.

Membership of the Exchange Rate Mechanism (ERM) of the EC in 1990 has made the Bank's role even more direct. It should first be remembered that the Bank's advice will have been the most important influence upon the rate at which we joined the mechanism. After that, it becomes the Bank's duty to maintain the parity. It is not possible to keep the exchange rate for long at a level that the market regards as quite unrealistic. Realignments in such situations are possible and necessary. Nonetheless, within a system such as the ERM, the attitude of the Bank is a major influence on the behaviour of the market. The Bank will intervene (and has frequently done so) in order to remind the market of the rate that it wishes sterling to reach. On the vast majority of occasions such activity is quite sufficient to maintain the parity. Is this enough to qualify the Bank as active manager of the currency? Within the ERM limits (set in part by the Bank), it probably is.

We said earlier that there were two aspects to the Bank's role as 'guardian of the currency'. The second is connected to, but even more far-reaching than, the activities outlined above. The currency also has an internal value. This is measured in terms of how many goods it will buy and depends, therefore, upon the domestic rate of inflation. As well as controlling the exchange rate, the Bank of England (in common, it would say, with any central bank) has a responsibility to combat inflation. In a sense this precedes its management of the exchange rate. We saw in Chapter 5 that the exchange rate depends in large part upon the relative purchasing power of our currency and others. This, in its turn, depends upon national rates of inflation. If our inflation is higher than that of

Germany, then sterling will fall against the Deutschmark. So, in a perfect world, the responsibility to combat inflation should relieve the need to do any separate currency management (this was the logic pursued by the government between 1979 and about 1983). Once we take on board the full implications of this, the Bank of England becomes a great deal more than just a bank. Indeed, it seems to enter wholeheartedly into the world of politics. For the past twenty years or so, anti-inflation policy has been arguably the most important part of the government's work. Where exactly does the Bank fit in?

This is not the place to launch a full-blooded analysis of policies that might be used to reduce inflation. High on any such list, though, would be control of the rate at which people spend money in the economy. According to the too-often repeated motto, inflation results from 'too much money chasing too few goods'. It is an over simplification. Nonetheless, it is surely true that control of monetary spending, and even, perhaps, control of the money supply, is bound to form a key part of anti-inflation strategy. This is where the Bank fits in.

One of the Bank's best-known functions is as the printer and issuer of banknotes in the economy. An entire department (the Issue Department) is concerned with this single chore. Whilst notes in circulation are no longer backed by holdings of gold in the Bank's vaults, the Issue Department must still hold assets (mostly gilt-edged securities) to balance the value of notes issued. At the moment the Bank prints and issues money to meet the demands made on it by commercial banks. If customers are withdrawing more cash, commercial banks demand more, and the Bank of England prints it. Some economists believe that more effective control of the money supply (and, thus, inflation) might be achieved by controlling the supply of assets to the Bank's Issue Department and thus limiting its ability to issue cash on demand.

As the agent of government monetary policy, the Bank of England takes its orders from the Treasury. The policies, though, are the Bank's and it is the Bank that executes them. The most ready example here is control of interest rates. By raising the cost of borrowing, governments hope to discourage it, and thus to reduce the rate at which spending in the economy uses. The Bank will not only advise on such policy but will also, through its position at the centre of the discount market, enact it. It can affect long-term rates through operations in the gilts market. Still in the gilts market, it can use its funding policy to absorb bank deposits and leave less cash available for direct spending. All these systems were explained in the previous chapter. In each of them the Bank is operating as a specialist technician and, if we are to believe what we are told, is acting under orders. It is still being more than just a bank.

Monetary policy does not end with interest rates. Over the years, various complex techniques have been employed in an effort to reduce the rate of growth of bank lending more directly. A prime feature of the deregulation of the 1980s was the abandonment of such procedures. No longer do banks have to hold given percentages of assets in specified liquid form. 'Special deposits' have not been employed since the early 1980s. 'The corset' arrangements are gathering dust. In their day, the Bank was directly responsible for this panoply of measures. In a sense it still is. It was in large part the Bank's advice that led to their abandonment and it is the Bank's job to determine whether or not they remain unnecessary. The Bank continually monitors the banking sector as part of its effort to control lending. Direct credit controls could easily be reintroduced. In one sense such controls have simply become less formal, anyway, We saw in an earlier chapter that the Bank put pressure on banks in the early 1980s to support corporate customers who were having difficulties during the recession. Similar pressures were exerted in the late 1980s. Whatever one may think of its success, the Bank of England has a direct influence upon monetary policy in the UK and, at least to some degree, makes that policy.

It is surely clear that the Bank of England is more than just a senior bank. It has a policy-making arm that extends beyond the technical field of banking and financial practice into the area that we are used to thinking of as political. It is through this that the Bank's status has come increasingly to be questioned. To whom is it, and to whom should it, be responsible?

The Question of Independence

In the speech following his resignation as Chancellor of the Exchequer in 1989, Nigel Lawson revealed that he had, in 1988, prepared a plan to render the Bank of England independent of political control. Mrs Thatcher had refused to proceed with the arrangements. All this came, apparently, as some surprise to the

Bank itself. Once raised, though, the issue has refused to die. In his bid for the Conservative leadership in 1990, Michael Heseltine announced his support for an independent central bank. Controversy over monetary arrangements within Europe, and about the possible establishment of a central bank for the EC, has encouraged further analysis of the Bank's position and role, and has prompted comparisons (usually unfavourable) with Germany's Bundesbank.

Political control of the Bank has always been controversial. The nickname of 'the old lady of Threadneedle Street' derives from an eighteenth-century cartoon in which the Bank was depicted as an old lady about to be ravished by the Prime Minister of the day, William Pitt. Political control was on the agenda then, and probably always will be (incidentally, at that time, the Bank was technically independent). The Bank of England was nationalised in 1946. The Act of Parliament is surprisingly short and gives little direct hint as to the Bank's role in policy-making. Clause 4 (there are only 6), Paragraph 1 comes closest:

> ***The Treasury may from time to time give such directions to the Bank as, after consultation with the Governor of the Bank, they think necessary in the public interest.***

The precise limits of the relationship between the Bank and the Treasury are still not clear. There is no doubt that the Treasury is the policy-maker, nor that the Bank has special responsibilities that relate to its role within the financial services industry. There is no danger of confusing the two institutions. But the Bank is not merely a tool of the Treasury. It does advise on monetary policy. It does advise on exchange-rate policy. Symbolically, perhaps, the Bank runs its own computer model of the UK economy, with which it produces forecasts of more than simple banking trends. It does not rely upon the Treasury model (as other government departments do) and voices proud faith in the superiority of its own forecasts. It does have a view of its own. The Governor did, for example, make speeches during 1990 in which he made arch references to membership of the ERM, described the depth of the economic recession and voiced the Bank's view of the need for tight monetary policy. Not only does the Bank have a view, but it is not reserved for Treasury ears. The Bank is more than just an agent of policy.

Lord Rees-Mogg, writing in *The Independent* in late 1989,

claimed that 'the record of political control of the Bank of England is a record of failure; the record is one of ignorance, inadequacy and manipulation for electoral reasons'. He went on to cite examples of various post-war Chancellors who had operated sloppy monetary policy, and thus risked inflation, because they lacked the political will to control the money supply with the necessary discipline. The argument can, of course, be extended to Chancellor Lawson himself. In 1987, fresh from a general election triumph and keen to keep the strong pound in line with the Deutschmark, Lawson cut interest rates. The policy continued, in the wake of the stock-market crash, well into the spring of 1988. It could be (and has been) said to represent the very sort of monetary indiscipline, culminating in inflation (in 1989 and 1990) that politicians cannot be trusted to avoid. If the Thatcher government – as ideologically pure as believers in monetary discipline are ever likely to see – cannot be trusted with the operation of monetary policy, then, the argument goes, no politicians can be. Scratch a politician, Rees-Mogg believes, and you are sure to find a 'dangerous inflationist' beneath. Inflation will only be satisfactorily controlled by an agency that is above politics. Only if monetary policy (including interest and exchange rates) is set with eyes firmly on the long-term defeat of inflation, rather than short-term electoral success, will the right policy be set.

Contrast with German experience appears to prove the point. Inflation has dogged German history in the twentieth century. The hyperinflation of the 1920s not only shattered faith in democracy but laid the foundations for Nazism. Inflation after the Second World War was less dramatic in its consequences, but no less serious for the German people. As a result, the West German Bundesbank (now serving the whole country) was designed to be above political manipulation and was charged by Act of Parliament with the very guardianship of the currency (with all its implications) that was described earlier. Germany's inflation record since the 1950s has been superior to that of any of her major industrial rivals, and has been vastly superior to that of the UK. The case appears proven. If you want low, stable inflation, you must trust your central bankers rather than your elected politicians. Speaking in 1989 of possible monetary arrangements for the EC, Karl-Otto Pohl, then President of the Bundesbank, said: 'Historical experience has shown [low inflation] can best be expected of a system which is independent of political influence'.

If the argument is as strong as this, why are there any dissenters? And why should Margaret Thatcher, one of the most vigorous of anti-inflationists, dismiss the idea? Our own example of the Lawson years may help to furnish a reason. The argument depends upon a belief that central bankers will be right where politicians are wrong. There is little evidence that the Bank was tugging at Chancellor Lawson's sleeve throughout 1987 and 1988, urging him to raise interest rates rather than cut them. The Bank has nonetheless gone on record since describing this period as one in which monetary policy was, in retrospect, too loose. So central bankers do not always do the right thing. The Bank, however, was an ally of Mr Lawson's in his desire to operate a controlled exchange-rate policy and, ultimately, to join the ERM. This policy was being resisted by the Prime Minister, Mrs Thatcher and her private adviser, Professor Sir Alan Walters. Independence for the Bank would have given Lawson a greater chance of being able to pursue it. The rights and wrongs of this particular issue need not concern us. The more general point that it throws up is that Mrs Thatcher's opposition to the idea was in part based upon a fear that an independent Bank might enact policy that she believed to be wrong, but for which she must take some responsibility, and within which she must govern. One may also question whether Mr Lawson would have been quite so keen to protect the Bank from political influence if it had not been happy to pursue a policy that he himself favoured.

International evidence is not entirely convincing either. It is true that Germany's inflation record is considerably better than that of the UK. Figure 8.2 shows that it is also considerably better than that of the USA. The Federal Reserve Board (the US central bank) is, like the Bundesbank, independent of direct political control. Japan's inflation performance can also be seen from Figure 8.2 to be superior to that of the USA. The Japanese central bank, like the Bank of England, is not independent. It is too easy to believe that independent central banks will always succeed in controlling inflation where politically dependent ones will fail. Germany's success may be due as much to her ghastly past experience of inflation, as to her system of central banking. Perhaps the British do not share this intense fear of inflation, and so are reluctant to subordinate all other aims to its control. The much-vaunted political independence of the Bundesbank can be exaggerated anyway. It may not be subject to political direction, but it feels political pressure. The plans finally adopted for monetary integration between East and West Germany in 1990 were not, apparently, those first favoured by the Bundesbank. They feared that a straight one-for-one swap between Ostmarks and Deutschmarks would generate inflation in the East. Nonetheless, there were sound political reasons for supporting the idea. The 'independent' Bundesbank was persuaded. Perhaps Germany's success with inflation is simply evidence of this same political will.

FIGURE 8.2
Comparative Inflation Rates in the UK, USA, Germany and Japan, 1975–89

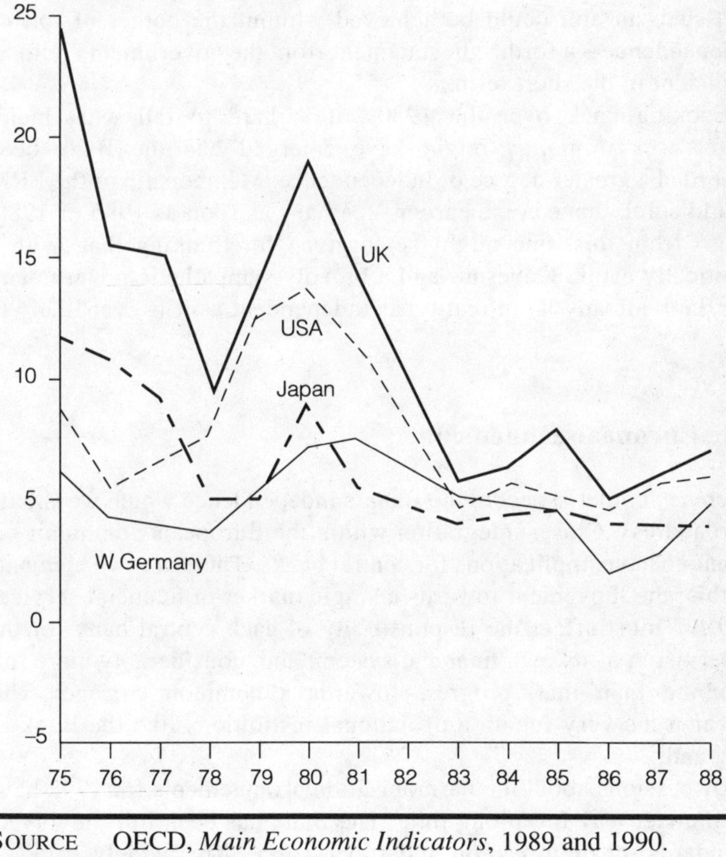

SOURCE OECD, *Main Economic Indicators*, 1989 and 1990.

The Bank of England itself has taken care not to seem too eager to grasp at the shadow of independence. Robin Leigh-Pemberton, Governor until 1993, clearly recognises strengths in the idea. In 1990 he was reported as saying:

> ***It would be easier for the politicians if this highly contentious matter of monetary policy, and therefore of how resolute the counter-inflationary stance is, were taken out of day-to-day politics and were seen to be the reponsibility of the central bank.***

He was at pains not to say that the Bank would do the job better without political direction, nor that he had any objection to the existing relationship between Bank and Treasury. He even observed that such an aim could be achieved without the bother of formal independence – a forthright statement from the government could be sufficient in the short term.

Looking back over the 1980s, it is hard to tell what major differences in policy might have emerged had the Bank been accorded a greater degree of independence. Membership of the ERM would surely have come earlier – perhaps as soon as 1985 or 1986. Apart from this, one might be forgiven for thinking that, with a politically astute Governor and a broadly sympathetic government, the Bank already is, in reality, as independent as it is ever likely to be.

The European Dimension

There is another aspect to the Bank's independence which we should also address. Closer integration within the European Community is bound to have implications for central banks. There are two elements of this: the movement towards a single market in financial services in 1992 must affect the responsibility of each central bank for the supervision of its own financial system; and, considerably more far-reaching than that, progress towards a common currency will threaten the very function of national institutions like the Bank of England.

Discussions about the harmonisation arrangements for 1992 have been under way for a long time. The Bank has been fully involved. Standards of authorisation and supervision differ widely between member-countries. Community-wide standards are to be adopted. Each central bank will remain responsible for the enforcement of such standards within its own national sphere of operations. Inevitably, the process towards harmonisation has not always been easy. The British financial system is more sophisticated than that of many of our European partners. Our experience of deregulation gives the Bank of England a fair amount of authority. There are likely to be a number of false starts before a satisfactory system emerges – possibly not until the later 1990s. There is an inherent problem that, while the enlarged market will attract new participants operating often at the limit of risk, the requirements of harmonisation will entail simpler and less-thorough standards for authorisation and supervision. The Bank itself has said that 'regulatory authorities will need to be that much more vigilant'. As we shall see later in this chapter, the Bank burned its own fingers in the 1980s in an effort to hit on the correct degree of vigilance for the newly deregulated banking sector. The advent of the single market will make this problem seem insignificant by comparison. It must also, to some extent, reduce the Bank's control over its own systems of supervision. The new standards are likely to involve some element of compromise. This could be said to chip away further at any independence that the Bank may claim. On the other hand, any process of internationalisation and liberalisation must require individual national authorities to sacrifice some of their autonomy. This is a price they should be happy to pay for the benefits of a larger, more-efficient market.

A common European currency is further away, but its full implications make the notion of an 'independent' Bank of England almost meaningless. We described the Bank earlier as 'guardian of the currency'. What is it to do if it has no currency to guard?

Before growing too apocalyptic, it should be remembered that the Bank's roles as banker to the government and to the banking sector, as well as its supervisory duties outlined above, would still need to be fulfilled. The operation of monetary policy, though, would no longer be a purely national responsibility. One of the Bank's executive directors observed in 1988 that 'with a single currency, many of the traditional functions of the national central banker will fall away'. Clearly some form of European central bank would have to evolve. The Delors plan includes provision for a 'European System of Central Banks' (ESCB) as a prelude to full monetary union. The Bank of England would be involved in such a system, but it would lose what little independence it has. There is currently a good deal of difference within the EC over the techniques adopted for monetary control. Some countries still use reserve requirements as a control on the banking sector. Others rely entirely upon activities within short-term money-markets. The Governor of the Bank of England made it clear in 1990 that he valued the right of each national central bank to pursue its own favoured system for as long as possible. 'However close we come to a common framework of Community monetary policy,' he said, 'I envisage flexibility in the instruments employed in individual centres.' In other words, he accepts that circumstances within the EC can determine the aims of monetary policy, but not that it should fix the techniques.

If the EC does go all the way towards a common currency, then even this slim measure of independence must be lost. The question then becomes one of where the new EC central bank is to be located, and upon what model it will be established. To those who regard the City as the financial capital of Europe, it would be the logical site for such a Eurobank. More than prestige is at stake. The existence of a central monetary authority might well attract a great deal of new banking and dealing business. London is an unlikely location, however, so long as the UK remains a reluctant traveller on the road to monetary union. The City's pre-eminence may be threatened. The question might be too simple, anyway; a central bank has many different functions and may, therefore, be able to have more than one location. America's Federal Reserve Board, for example, has a policy-making division in Washington (near the politicians) and an operational division in New York (near the money-markets). Talk of this simply leads the Bank of England to fear a future as the operational arm of a policy-maker located somewhere on the continent.

Inevitably, the Bundesbank is most commonly put forward as the model. It would be small consolation for the Bank of England to sacrifice what little independence it has, to a new institution, built along German lines, that will have a good deal more. In fact, it may be premature to regard the Bundesbank as a blueprint for a European central bank. Membership of the ERM, in which the Deutschmark is the strongest currency, effectively requires EC finance ministers to set interest rates and monetary policy according to a standard laid down by the Germans. A number of them are tired of the remorselessly tough policy that emanates from Frankfurt, and would like to exert rather more influence over their own monetary affairs. Perhaps the new bank will be more open to political influence than many suppose. Perhaps, most ironically of all, the Bank of England will sacrifice its small degree of independence to an institution that is even more subject to political pressure – and to the complex pressure of twelve European governments rather than just one.

The Bank and the City

It is not only the Bank's overseas relationships that are of interest. It has an even more schizophrenic relationship with the remainder of the City. It is, as we know, a banker in its own right. It is a major player in various City markets – the discount market, the gilts market and the foreign exchange market at least. It should be remembered too, that, while its motives for dealing in these markets will differ from the other institutions involved, the actual manner of its dealing is, in most cases, indistinguishable. To this extent, then it is like any of the major banks in the City.

The Bank also supervises these markets, reporting on them to the Treasury or, in some cases, to the Department of Trade and Industry. Its particular field of responsibility is the banking sector, but the changing nature of the Bank's influence is another of the stories of the 1980s. The Bank acts as the government's eyes and ears in the City.

Already we see the ambiguity of the Bank's role. On the one hand it is a major element of City markets, on the other it is a supervisor and overseer of them. It is referee, centre-forward and goalkeeper at the same time. It even keeps the score.

In the days of exchange control, any significant transfer of money out of the country required the permission of the Bank of England. This gave it enormous power. The authority was fully delegated from government, so the Bank could effectively make its own rules as and when it liked. Any international financial operator relied upon the goodwill of the Bank. Inevitably, when you have direct power of this kind, you do not need to use it. The Bank could influence City behaviour simply by the central banker's equivalent of a raised eyebrow or a quizzical frown. This came to be known as the Bank's 'moral authority'. It was in this way that the Bank was able to enforce such tight rules for the conduct of sterling business, whilst at the same time relaxing exchange controls almost completely as far as business in foreign currency was concerned. It was this that attracted the Euromarkets to London. The Bank's flexible approach to City management can, therefore, be said to have saved the City in the 1960s and 1970s, which might otherwise have been its darkest hour.

The abolition of exchange controls in 1979 changed the role of the Bank considerably. Flexibility was, in any case, no longer as fruitful as it had once been. The rapid influx of foreign bankers had stretched the Bank's 'moral authority' to the limit. It was coming to rely increasingly upon statute law. The first impact of abolition was to make almost 700 of the Bank's staff redundant (the exchange control department had been one of the busiest) – 400 of them were found jobs elsewhere in the Bank. It also required the Bank to establish new relationships with its City colleagues. Its formal authority over the City came to an end with abolition. What has taken its place has been the urge to watch and listen and report back. For example, in the days of exchange control it had effectively supervised the London Metal Exchange (LME), since all international deals required Bank permission. This had to end. But the Bank was still the first institution to express its concern over the LME tin market in the middle 1980s – about eighteen months before the market collapsed. It was very quick to replace the direct authority (moral or not) that it had enjoyed under exchange controls, with a less formal role as watcher and listener. The new arrangement is ideally suited to the more flexible procedures of the new City. The Bank showed an adaptability that surprised many of those who thought of it as the very symbol of the old way of things.

In fact the Bank was not just adapting to changes. It was instrumental in making them. The story behind the Stock Exchange's Big Bang reveals the Bank's contradictory – or changing – values remarkably well. When the Restrictive Practices Court threatened proceedings against the Stock Exchange in the early 1980s, the Bank was wholeheartedly opposed to the idea. Its motives here were surely a desire to preserve the special, cosy atmosphere of the City of London where self-regulation was the order of the day and within which the Bank saw itself very much as the top dog. This smacks of the old City, where the Bank could exert its 'moral authority'. The Bank, though, was also quick to realise the threat being posed by international competition. Business was moving rapidly from banking markets (in which the City was highly efficient) into securities markets (in which the reverse was true). Wholesale reform at the Stock Exchange was required. The Bank pressed the case, informally, to the government. In the end, it could be regarded as the author of the Big Bang solution. This was, of course, nothing new. It was the same Bank that had been keen to encourage the development of Euromarkets in the 1960s.

The change in the 1980s has seen the final demise of that part of the Bank that was the centre of old City cosiness and was happy to rely on moral authority. The new Bank – in many cases indistinguishable from the old one – could be seen as the founder of the new City. Whatever might be the limits to its formal authority, it is deeply committed to a successful financial services sector and has clearly recognised that deregulation is an inevitable trend. Whether it explained this to its political masters, we do not know. It certainly had to explain it to many of its friends in the City, who required a good deal of convincing.

The irony of all this, as we shall see in the next chapter, is that the progressive deregulation of the 1980s has strained systems of regulation to the limit. The Bank's sphere has been formally narrowed. Most ironically of all, it has been in the area of its most traditional involvement – the banking sector itself – that the Bank has met the greatest problem.

The Johnson Matthey Affair

Of all the Bank's various roles, supervision of the banking sector looks likely to be amongst the most straightforward. It is itself a major and important bank. It has daily contacts with other banks. It understands banking. It stands at the pinnacle of the banking system. For many years, it really was that simple. The Bank hardly even needed a formal structure within which to carry out its supervisory duties. Moral authority was enough.

The opening of the City changed all that. Supervision must have been growing harder throughout the 1960s and 1970s. The new foreign operators, who had been attracted to London by the Euromarkets, were not hamstrung by the complex network of regulations that applied to British banks. Nor were they as naturally respectful of the Bank of England. As long as exchange controls kept the domestic and international banking markets apart, this may not have mattered too much. After 1979 the separation was no longer possible. The Bank entered into a new phase in its operations.

We know from earlier chapters that the 1980s saw a surge in banking activity in the City (and elsewhere). This did not come as a surprise. Deregulation was bound to have such an effect. It did call for a more stringent system of regulation, though. The Bank was quick to foresee the need for this. The Banking Act of 1979 was designed to cope with the new arrangements. It divided banks into two groups: recognised banks and licensed deposit-takers. The top tier (mostly experienced and well-known banks) would be only lightly supervised, while the others (relative newcomers) would receive the bulk of the available attention.

The new system failed. Whether this was because the planners underestimated the changes in banking behaviour, or simply because it was a bad system, it is hard to say. The issue of banking practice was raised in Chapter 4. In the newly deregulated, harshly competitive world of the 1980s, traditional banking prudence became an unprofitable commodity. Perhaps the Bank of England was not prepared for this. In that sense, the Johnson Matthey affair was a scandal waiting to happen. If it had not been that bank, it would have been another.

Johnson Matthey Bank (JMB) was a well-established City presence with over a century's experience in the precious metals business. It was a member of the circle that met daily to fix the world gold price. It had added banking to its activities in 1965. Inevitably, it was classified as a top-tier bank under the 1979 Act. The directors decided in 1980 that JMB should expand its banking activities – loans at that time accounted for less than 4 per cent of the bank's assets (the remaining 96 per cent were related to bullion-dealing). A more aggressive lending policy was pursued. Between 1980 and 1984 JMB increased its lending from £34 million to £309 million. Its banking profits halved over this period. Almost all the increased lending – amounting to 115 per cent of the bank's own capital – was to just two borrowers. Predictably, they were unable to repay the loans. JMB had made virtually every mistake in the banking book. It had lent too much. It had lent to customers about whom it knew too little. Far too much of its risk was concentrated on a few customers. Worst of all, it had thrown good lending after bad in the desperate hope of recouping its initial investment. It was a simple example of appallingly imprudent banking practice.

It is such a simple example that it seems extraordinary that a sophisticated system of banking supervision allowed it to happen. The collapse was almost as much of a disaster for the Bank of England as for JMB. It revealed that the Bank's Supervision Division was frantically overworked and unable to look at bank returns in sufficient detail. It revealed that the distinction made in the 1979 Act was unsatisfactory – recognised banks needed just as much supervision as anyone else. It also implied that the Bank was too much the gentleman – JMB's management had flannelled and misled the supervisors, but the Bank had simply 'expressed concern'. By the time the problem reached crisis point it was too late. After a rash of secret emergency meetings, it was decided that the Bank would take JMB in itself – for the outlay of £1. This was criticised too. A bank that had been seriously mismanaged was apparently being bailed out. In reality, the Bank was trying to protect the other British banks in the bullion market – particularly the Midland (represented by its merchant subsidiary, Samuel Montagu) which was probably the UK's weakest clearer at that time.

The JMB affair led ultimately to a new Banking Act in 1987. The Bank will insist that this was because it was by then able to convince others of weaknesses that it had recognised for some years. Under the 1987 Act the Bank of England must authorise all deposit-takers, setting rules to cover capitalisation, quality of management and so on. The Bank's Supervision Division has been expanded and a Board, which includes outsiders as well as a team from within the Bank, has been set up to monitor the process. The Board will be quick to recommend changes in procedure to the government. The hope is that this will enable the supervisory system to match the pace of developments within the banking sector itself.

There have been no further JMB-type scandals since 1984. Perhaps this proves that the Bank has got it right. Or perhaps it is just luck. The JMB affair might be described as the day when the old lady came to terms with the new City. The days of a nod and a wink between friends were over. The Bank could no longer be sure that it should trust even its traditional friends. The world was more ruthless. Perhaps the Bank has become more ruthless too.

9 From Deregulation to Regulation

The Paradox

From all the developments and reforms that have come together over the 1980s to constitute the new City, there now emerges an extravagant and confusing paradox. The basis of the new regime has been the wholesale relaxation of various systems of rules that controlled and distorted financial activity both in the City and elsewhere. This process of deregulation, or liberalisation, has been hailed as a return to the freedom of market forces. It has also given rise to the most comprehensive overhaul of regulatory systems ever seen in the City of London. It has ushered in the most complex and far-reaching programmes of supervision and control that UK financial markets have ever endured. Whole rafts of financial operators who, ten years ago, could go about their business with never even a backward glance, are today subject to extensive programmes of regulation. The process of deregulation appears to have left us with a regulatory system so cumbersome and complicated as to make the old City seem positively permissive. On the face of it, it looks rather like Lenin choosing to dismantle capitalism by means of a deliberate extension of private property; or Mary Whitehouse fighting for public morality by the distribution of pornographic magazines.

The paradox of financial regulation goes something like this: over-regulation diverts business to other financial centres, where firms can operate more freely; under-regulation gives rise to financial scandals which divert business to other financial centres where investors feel that their money will be safer. A successful financial centre therefore, needs, to be both regulated and deregulated.

There are those on both sides of the regulation debate who would argue that this is actually possible. Deregulation is necessary to allow free movement of money. Regulations should protect investors from fraud and sharp practice. The two are not incompatible. One refers to the context within which national markets operate, the other to behaviour within the markets. It sounds very neat. UK experience over the 1980s suggests that the balance is actually extremely hard to achieve. As we shall see, the systems developed have met with almost universal scorn. The issue that must dominate this chapter is whether or not there is a workable alternative.

The 1980s have highlighted a further paradox that has dogged financial regulation in the UK for centuries. It is a greater source of controversy now than ever before. In the old City people who worked at the Stock Exchange, or at Lloyd's, or the Baltic, were effectively members of a club. The City was a series of such clubs. They set their own rules, which were enforced by respected older members. Anyone in breach of the rules would be taken aside and spoken to quietly. If he (for members were bound to be men) persisted, then he might have to be blackballed. It would all be carried out most discreetly, for the honour of the club must be protected. The 'clubby' atmosphere of the City has largely passed.

The system still remains – to an extent. It is known as self-regulation. The institutions of the City are responsible for their own policing. They establish rules which are enforced by their permanent staff. There are a number of arguments in favour of such an idea. The institutions should have a powerful interest in their own sanctity and so should be keen to root out offenders from within their midst. At the same time, they may well be best-placed to catch fraudsters, since they understand the markets so well. Also, and perhaps most tellingly, markets are developing so rapidly that no external authority could keep pace with the changes. If such an authority were effective, it would be rigid and would thus hold back the market's ability to adapt. Business would be lost. According to these arguments, the system of self-regulation helps to account for the City's success over the past century. Our markets have not been held back by the cumbersome systems favoured by other countries. As a result, we have gained more business, and our markets have remained honest, secure and well-organised.

There is another view. Self-regulation can be seen as a paradox in itself or, at least, as a contradiction in terms – no better than the lunatics running the asylum or the animals managing the zoo. First, there is the doubt that internal regulators will be genuinely strict with their own colleagues and friends. They may also have a powerful incentive to cover up. After all, their strongest desire is to give the impression of a safe and secure market. This might be achieved by ignoring wrong-doing rather than by exposing it. There is the further point that, however successful it may be, self-regulation fails because it does not inspire the confidence of outsiders who use the markets. It might also give the impression to operators that malpractice is a mild misdemeanour rather than a serious offence – after all, serious rules would be laid down by law. Finally the City is no longer the club that it once was. The abolition of exchange controls, Big Bang on the Stock Exchange, the reform of the money-markets have all attracted to the City an influx of operators who might not have been granted membership in the old days. The rules of the club are no longer enough.

Before looking at the manner in which the current system attempts to fuse self-regulation with external authority, it is instructive to look at the particular experience of Lloyd's insurance exchange. Both the nature of malpractice there, and the response to it, may provide lessons for the rest of the City.

Rape at Lloyd's

Lloyd's was the most club-like of all the institutions of the old City. Its organisation of brokers and underwriting syndicates seemed particularly well-suited to the quiet, self-regulatory systems described above. It had originally been just such a club of individual underwriters. From its incorporation in 1871 and through the changes of 1983, Lloyd's has been run by an elected committee of its own members. In the 1970s and 1980s, the system appeared to be under strain.

The experience of Lloyd's over these years seems to offer a miniature representation of what was about to happen to the entire City five or ten years later. Having been a major success on the international insurance scene for many years, the post-war period was one of steady decline for Lloyd's. By the mid-1980s its share of world insurance business had fallen below 1 per cent. Marine activity had once been its staple diet, but, over the 1960s and 1970s, re-insurance took over. This is rather more risky. If it were to maintain its share of a rapidly growing market, Lloyd's needed more and more syndicate-members to provide financial backing for underwriters. The corporation was happy to see a recruitment drive. These syndicate-members are called 'names'. It is their private wealth that actually underwrites risks (the organisation of the market is more fully explained in Chapter 2). The number of names tripled between 1970 and 1980. This increased the liquidity of the market, but it also changed the relationship between underwriters and their syndicates. Rather than risking the fortunes of their family and friends, underwriters now relied upon groups of remote and rich individuals who played no part in the business of the market itself. The club had grown a great deal more diverse.

There are two classes of person on the floor of Lloyd's: brokers, who bring the business to the market, and underwriters, who actually insure the risks. Another important development of the 1970s was the increasing fusion of these two. Large brokers – the 'broker barons' – had come to dominate the market. Their business was less risky and often more profitable than that of underwriters. Some of them expanded by buying underwriting companies, forming insurance conglomerates similar to those that developed in other financial markets later in the 1980s.

If we put these developments together, we get a transformation of the Lloyd's insurance market that is remarkably similar to the Stock Exchange's Big Bang. It did not entail formal deregulation, and it did not capture the popular imagination. It still managed to produce a larger market, with more outside members, conducting riskier business. It was also a market dominated by large operators who practiced 'dual capacity' – they not only won business from customers but also stood prepared to execute that business. Just as with the breakdown of the broker/jobber distinction in equity markets, dual capacity offers the opportunity to profit by diverting customers' business directly to one's own subsidiaries. It is to be hoped that the Stock Exchange has learned from the experience of Lloyd's.

The first major scandal to hit the market seems fairly insignificant in the light of what was to follow. A syndicate led by the underwriter Tim Sasse incurred losses of some £20 million on US property business. The unfortunate names who had to pick up the bill alleged that the underwriting had been in breach of the market's rules and that the committee should have provided stricter regulation.

This prompted plans for a revised disciplinary system for Lloyd's. The Bank of England, interestingly, was prominent in pushing for changes despite its lack of any formal authority over the insurance market. A new Lloyd's Act was already through Parliament when the next scandal broke.

In 1982 an American broker who had recently acquired the Alexander Howden Group, alleged that $55 million had been diverted from this Lloyd's brokerage company and its underwriting subsidiaries into the personal fortunes of certain directors. One of the men named, Ian Posgate, was the most celebrated underwriter at Lloyd's. Posgate was acquitted of serious malpractice by a disciplinary committee. Inevitably, there were those who said that the self-regulatory system of Lloyd's was not best-placed either to deter or to punish such malpractice.

Worse was to come. Later in 1982, disclosures began to leak about a Lloyd's broker named Minet Holdings, which also owned underwriting subsidiaries. By late 1990 investigators at the Department of Trade and Industry had still failed to plumb the depths of the Minet saga. It revolves around misuse of reinsurance premiums. The names had not only suffered misappropriation of their funds, but apparently faced an additional trading loss of over £100 million.

There can be little doubt that, if the Minet and Alexander Howden affairs had broken sooner, the new system introduced at Lloyd's would not have continued to rely upon self-regulation. It is very likely too that, if Lloyd's had been forced to accept external regulation in the early 1980s, then the schemes devised for the remainder of the City in the middle of the decade would also have favoured such authority.

The changes actually introduced in 1982 were still along self-regulatory lines. A Council is now elected, both by the market's working members and by the non-working names. The Council also has some external members. The most significant change was a last-minute addition by the Bank of England. In the light of the Alexander Howden affair, the Bank added the post of permanent chief executive to the Lloyd's Council. It was filled by Ian Hay Davison, an outsider who has also helped to clean up the Hong Kong financial sector. Under his authority, underwriters were forced to disclose their financial positions, and brokers had to 'divest' themselves of underwriting businesses. Davison's reign was not popular within Lloyd's itself. He resigned in 1986.

The continuing ramifications of the Minet scandal led to pressure on the government to include Lloyd's in the provisions of the 1986 Financial Services Act that redesigned regulatory systems for the remainder the City. The limits of time prevented this. Lloyd's carries on as a self-regulating body. Its experience appears to show only too clearly what happens when an institution is liberalised without a satisfactory regulatory system in place to maintain discipline. It should have provided an object-lesson to the regulators of the remainder of the City. Perhaps it did. We shall see in the next sections.

Altogether, it is reckoned that various members of Lloyd's – mainly external, non-working names – have been plundered to the tune of some £100 million by their supposed colleagues. It was described by one old hand as 'the rape of the greedy by the very greedy'. A common defence of City crimes of this kind is that they are, in some sense, victimless – or at least that the victims are sufficiently rich not to notice. It surfaced at the Guinness trial of 1990. It is a dangerous view. Quite apart from the direct victims (who clearly do suffer), malpractice of this kind threatens the future of the very markets in which it occurs. A leading article in *The Independent on Sunday* at the time of the Guinness trial in 1990 used the example of Lloyd's, arguing that:

> ***much of [its] reputation has been lost, because investors were looted by insiders whose names are known to the authorities...but none of whom has ever been convicted in a court of law. Lloyd's...suffered from too little regulation. Had the cheats who exploited investors been put behind bars, the market would now be in a healthier state. Here is a practical market-led argument for honesty.***

The argument is sound and telling. We should be careful, though, not to condemn the post-1983 system of self-regulation at Lloyd's too hastily. The scandals date from a period when the club's rules had clearly failed. It might not be self-regulation itself that accounted for this. It might have been over-reliance on respect for the club. That is surely what the government must have thought – or hoped.

Their new systems for the rest of the City are remarkably similar to that in use at Lloyd's.

The New System

The Financial Services Act was passed in 1986. It came into operation in 1988. The regulatory system that it introduced was designed to combine the strengths of self-regulation with the need for firmer external control. It is immensely complicated and, predictably, satisfies no one. Believers in self-regulation despise it for its formality and bureaucracy. Advocates of a statutory system complain that it is weak, ineffective and unfathomable. Even David Walker, the chairman of the Securities and Investments Board (SIB) that stands at the head of the new system, has admitted that the changes were too rushed and have caused 'widespread hostility' amongst the practitioners they are meant to regulate.

Self-regulation remains the basis of the system. The Act established a series of Self-Regulatory Organisations (SROs) to cover the entire financial services industry. They are:

- The Securities Association (TSA) which covers all firms dealing in bonds, equities and so on.
- The Investment Management Regulatory Organisation (IMRO) which looks after fund managers.
- The Financial Intermediaries, Managers and Brokers Regulatory Association (FIMBRA) which supervises the activities of all the various financial advisers and salesmen at work in the UK.
- The Association of Futures Brokers and Dealers (AFBD) which authorises membership of futures and options markets.
- The Life Assurance and Unit Trust Regulatory Organisation (LAUTRO) which oversees companies in these fields.

Any firm (or, in the case of FIMBRA, private individual) who wishes to operate in any of these markets must first be authorised by its (or his/her) relevant SRO. Authorisation will depend upon certain 'prudential standards' being met – most importantly, proof of adequate capital backing. This alone caused an immense workload when the system was set up in the late 1980s. The SROs were established in 1986 (even though their work did not formally begin until 1988) in the hope that the bulk of their authorisation chores would be over before the new era began. The start was inauspicious. Thousands of firms chose to delay application until they were sure of the full implications. By 'A' Day in April 1988, authorisation was a long way from completion. The system began, therefore, with a large number of companies claiming 'interim authorisation'. This meant, in effect, that they were allowed to operate but had not been authorised in any way – the very reverse of what the planners had intended.

The SROs are also responsible for setting rules for their members. In the period between 1986 and 1988 they were busy devising rule books. They did not have an entirely free choice, however. Their rules must be in line with the overall rule book laid down by SIB. This is not a slim document. It weighs four and a half pounds. The bureaucracy involved in preparing and administering these sets of rules has been immense.

The cost of all this is substantial. SROs are financed by their members, the SIB by a levy upon the SROs. So the industry is paying for its own regulation. One estimate has put the cost at around £100 million.

This seems fairly elaborate, but it does not stop here. As well as the SIB and the five SROs, the Department of Trade and Industry (DTI) is still concerned with a variety of areas including insider dealing, and the establishment of new unit trusts. The Bank of England supervises the banking sector. The Stock Exchange and Lloyd's have control over their own markets. Mergers and takeovers in any of the sectors may be referred to the Monopolies and Mergers Commission. The Takeover Panel has an input here as well. Lastly, of course, the Fraud Squad can make investigations of its own. Simply calculating which organisation is responsible for a particular activity can be time-consuming.

It is also worth noting that, of all of these various bodies, only the DTI and the Fraud Squad actually have the power to initiate a prosecution. The others can do no more than recommend cases up the ladder. SROs can withhold authorisation, but this might not be much of a deterrent to multi-million pound fraud.

It is easy to poke fun at the scheme. It is worth remembering the paradox with which regulators are faced. Aggressive regulation deters operators. Weak regulation deters customers. The Financial Services Act attempts to find a middle way. It was clearly felt that self-regulation should not be sacrificed. It is widely held in the City that self-regulation is essential if markets are to remain sufficiently flexible and adaptable. Its abandonment would have been very unpopular within the industry. It might have caused a serious outflow of firms and thereby threatened the City's ability to dominate the European market. We should not forget that the new City's very existence is founded on the success of the Euromarkets, which is itself directly attributable to the low-key regulation that they attracted in London.

Whilst self-regulation was to form the basis of the system, there was also no doubt that policing must be a good deal tighter than it had been in the past. The experience of Lloyd's showed what could happen if a market were allowed to expand rapidly without satisfactory discipline. *The Financial Times* had no doubt that 'in the aggressively competitive climate that followed Big Bang in the City, a tougher framework of enforcement was bound to be necessary'. The establishment of the SIB, the need for authorisation, the writing of rule books, even the financing arrangements, are all evidence of a desire to impose a rigorous discipline upon the industry.

It could be argued, then, that the scheme is a clever compromise that manages to tread the narrow line between under- and over-regulation with considerable skill. It could be argued. Nobody has.

Still in the Club

The kindest way of looking at the new system is to treat it as an experiment. There are bound to be teething troubles. You cannot expect to get it right first time. There have been and they did not. Even the SIB recognises that the volume of rules is absurd. In 1989 David Walker announced the need for a thorough review of the arrangements with the distinct intention of simplifying the rule books. It has been stated on many occasions that the very complexity of the current system is sufficient to divert prospective entrants from the market – the 'advantages' of self-regulation are more than offset by the elaborate maze within which SROs and their members have to operate. The intricacies all serve to make the system more expensive too. Participating companies feel themselves doubly disadvantaged: not only are they labouring under a complex and bureaucratic system, they are also having to pay for it. The bill to cover schemes compensating investors in the event of company failure, rose from £7 million in 1990 to £12 million in 1991. This cost is entirely met by member-companies. The financial burden has given rise to a further problem, which is more far-reaching and may threaten the whole notion of self-regulation.

If companies within an industry are invited to subcribe towards an agency, like an SRO, that covers that industry, it is tempting for them to think of it as a sort of trade association. It is supported by their contributions. They might expect it to represent their wishes. Nothing, of course, could be further from the minds of those who framed the legislation. There is a danger, though, that the SROs come to be seen as protectors of their members rather than of investors. This would mean that the new system had simply replaced one type of club with another – a movement, if you like, from the Garrick to a trade union for financial service dealers. Although this is an exaggeration, the danger is genuine. Discussions about regulation of European financial markets after 1992, led some of representatives to suggest that the UK's SROs should not be approved throughout the EC since they amount to little more than trade associations.

Recent developments at FIMBRA illustrate the point only too well. The members of FIMBRA are mostly small, often one-man, businesses and are spread all over the country. They offer independent financial advice to their clients. Before 1988, they were subject to no regulation at all beyond the laws of fraud. In one sense, then, the new scheme has been helpful. It has laid down standards of good practice that were not always being followed before. It has done the investor a good turn. However, its members also believe that it has cost them a great deal of money – costs which have continued to escalate as extra items of regulation have been added. Such high costs have led to a steady decline in FIMBRA membership. By early 1991, the organisation was actually facing insolvency. A programme of redundancies solved its immediate problems. The attempt to protect investors appears, therefore, to have threatened not only the supply of financial services, but also the the viability of the protection itself.

The problems of FIMBRA go further. In 1990, the council intended to introduce a compulsory insurance scheme for all member-firms. The cost would, of course, be met by those firms. It probably would have benefited the investor. The members were outraged at the additional cost. They saw it as tiresome and expensive interference from a body that should be more sensitive to their interests. An extremely rancorous annual general meeting ended with the premature retirement of the chairman of FIMBRA (Lord Elton) and the scrapping of the insurance scheme. The members were well-satisfied with the result. They had apparently succeeded in proving that the regulators could themselves be regulated. Quite apart from the pros and cons of the particular scheme involved, the development has a dangerous side. If the regulators quake when members put pressure upon them to relax the system, then the SROs do become little more than trade associations.

You might wonder who comes at the top of FIMBRA's protection list – its members, their investors or itself. The members may yet have cause to regret their action. The government will face considerable pressure from within the EC as the need to harmonise regulatory systems becomes more pressing. Any hint that UK operators are able to influence their SROs is bound to damage the case for self-regulation. A return to clubland can only be temporary. Its final replacement might turn out to be a lot more threatening than the likes of FIMBRA.

Insider Dealing and Slippage

If the financial pages of the early 1980s were dominated by stories of scandals at Lloyd's, it was the Stock Exchange – or, at least, sharp practice involving shares – that provided copy for the second half of the decade. The most well-known scam of this kind is insider dealing – illegal dealing in shares by those who have privileged access to price-sensitive information. Twenty years ago it was not even frowned upon. It has been a criminal offence for ten years. It is generally believed to be a fairly common practice, though it is hard to see on what the belief is based. It is also notoriously difficult to track down.

Big Bang has made a number of changes to the world of insider dealing. It has made it a great deal more likely to occur. The formation of financial conglomerates means that stockbrokers and market-makers can be working for the same company as corporate bankers, who have access to highly sensitive information. The information may leak between the two branches.

Big Bang also led to a dramatic surge in share prices, which itself fuelled a boom in company takeovers (which could be financed by the issue of highly priced shares). Takeover plans offer the most fruitful source of information to the insider dealer. Shares in a firm threatened by takeover are bound to jump in value as the rivals compete for ownership. Anyone who buys these shares before the bid is public knowledge is sure to make a tidy profit. The effects can be far-reaching. In late 1989, the Kingfisher group of companies (consisting of Woolworths, B & Q, and Comet) planned to bid for Dixons (the electrical retailer). Inevitably, about 400 merchant bankers, accountants and lawyers knew of the plan a few days before it was due to be announced. Someone thought the chance was too good to miss. On 5 December 1989, the price of Dixons' shares jumped 11p as rumours swept the market. By 8 o'clock the next morning, Kingfisher were obliged to disclose their offer (earlier than they had intended). The bid failed. The dealing may not have been by a mischievous member of Kingfisher's support team. Just as likely (if not more so) is the possibility of 'slippage' – this is where price-sensitive information is accidentally passed on, perhaps in casual conversation, and a third (or fourth or fifth) party acts upon it. The result is the same as with simple insider dealing, but the offender is difficult to track and the crime impossible to prove. The dealer may not even be aware that access to the information is restricted.

The rash of takeovers in the middle 1980s generated the sort of information upon which insider dealing thrives. The new market arrangements following Big Bang may have made it easier to pass this information into the market. The planners were well aware of this danger. As early as 1983, instructions were being issued for the erection of 'Chinese walls' between the different departments of the new financial conglomerates. These are artificial barriers which, though they cannot prevent the passage of information, can at least make it a good deal harder. An example might involve establishing the banking and market-making branches of a business in separate premises. Some companies have complicated arrangements of communicating doors that are locked to all but those sufficiently trusted to have access to electronic 'passwords'. For all the effort, though, no system can be foolproof. Colleagues are bound to drink together, and, even if telephone conversations are recorded (as they are in some companies), there are other ways to keep in touch.

While Big Bang initially increased the likelihood of insider dealing, it also increased the possibility of catching offenders. Now that the market is computerised, every deal is recorded and time-logged. The Stock Exchange employs a large staff who study this data on the look-out for evidence of heavy dealing in advance of information becoming public. In the case of Kingfisher and Dixons, for example, they will have tried to establish the identity of the early traders on 5 December. It is still fairly easy for determined offenders to cover their tracks. The Surveillance Department at the Stock Exchange passes its suspicions on to the DTI. During the 1980s, the first decade in which insider dealing has been a criminal offence, 180 suspected cases have been reported to the DTI. Only twenty-six have resulted in prosecution and just ten of these led to conviction. In each case the defendant pleaded guilty. None of them received a prison sentence. One of the most severe cases was that of Geoffrey Collier, an executive at Morgan Grenfell, who in July 1987 was fined £25 000 and given a twelve-month suspended prison sentence. The hope was that this would be sufficient to deter others.

The public reaction to the sentences passed in the Guinness proceedings of 1990 suggest a wide belief that fines alone are not an adequate deterrent in City cases where such vast sums are involved. The case concerned illegal share dealing (although there was no insider dealing as such). Guinness was trying to outwit the Argyll Group in its efforts to take over the Distillers company. It planned to finance its bid with an offer of shares in Guinness. The case revealed a series of attempts to bribe share-dealers to buy huge quantities of Guinness shares – often using Guinness's own funds – in an effort to 'ramp' their price. The high share price would make their offer for Distillers seem more generous than that of Argyll. The plan succeeded so far as the takeover went. It was less of a success for those directly involved: Ernest Saunders (former chairman and chief executive of Guinness) was sent to prison for 5 years; Gerald Ronson and Anthony Parnes (who had helped to force up the price of the shares) also received custodial sentences. The newspapers variously described the result as: 'a triumph' (*The Independent*), 'salutary and symbolic' (*The Times*), 'welcome' (*The Daily Telegraph*), 'a blessing in disguise' (*The Independent on Sunday*). There was no doubt amongst many observers of the City that a genuine shock had been needed to prove to practitioners that they did have to go in fear of the law. Regulation and punishment before the Guinness affair had not been sufficiently fearsome. It is no consolation to Mr Saunders and his co-defendants that they have become the City's equivalent of the severed heads of traitors impaled on spears in the Middle Ages. Nonetheless, they may have served a useful purpose. Andrew Hugh Smith, chairman of the Stock Exchange, commented that 'the publicity surrounding the Guinness case...has been a highly visible warning of the innate risks in activity of this kind, let alone the outcome of the trial'.

It is clear that the City authorities wanted to see the Guinness case as proof that the existing system can root out wrong-doing and punish the offenders. The offences were committed before the new arrangements came into force in 1988. Nonetheless, the case was looked upon to justify the amalgam of traditional company law, self-regulation and extensive bureaucracy that had been introduced. The affair showed that tightening up had been necessary and that the authorities were serious in their desire to stamp out malpractice. It was used by the likes of Andrew Hugh Smith to justify the *status quo*.

The Guinness sentences gained much publicity for a week or two. They will be quickly forgotten. Only a matter of months after the case, there were allegations of 'bear raiding' in the equity market. The collapse of the Polly Peck corporation (whose financial position was dire) was said by its chairman to have been precipitated by the deliberate circulation of inaccurate rumours that were calculated to drive down the share price (it was even suggested that the chairman had been shot). Traders sell shares that they do not yet own, drive the price down by this rumour-mongering, and then buy shares (to settle the earlier deal) at a far lower price. Polly Peck shares fell so dramatically that dealing was suspended. Such raiding is not significantly different from the practices for which the Guinness defendants were sent to prison. It involves the deliberate distortion of market prices in order to produce circumstances which will generate a private capital gain. It is very hard to prove, for it is based upon the circulation of rumours rather than dealing. If it did happen, then it makes the hopes of Andrew Hugh Smith seem particularly pious. Perhaps the truth is that, in a deregulated market, the possibilities of profit can seem so huge that no viable sentence could be an adequate deterrent to sharp practice.

There is a simple alternative to the hybrid system that seeks to regulate the City. Other countries seem happy with statutory control of financial markets along the American model. There are many who have not ruled this out for the UK. The leading article in *The Times* on the day following the Guinness sentences ended by suggesting that: 'Further statutory regulation must still be kept as a threat hanging over the City.' What form might such control take?

The American Way

It is ironic that some of the key evidence that put the DTI investigators on the trail of the Guinness offenders in London, was actually collected by the regulatory body of the American financial sector – the Securities and Exchange Commission (SEC). The SEC was investigating the case of Ivan Boesky, one-time king of Wall Street, later proved to be king of the insider-dealers. Boesky had been recruited by Gerald Ronson to spend millions of dollars on Guinness shares. He was handsomely paid for his trouble. His sworn statement helped the DTI to build the case that they needed.

So the case which the British treat as the final proof of their regulatory system's ability to bite, might in fact have been made possible only by the genuine toughness of the American system. The SEC is a statutory authority. It is established by federal law and financed by the tax-payers. It is a form of specialist fraud squad for the financial markets – a far cry from the cosy self-regulation that has dominated the City for so long. Its powers extend through a combination of civil and criminal law. The SEC can enter into litigation on behalf of the investors who have suffered through financial malpractice. It can also bring criminal prosecutions. Boesky, for example, was fined $100 million before he was sent to prison. This has a number of advantages. The body clearly has teeth. It also has the flexibility to choose the course most likely to bring the desired result – to frighten potential wrong-doers. As one of its officials, Richard C. Breeden, has put it: 'We like to put them in jail.' If a civil action will get a quicker or more secure result, however, that route will be used. This overcomes another problem that dogs the British system. Financial frauds are frequently extremely complex. A conventional jury may find it hard to understand the case, let alone to judge it. There is a motto in the City that, if you are going to try your hand at fraud, you should make it as elaborate as possible. By the time the DTI investigators have grasped it (if they do), they will probably advise against prosecution, doubting their abilty to secure a conviction in what could be an absurdly long and costly trial. Some have suggested specialist juries. The SEC's flexibility is a simpler method.

There is a further, unlooked-for, benefit from the SEC's powers to prosecute – it has become self-financing. In every year from 1983 to 1990, more was taken in fines and seizures than it cost to run the organisation. By 1990, earnings were actually twice as large as costs. It was one of the most profitable elements of US government activity.

The City's SIB is a half-way house between the SEC and the pure self-regulation that existed before. It has been disparaged by some for wanting to turn itself into a British SEC. If it were to take over the powers of investigation and prosecution currently held by the DTI, it would be well on the way towards becoming such a body. The DTI's record is not especially good: their investigators were misled by the Al Fayed brothers in their battle for House of Fraser; despite warnings, the DTI granted authorisation to the Barlow Clowes investment group which was later revealed to have been misusing its investors' funds; after seven years the DTI has still failed to get to the bottom of the Minet scandal at Lloyd's. Some criticised the Guinness investigation for being clumsy and excessively long drawn-out. Perhaps a beefed-up SIB (along SEC lines) would do better. David Walker has certainly admitted that the SIB currently fails to inspire fear in the way that the SEC seems able to do.

The next stage in the development of the UK's regulatory structure will be the simplification of the rule books of the SIB and its SROs. The intention here is not to make the rules softer but rather, by making them clearer, to see them more readily enforced and, thus, more effective as a deterrent. We should not expect any relaxation of the principle of self-regulation. It is still widely held in the City that such a system can and will work. Much of the publicity given to the SEC ignores the fact that a large proportion of its work is actually based upon self-regulatory organisations, such as the New York Stock Exchange and the National Association of Securities Dealers. Experienced City regulators think it mistaken to regard the issue as a choice between self-regulation and a powerful external authority such as the SEC. Any system, they say, will involve some self-regulation. There is no other way of covering the sophisticated financial sectors of today. The question really concerns the precise limits of this self-regulation, and the nature of the organisation to which the SROs are responsible. Should the SIB be the quasi-independent body with limited powers that it currently is? Or should be it be more like the SEC – a branch of government with less independence but greater power? The simple answer at the moment is that not even the SIB can make up its mind.

It is, anyway, possible to become hysterical about City malpractice. The fact that few cases are brought to court may mean that the markets are largely clean. Nicholas Ridley, Secretary of State for Trade and Industry in the late 1980s, believed that insider dealing was far less widespread than was popularly thought and that the absence of cases coming to court was proof that self-regulation was successful in discouraging such activity. While this may be over-optimistic, we should be wary of jumping to sensational conclusions.

Similarly, the fact that the SEC succeeded in punishing Boesky does not prove that it has stamped out financial malpractice. There might be much going on undetected. And there is a cost involved in regulation. Its aim is to protect investors without damaging the efficiency of the market. City operators will say that the very fear that the SEC is said to instil in traders in New York makes it harder for them to react as quickly or flexibly as their City counterparts. A beefed-up SIB would cause the same problems in London.

The European Way

The fear is that heavy-handed regulation erodes competitive advantage. One solution might lie in international harmonisation. If all countries were to adopt the same standards and the same methods of enforcing them, then the playing field would be well and truly level. Discussions within the EC preparatory to a single market in financial services in 1992 have provided an authentic opportunity for this. If their progress is anything to go by, global optimism would be premature.

There are three broad elements to financial regulation: prudential standards (conditions which must be met before a firm can seek to provide financial services); the enforcement of these standards; and rules to cover the conduct of day-to-day business. EC countries have agreed to seek harmony over the first category only. This has proved difficult enough. Standards of bank authorisation for example, are, higher in the UK than in many other countries. We have been reluctant to accept lower standards in the interests of compromise. Once these standards are agreed, any firm authorised within its own country will be free to operate throughout the EC. Processes of authorisation and the policing of actual business will be the responsibility of individual countries. Some nations have been surprised by our reliance on self-regulation. The final outcome is still uncertain. Some believe that our hybrid system will seem more friendly than the American-style schemes that operate in other centres, and that the City will therefore play host to a rapid inflow of European operators. Others fear that the uneasy mixture of overcomplicated and costly rule books with a topping of law, will not only deter entrants but will also hold back City firms in their efforts to win European business. It may even encourage them to seek a simpler environment elsewhere, when the European market is opened.

The chapter ends, then, as it began, with a paradox. This one runs to the very root of financial markets. The industry moves at an extraordinary pace. Efficiency and competitive success depend upon flexibility, adaptability and split-second judgement. International deregulation has placed even greater stress upon these qualities. Any system of regulation must slow down the market that it regulates. It therefore makes it less efficient and less competitive. Regulation is essential if these industries are not to be beyond the law, and yet there will always be an advantage in being the least regulated market in the world. Whilst it would be too strong to say that authorities have to choose between a trustworthy industry and a successful one, it is nonetheless true that the admirable desires of the SIB and the SROs and of the Labour Party (who are pledged to tighter controls on the City) are bound to put the UK financial services industry (a major foreign-currency-earner) at a competitive disadvantage. In the face of an open European market in 1992, such a disadvantage could be serious. Much of the City's success lies in its dominance of the European time-zone. At the risk of repetition, we should not forget that the City's past success has been founded upon a flexible, if not relaxed, attitude to regulation. There are those who say that we cannot afford to beef up the system. The issue really is to what extent we dare to doubt the City's honesty. The consequences of a perfectly safe market could turn out to be even more alarming than those of a dishonest one.

10 City Limits?

The Story So Far

The 1980s saw a quiet revolution in the City of London that was entirely without precedent. Everything has changed.

The firms are different. The City is no longer the domain of small specialist operators. Stockbrokers and jobbers, investment bankers and securities dealers have been subsumed into huge conglomerates. Ten years ago, the typical City firm was a partnership (unless it was a bank). Now it is a publicly quoted company. We can no longer assume that it is British. The Americans and, especially, the Japanese have a major presence in today's City markets. Many of the new operators are types of firm that did not even exist ten or twenty years ago. Market-makers on the Stock Exchange, inter-dealer brokers in money markets, competitors for the discount houses, dealers in financial futures would have seemed exotic species to the observers of the 1970s.

The way in which they do business is different. Technological developments have made traditional face-to-face trading a thing of the past. Securities are bought and sold by telephone, telex and computer. Trading is international. Global markets never close. The volume of business has increased phenomenally. The environment is infinitely more competitive. Traditional businesses, such as banking, have found themselves in a new and tougher market-place. They have adapted themselves to the conditions. Business that was once based on steady relationships developed over years, has become a ruthless speculative trade. The nature of the business conducted is different. In London today, products which hardly even existed in 1980 are being traded in their millions. Futures, options and swaps contracts have grown out of specialised, fringe markets into billion-pound businesses. Traditional products have changed. The range of borrowing opportunities is immense. Securities can now be issued in forms calculated to cover every need.

Customers are different. Just as the dealers are likely to be large, multinational corporations, so are their clients. In an increasing number of markets, it is hard to tell the dealers from the customers. Many large companies have established specialist departments who are responsible simply for the manipulation of the firm's financial reserves. They will move millions of pounds worth of currency within the world's money markets, lending to other companies or to banks in the search for profit. Money has ceased to be the preserve of financial specialists. Every firm with funds aims to be a financial specialist now.

The relationship with government is different. Deregulation has removed the network of rules that limited much of the free flow of capital. New and more technical rules have been imposed. And, perhaps more significantly, government policy-making has come to rely more heavily upon these financial markets. A return to fixed exchange rates and an overriding concern with monetary spending have combined to make the setting of interest rates, the conduct of bank lending and the behaviour of currency markets more important to the economy than ever before.

The people employed to do the work of the City are different. Thousands more are now employed in this sector than there were in 1980. Their average age is far lower. A greater proportion of them are women. Formal educational qualifications range more widely, from first-class degrees to a GCSE or two.

Even the premises in which they work are different. There is an extraordinary new Lloyd's building. Older, more traditional work-places have been gutted and transformed. The City is now extending eastwards with the development of the old London docks at Canary Wharf.

The list could go on. Any industry will develop over a decade. Some of the changes that the City has witnessed can be put down to no more than the natural expansion of a particular sector during a period of fluctuating economic activity. These developments go beyond that, though. The new City has appeared to prosper through boom and slump. In the first place, it is the result of deregulation. The abolition of exchange controls and the relaxation of reserve requirements for banks were among the major factors that gave the industry the freedom to grow in the early years of the decade. The impact of deregulation in the UK was made all the more significant by similar developments in other financial centres. Once this had begun – and the City was in the forefront (though not the only leader) – the internationalisation of the market was bound to speed its growth and hasten the evolution of new products. The other factor that enabled the growth to be as alarming as it turned out to be, was the availibility of computer technology. Deregulation expanded the potential market considerably, microelectronics allowed operators to reach every part of this huge market and to do so in seconds. The rest is history.

Deregulation can only happen once. Some markets were already feeling a chill before the end of the decade, as the first flush of deregulation gave way to the cold reality of cut-throat competition. Technology will continue to develop, but it can surely never again have the impact that it managed in combination with the liberalisation of the early 1980s. Was the decade, then, a freak in the history of the City of London? Have the limits of the City now been pushed as far as they will go?

The Single Market

It seems as though the City may lead a charmed life. Deregulation, it has just been said, can only happen once. Yet the planned fusion of European markets after 1992 could, on the face of it, provide a second dose of deregulation within less than ten years. British suppliers of financial services will have free access to the markets of all twelve EC countries. Surely this provides the very opportunity to push the City's limits ever further?

The Cecchini report on the probable effects of the single market was published (on behalf of the EC Commission) in 1988. It includes a section that estimates the gains for the financial services sector. The extra competition should reduce prices. The largest falls will be experienced by the countries whose sectors are least efficient when the single market opens. Spain, for example, is reckoned likely to benefit from price falls of 34 per cent on financial services. The UK has a highly efficient sector. Its price falls are estimated at about 13 per cent (still a major benefit for customers). Nonetheless, Signor Cecchini believes that the UK's overall gain will be the greatest, since our highly developed financial services industry will be able to exploit the opportunities offered elsewhere in Europe. The report puts our likely gain at ECU 5.1 billion – about £3.3 billion. This sounds most encouraging. The mathematics must be highly speculative, though. There is harder evidence to suggest that the single market may expose the City as well as boost it.

Wholesale financial markets are already more or less global. The City has a large share of them, but there seems little evidence to support the view that European liberalisation can help it to expand its share dramatically. Retail markets (those serving private customers), on the other hand, are highly fragmented along national lines. It seems, though, that this is set to continue for a good deal of time. It is 'cultural' factors that account for the idiosyncracies of individual markets. Spanish farmers are not about to bank at Barclays simply because they are able to do so. There may be a movement towards cross-border joint ventures and even mergers – but this will be a gradual process. The Royal Bank of Scotland has formed links with Spain's Banco Santander. The NatWest has opened a few branches in Spain. This, though, is a strictly experimental process.

National operators are preparing for the competition too. There are plans to merge all 584 of Germany's individual savings banks and 11 investment banking subsidiaries (known as *Landesbanken*) to form a single nationwide institution that should be able to withstand the onslaught of, amongst others, the British. Banking authorities in Italy and Spain are keen to see similar mergers in their commercial banking sectors, which are particularly fragmented. They are also intending to improve the quality of their products (offering interest-bearing current accounts, for example) in order to ward off competition. This is, of course, excellent news for the customers of German, Italian and Spanish banks. It does not support the view that the City is about to cash in.

Euromarkets will be virtually eliminated. The harmonisation of regulatory arrangements will remove the incentive to hold deposits outside domestic centres. At the moment, about 30 per cent of the turnover of German government bonds, 50 per cent of normal

Deutschmark bond issues, up to 90 per cent of floating rate Deutschmark bond issues and 20 per cent of dealing in German shares takes place in London. In time we might expect to see most of this find its way back to Frankfurt. The Dutch have been particularly ambitious in their planned regulatory reforms and, in early 1990, expressed a desire to make Amsterdam 'the financial gateway to continental Europe'. Half of all bonds denominated in Dutch guilders are currently issued in London. Much of this business is likely to return home. The Paris *bourse* will finally abolish fixed commissions on share dealing. A third of trade in the most highly regarded French equities currently takes place in London. It will not do so for ever. It has, however, been extremely hard to convince the French that further reforms – giving outsiders greater access to trade in French equities – would be beneficial. The Stock Exchange's deep desire to establish an extra (electronic) market to cover the whole of Europe, enabling it to win business from all the national exchanges, has gone down very badly.

There is a distinct danger, then, that other countries may have a good deal more to gain than the UK. A level playing field is most attractive to those who are currently having to play uphill. The City is used to playing downhill with a following wind. Competition after 1992 will be a good deal more fierce. There is a fear, too, that further relaxation of regulatory systems in the USA might deflect business (and operators) away from a single Europe altogether and towards New York instead.

American competition will extend beyond this. The attraction of the huge, lucrative EC market is bound to attract operators from elsewhere – particularly from the USA, Japan and Switzerland. A 1989 survey conducted by the Bank of England into City attitudes to the single market revealed far greater fears about this influx than about competition from within the EC. Since 1989 the banking sectors of both the USA and Japan have experienced considerable setbacks. Perhaps the fears will not be realised. The Bank has still felt the need to warn that it will guard the UK banking industry from foreign takeover. The very liberalisation of UK equity markets might serve to help takeovers of British institutions.

Predictably, respondents to the Bank's 1989 survey took the opportunity to complain about the City's regulatory structure and to claim that it will hold back British companies in their efforts to compete. At the same time, they feared the impact of regulation from within the EC. A cynic might conclude that they are opposed to regulation of any kind. Nonetheless, the imminence of the single market has surely been a factor in persuading the authorities to simplify the SIB's rules.

The Bank itself refers optimistically to the opportunities for exploiting overseas market and the benefits to customers of increased competition. Big Bang can be said to provide a precedent for the sort of developments we are likely to see. This led to an increase in market capacity that was later revealed to have been far too large. It also encouraged ill-advised expansion by some relatively inexperienced operators. The single market could have exactly the same effects. The banking and insurance industries of Europe are already highly fragmented. There is bound to be a considerable increase in concentration. A number of the companies entering the market in 1993 are unlikely to remain independent within it for very long. In the end, customers may well benefit. On the way a number of national operators will be swallowed. Even the ever-cheerful Bank of England is prepared grudgingly to accept that 'these negative effects...of increased competition could appear before the potential benefits begin to be felt'.

The Cecchini report begins to look a touch over-confident, then. There will be costs involved in the single market and, while the City is as well-placed to face the future as any other centre, it would be naive to pretend that there are no risks. The European financial sector in twenty years' time will be dominated by a smaller number of multinational operators. Some of them will be based on the expansion of successful British firms. Others, though, will be based on German or French, Japanese or Swiss companies – at the cost of the British. It is bound to happen.

The last and most troubling implication of the single market lies a few years beyond 1992 in the possibility of a single currency for the EC. Such a development will allow big EC corporations to arrange their financial business in any European centre they choose. If the UK is slower than her main rivals, (particularly the Germans and French) to adopt the currency, then the City's ability to win its share of this business may be seriously impeded. However strong the government's reasons for resisting the single currency, there must be those in the City who fear the UK being in the worst of all worlds – slap in the middle of a highly competitive single market, without the wherewithal to compete.

City of the Future

It would be rash to offer firm predictions of the next stage of City development. Clearly, much will depend upon the actual progress of the European single market, which, as we have seen is fraught with uncertainties.

We can, however, isolate some of the strengths and weaknesses that the City carries into the years ahead. The markets, for example, in which it is currently at its strongest are said to be Eurobonds, foreign exchange, syndicated lending and interest-rate swaps. In each case there are grounds for both pessimism and optimism.

The decline of Euromarkets and competition from Japan will affect London's Eurobond market. At the same time, the uncertainty engendered by volatile stock markets may well generate a further bout of securitisation, to the benefit of all bond dealers, certainly those in the City.

The movement towards fixed exchange rates within Europe may reduce the volume of foreign exchange activity. It is sure to reduce the use of futures contracts. Progress towards a single European currency will have an even greater effect. But currencies will still have to be exchanged. Dollar and yen business will continue to expand. The opening of eastern Europe will create trading opportunities and will, therefore, generate foreign exchange business. London is sure to be directly involved in these developments. In the long term, though, the success of this City market may well hinge upon the UK's attitude towards a common currency for Europe.

Syndicated lending may turn out to be among the most fragile of these leading markets. Whilst there will continue to be a demand for very large loans, the exposure of all banks to bad debt from Third World borrowers must reduce their ability and willingness to become involved with similar lending in future. The late 1980s and early 1990s have seen a crisis for international bankers in general, caused both by this exposure and (particularly in the case of US and Japanese banks) by too rapid a growth of lending to domestic and European customers. Taken together with the Basle Capital Convergence Accord, this suggests that we are likely to see a quiet period for international banking. There may even be one or two bank failures. This cannot be very good news for the City.

Interest-rate swaps are a particularly risky area. They are, nonetheless, a sector that has shown staggering growth, and where such growth is set to continue. The only doubt here must reflect the general fear about the banking sector that was considered above. Swaps are put together by banks. One side-effect of a general decline in the banking sector might be slower growth in swaps markets.

Fears for the future must centre on the insurance market, where competition from the USA, Germany and Switzerland is particularly fierce, and the general restructuring of Euromarkets and of international lending, that will follow from continued deregulation. Altogether, pessimists may feel that they have the edge in the argument. It should not be forgotten, however, that the accumulated experience that the City can boast gives it an inherent advantage over many other financial centres that will count for a good deal.

There is another side to the City's future as a financial centre that it would be unwise to overlook. In a newly deregulated world and, particularly, in an open Europe, operators have a wider choice of location. Factors such as the cost of accommodation, the efficiency of communications, the cost of staff and the life-style that a country can offer to senior managers, all enter into this decision. They may be crucial.

Table 10.1 shows rental charges per square foot of office space in various international centres, calculated in spring 1989. The City was a good deal cheaper than Tokyo, but very much more expensive than the other cities shown. The impact of the national business rate has increased the running costs of City premises further. Most worrying, perhaps, is the comparative bargain that Frankfurt offers. The unification of Germany and the increased influence of the Bundesbank on pan-European monetary policy must make Frankfurt a more frequently considered centre than it once was. It is widely hoped in London that new sites available through the development of docklands will help to tip the balance back towards the City.

Docklands may also help to overcome the City's traffic problems. Its network of narrow streets was never intended to carry the huge volume of traffic that passes through it today. This can be a serious disadvantage to international dealers to whom time spent travelling may be time wasted. The development of the City Airport at docklands was an attempt (strongly pressed by the Bank of England) to overcome this weakness. Disagreements with local residents over noise levels have so far prevented it from offering the sort of liberation that had been hoped.

The proliferation of electronic information systems in the City is

TABLE 10.1
Rental Cost per Square Foot of Prime Office Space in Major Financial Centres, Spring 1989

Location	*Rent (£ per sq. ft)*
City of London	65
Downtown New York	25
Midtown New York	36
Tokyo	99
Paris	34
Frankfurt	22

SOURCE *Bank of England Quarterly Bulletin*, November 1989.

advantageous, though. International companies are seeking markets that offer the most efficient dealing and settlement systems. London can, increasingly, compete with the world. Dealing systems are among the most sophisticated anywhere. Settlement has been slow to catch up, but the establishment of the Central Gilts Office and, now, the Central Moneymarkets Office have done a good deal to restore the City to some sort of primacy. It is disappointing that the TAURUS system for computerising Stock Exchange settlement has been so frequently postponed (planned now for late 1991). Such technology is an especially fast-moving area and it is dangerous to grow complacent after a single electronic system has been set up. There is a race now to hit on new arrangements to reduce the cost of small-scale share-dealing by matching sales directly to purchases. Paris, Toronto and Frankfurt are all experimenting with systems of this kind. The City's current advantages might prove to be strictly temporary. The Bank of England has been particularly keen to press for increased efficiency in these areas, recognising that it may, in the end, determine the City's future.

Staffing is reckoned to be easier in London than in many centres. There seems to be a ready supply of young and talented people, many of whom already have valuable experience. Salaries are rather lower in the UK than elsewhere. However, bonuses make up a smaller proportion of average salaries here. This makes the salary bill less flexible in periods of downturn.

Surveys suggest that costs of living do not differ greatly between the world's financial centres – apart, that is, from Tokyo, which is half as expensive again as London, Frankfurt, Paris and New York. London is also reckoned to have benefited in the past from its ability to offer a life-style that appealed to international senior managers – the so-called 'Ascot factor'.

Put all these elements together, adding the useful fact that English is the language of modern finance, and it can be seen that, whilst the pressure upon London is bound to become more severe in the next few years, it would be naive to think that the City's days are numbered. We can be sure that London will remain one of the world's leading centres. The threat from Europe is real, though. Commentators in Frankfurt, Paris and Amsterdam are sure to be predicting significant growth for those cities. At issue is the extent to which that growth turns out to be at the expense of the City of London.

Too High a Price?

The progress of the 1980s has not been without its costs. It is widely believed by outsiders that the new City is little more than a playground for the unscrupulous. Deregulation has fostered a world in which pursuit of profit dominates all market behaviour. There is no money in scruples.

There are a number of examples in this book of the new City doing its job less well than might have been expected. For all the boasting of politicians, the 1980s has not been the decade of the small investor. There may be more private shareholders, but most of them have only token holdings in privatisation stock. It is the investing institutions that have benefited from the liberalisation of the Stock Exchange. Their dealing costs are the ones that have been reduced. It is harder today for small investors to find brokers who will take their business than was the case before Big Bang. Should they find them, the commissions will be higher.

A deregulated banking system has lent, not wisely, but too much. The decline of traditional banking prudence has created greater risks and more fragile companies. The failure of firms such as Coloroll and Sock Shop in the late 1980s might have been prevented by bankers who had been a little less keen to lend. More seriously, perhaps, burgeoning inflation and the resulting policies of high interest and mortgage rates might also have been avoided by more restrained lending by banks and building societies. Deregulation of banking could surely be said to have put greater pressure on interest rates as a tool of government policy. We may have to grow more accustomed to unpleasant volatility in mortgage and loan repayments.

Internationalisation is bound to make markets more volatile. The crash of 1987 showed how share prices could become trapped in a cycle of pessimistic expectations that swept from centre to centre. Electronic dealing and programme trading seem to have served to increase this volatility. The value of individuals' savings, and of the investments that we all make through pension funds and investment trusts, is made less secure as a result.

More active and more volatile markets encourage speculation and may give rise to sharp practice. International markets are hard to police. We saw earlier how difficult it has been to devise a satisfactory system of regulation for the financial services industry of the UK. Even were such schemes in operation, the increasing size and sophistication of the markets must still make it easier for fraudsters to hide – and more attractive for them to try. So the markets may be less safe than they were ten years ago. Holders of Guinness shares who saw their price fall after the illegal syndicated buying was over, cannot have been full of praise for a new market that encouraged firms to finance ambitious takeovers in this way.

The Guinness example also shows how the greater liquidity and flexibility afforded by the markets of the new City encourage takeover and merger activity. This may put long-awaited pressure on directors to operate efficiently. It may also encourage lucrative asset management at the expense of productive efficiency. Acquisition may take priority over production. Valuable independent companies may be lost. As we saw earlier, a number of independent entrepreneurs have criticised the preoccupation of the new City with short-term results and simple profit data. If markets do not understand the real strengths of businesses, then the wrong companies may be rewarded.

The efficiency of a financial centre depends upon the efficiency of its markets. The proudly deregulated new City boasts markets that can respond more directly and more openly than used to be the case. However, if they are responding to the wrong things, there is nothing much to boast about. A leading article in *The Independent* after the Guinness affair stated baldly: 'Markets tend invariably to excess.' If this is true, then the liberation of markets in the 1980s may actually have reduced their efficiency. There is a leap of faith in the application of free-market principles to the financial sector. The theory is that these markets will always manage to produce a true equilibrium price in the long term, even though short-term behaviour is determined by no more than rumour and speculation. It is difficult to see how the combined efforts of a market-full of traders intent only upon short-term results can so reliably predict a true long-term price trend.

Deregulation has come at a price, then. It has not been a universal benefit. The new City falls some way short of the garden of Eden. It does not follow from this, though, that we were better off before. The old City had weaknesses and inefficiencies that were, if anything, more alarming. Robin Leigh-Pemberton, the governor of the Bank of England, referred to this in a speech in 1988:

> ***Some people mourn the old City, and would hold that standards were higher then and more easily enforced. I am not at all certain that I agree, and, in any case, there were patent inefficiencies that without doubt impaired the range and quality of services provided to the City's customers.***

The Governor is, of course, right. He might have added that technological developments and the attitudes of other financial centres meant that deregulation was both inevitable and essential. We had no choice. Without the changes of the 1980s, the City would have become a backwater. There are inefficiencies and inequities in the new City. If we had not responded to the challenge presented in the 1980s, we would still have bought our financial services from markets that were inefficient and inequitable. They would, however, have been in New York, Tokyo, Frankfurt and Zurich. The development of the new City was a broadly successful response to changed circumstances and increased competition in the market. It is not only an arena for the free play of market forces, it is the child of them.

[illegible]

[illegible]

[illegible]

[illegible]

Index